SPORT

FOUNTAINHEAD PRESS V SERIES

Edited by
Cassie Anne Wright

FOUNTAINHEAD
PRESS

Our green initiatives include:

Electronic Products
We deliver products in non-paper form whenever possible. This includes pdf downloadables, flash drives, and CDs.

Electronic Samples
We use Xample, a new electronic sampling system. Instructor samples are sent via a personalized Web page that links to pdf downloads.

FSC Certified Printers
All of our printers are certified by the Forest Service Council, which promotes environmentally and socially responsible management of the world's forests. This program allows consumer groups, individual consumers, and businesses to work together hand-in-hand to promote responsible use of the world's forests as a renewable and sustainable resource.

Recycled Paper
Most of our products are printed on a minimum of 30% post-consumer waste recycled paper.

Support of Green Causes
When we do print, we donate a portion of our revenue to green causes. Listed below are a few of the organizations that have received donations from Fountainhead Press. We welcome your feedback and suggestions for contributions, as we are always searching for worthy initiatives.
Rainforest 2 Reef
Environmental Working Group

Cover Image: © Wikimedia Commons

Design by Susan Moore

Books may be purchased for educational purposes.

For information, please call or write:

1-800-586-0330

Fountainhead Press
Southlake, TX 76092

Web site: www.fountainheadpress.com
E-mail: customerservice@fountainheadpress.com

First Edition

ISBN: 978-1-59871-482-1

Printed in the United States of America

INTRODUCTION TO THE FOUNTAINHEAD PRESS V SERIES

By Brooke Rollins and Lee Bauknight
Series Editors

The *Fountainhead Press V Series* is a signature collection of single-topic readers that offer a unique look at some of today's most pressing issues. Designed to give writing students a more nuanced introduction to public discourse—on the environment, on food, and on digital life, to name a few of the topics—the books feature writing, research, and invention prompts that can be adapted to nearly any kind of college writing class. Each *V Series* textbook focuses on a single issue and includes multi-genre and multimodal readings and assignments that move the discourse beyond the most familiar patterns of debate—patterns usually fettered by entrenched positions and often obsessed with "winning."

The ultimate goal of the series is to help writing students—who tend to hover on the periphery of public discourse—think, explore, find their voices, and skillfully compose texts in a variety of media and genres. Not only do the books help students think about compelling issues and how they might address them, they also give students the practice they need to develop their research, rhetorical, and writing skills. Together, the readings, prompts, and longer assignments show students how to add their voices to the conversations about these issues in meaningful and productive ways.

With enough readings and composing tasks to sustain an entire quarter or semester, and inexpensive enough to be used in combination with other rhetorics and readers, the *Fountainhead Press V Series* provides instructors with the flexibility to build the writing courses they want and need to teach. An instructor interested in deeply exploring environmental issues, for example, could design a semester- or quarter-long course using *Green*, the first of the *V Series* texts. At the same time, an instructor who wanted to teach discrete units on different issues could use two or more of the *V Series* books. In either case, the texts would give students ample opportunity—and a variety of ways—to engage with the issues at hand.

The *V Series* uses the term "composition" in its broadest sense. Of course, the textbooks provide students plenty of opportunities to write, but they also include assignments that take students beyond the page. Books in the series encourage students to explore other modes of communication by prompting them to design websites, to produce videos, posters, and presentations; to conduct primary and secondary research; and to develop projects with community partners that might incorporate any number of these skills. Ultimately, we have designed the *Fountainhead Press V Series* to work for teachers and students. With their carefully chosen readings, built-in flexibility, and sound rhetorical grounding, the *V Series* books would be a dynamic and user-friendly addition to any writing class.

TABLE OF CONTENTS

INTRODUCTION: SPORT AS SPECTACLE

By Cassie A. Wright

I can still remember the deafening thunderclap, amplified by the acoustics of the Pasadena Rose Bowl, immediately following the faint swoosh of the ball as it soared past China's goalkeeper into the back of the net. In that chaotic historic moment, Brandi Chastain, and her iconic if accidental Nike sports bra advertisement, changed the trajectory of women's sports, and the sports apparel industry, forever. In clinching the U.S. National Team's victory in the final match of the 1999 FIFA Women's World Cup, Chastain immediately became both fledgling soccer hopefuls' idol, myself included, and Nike's answer to a growing female sports apparel market. As an attractive white woman who had just revealed her spectacular ripped physique in front of millions in an extemporaneous moment of joy, Chastain had also become a national spectacle and the center of media buzz for months to come. Meanwhile, hopefuls like myself awaited the day we too could get a scholarship, and wearing our own Nike apparel, join the growing ranks of budding female soccer stars, who, day in and day out, sweated it out on grassy patches. They were our version of postmodern "girl power."

Like millions of other Americans, I grew up breathing, eating, sleeping, and playing sports. Soccer, track, volleyball, cross-country, basketball, swimming and diving—you name it, I played it. Of course, I had the benefit of being a girl born in the United States well after the establishment of Title IX in a household that was likewise supremely physical and sport-oriented. Thus, I had the privilege of growing up naive to the notion that sports were "a boy thing." My own mother, very athletic in her own right, married and had children early, yet she continued to play softball and soccer throughout my childhood, serving as a model and inspiration for my own sporting interests. I can still remember attending many of her games on the weekends and watching her take joy in the physicality and camaraderie of team sports. Or the ceremonious summers and winters when our family would spend nights together glued to the television screen watching U.S. Olympians compete for gold. My mother's commitment to the demands of being a "soccer mom" also meant both our days were engulfed by the love for and logistics of sports. And so, as a child, sports were my life. If I wasn't at practice, I was in the gym or training somewhere, doing sprints on a dusty graveled high school track (before the days of the high tech all-weather stuff), or training slow twitch muscles and logging miles in the soft sand at the beach. And let's not forget the injury rehabilitation protocol for torn ligaments and broken bones that began long before my stint in Division I ball. Almost always, there was a soccer ball at my feet. When I wasn't training, I was fidgeting, squirming, counting down the minutes until I could get back out and have at it again: a body perpetually in motion.

As a lover of team sports and a tomboy, I grew up with dozens of girls and boys who seemed to feel similarly, who passed away hours after school and during summer enjoying the wonders of cultivating an athletic form. Of feeling our bodies tighten and harden, our lungs burn and adapt, our minds sharpen in focus and determination, our bonds deepen with our teammates as we succumbed to the rhythm and repetition of sporting competition.

Western culture has been fascinated by athletes since at least as early as the ancient Greek and Roman times. Indeed, athletes were thought to encompass many ideals of the human form, and the ancient Olympics were an important moment for celebrating athletes' bodies and their spectacular feats. But, athletes are controversial as are the spaces they inhabit: pitches, courts, tracks, greens, fields, slopes, courses. Sports and their bodies are spectacles. Spectacular. Public. They have a way of drawing attention to themselves and their performances, both on and off the pitch. Perhaps nothing speaks more strongly to this than the notion of the athlete as celebrity or role model. The iconic status of modern athletes is in part a response to a growing sports media industry, as are growing sports fandom and sports journalism sectors. All are enmeshed in a lucrative if nuanced industry whose success depends largely on sport's bedazzling hold on American culture, leading some skeptics to argue sport is, borrowing a term from Karl Marx, America's great "opiate of the masses."

Sports also draw money—lots of it. They compel large scales of economy and production that globalize certain cultural values and bodies, often at the expense of others. Sports dictate cultural norms, policy, reform, and research—expensive research in biotechnologies and performance enhancement, and nutrition and exercise genetics. Too, sports channel public funds to revitalize urban development through sports stadia construction, outreach and urban development programs, and they inspire international policy and foreign diplomacy initiatives that use sport as a low-cost high-impact tool for international socioeconomic development and promoting gender equality. Sports also serve as an interesting backdrop for ruminations on the complexities of a postcapitalist society driven largely by celebrity culture. As media blitzes surrounding the incivilities and criminal actions of athletes from O.J. Simpson to Aaron Hernandez to Michael Vick go viral through mass, micro, and social media alike, many question the tangled threads that weave sports into a broader tapestry of social ills: violence, homophobia, racism, sexism, and classism. Finally, sports are an interesting place to examine the ways in which cultural perceptions of gender, sexuality, and race are normalized and or resisted, as evidenced by the recent Michael Sam and Donald Sterling controversies.

And, so, sports, and their spectacular athletes, do not always make for good news. Nor, it seems, do sports whet the appetite of those who feel conflicted over the endless wake of "beer and circus" splashed across a global stage by sports' jocks and its media. But, when organizations like the United Nations declare 2005 the International Year of Sport and Physical Education and use sport as a strategic part of their Millennium Development Goals, when sports continue to be lauded as a mainstay for personal, professional, social and economic well being, one is compelled to ask, can sports and their bodies really be all that bad? Throughout this book, we'll think about questions like these as we read and write and think hard about the complicated and controversial terrain of sport, its spectacular doings and its spectacles, its spectacular and its deviant bodies, and its spectacular claims and research that are changing the way we understand our relationship to sport as athlete, fan, and consumer.

A NOTE ON TERMINOLOGY: "SPORTS" VS. "SPORT"

Rather than the word sports, the term used throughout the remainder of this book is the singular form, *sport*. By sport I mean an institution with a certain set of ideologies and practices that shape the way we act in and come to understand our society. Individual sports are therefore a part of the larger institution of sport. One goal of this reader then is to help us think critically about sport and the way it impacts our everyday lives and identities.

READING SELECTION

As we work our way through the readings and assignments in this book we will be prompted to reconsider our assumptions about sport and the role it plays in contemporary American society. From the normalization of bodily ideals, to the technologization of the athlete's body—part machine/performance enhancement, part human—to the intertwining of racial, gendered, classed, able-bodied, and heterosexual privilege in sport culture, sport powerfully shapes the way we come to understand and value certain bodies and bodily practices over others. Sport also influences the way we socialize and the identities we assume in society, be it by way of directly playing a sport and identifying as an athlete, or by sharing in the joy and pain of spectating sport as a fan, playing sport video games as a gamer, even protesting against or advocating for sport as an activist. All of these identities are tied up in and contribute to the heartbeat of modern sport culture and its influence on American society.

To wit, working within the spatial limits of a textbook, *Sport* cannot cover everything interesting or important about sport. *Sport* also focuses, for the most part though not unproblematically, on American sport culture, as American sports remain the "center" of modern sporting culture, business, and ideology writ large. While not intended as an exhaustive overview of sport, included readings nonetheless present a diverse range of contemporary and important sporting issues and encourage you to reflect on your own relationship to sport and to reconsider your assumptions about both sport and sporting bodies.

To do so, selected readings and images connect sport to broader social issues: modernity, racism, sexism, homophobia, economic and international development and globalization, to name a few. A glance at the Table of Contents reveals readings have also been strategically arranged to introduce you to various genres of sports writing and rhetoric as well as to provide a balanced discussion surrounding some of the more controversial topics in sport, from "Pay for Play" to advancements and applications of sports genomics. The book thus begins with an invitation to reflect on how "sports talk" and its dominant metaphors shape our understanding of everyday cultural values. We continue our appreciation of language and sport with a survey of a few of literary sports journalism's most iconic and anthologized pieces, Giamatti's "Hyperbole's Child," Thompson's "The Kentucky Derby is Decadent and Depraved," and Williams's "The Crowd at the Ball Game." The book then shifts to readings and discussions surrounding sports and identity, focusing on opinion editorials, feature articles, magazine cover images, and scholarly articles and blogs that survey the complex landscape of sport and identity. From issues surrounding ritual, culture and sport fandom to discussions of sport and race, including the role of black athletes in historical activist movements (see Carlos, "1968") and the much heated debate over the ethics concerning "Pay for Play" in college athletics, readings, visuals, and activities push our thinking about how sport and identity and language are intimately bound. Likewise, they provide an opportunity to reflect on timely issues concerning sport as a gender-segregated institution, from the historical consequences of Title IX for women as well as current debates over how sport impacts LBGQTI communities. In "Either/Or," for example, Levy depicts the fascinating if tragic struggles of intersex track athlete Caster Semenya and her struggles to "fit in" to the binary gendered logic of Olympic-level sports. These kinds of ethical complexities also inform discussions around sport for disabled communities, and Keith Storey's "The Case Against the Special Olympics" provides a compelling if unexpected critique of the disabled community's major global sport platform. Likewise, Behar's "Will Genetics Ruin Sports?" and Macur's "Born to Run?" introduce us to current and fascinating discussions around advancements in the burgeoning world of sports genetics. Closing materials prompt us to consider the limits and potentials of sport in a global world, including the ethics of global sports markets and the use of sport and events like the World Cup as opportunities for activism concerning international development and human rights. The judiciously selected texts included herein provide both powerful critiques and celebrations of sport in a vast array of contexts so that you might consider and, ultimately, come to appreciate the complexity of modern American sporting culture and its growing impact on the world.

WRITING PROCESS

We might imagine sport as a metaphor for the writing process. Like an athlete, a writer becomes a writer by way of practice. Through what Debra Hawhee calls the "3 R's": *repetition, rhythm,* and *response,* athletes' develop a habitude in sport that makes them proficient at their craft. If we apply Hawhee's heuristic to writing we come to understand writing as a rhetorical process—a game?—that equally requires the honing of the 3 R's: repetition (invention and drafting), rhythm (style, voice, and delivery), and response (logical argumentation and evidence). And, just as with any athlete, there are good days and bad days. Some days we simply can't perform. Just as our most beloved athletes have the occasional bad games, as writers, we can also encounter days where the dreaded writer's block creeps in, or we simply flub a draft.

But, also like any good athlete, if we believe in and abide by the 3 R's, then we continue to write and revise and polish our performance, and slowly, steadily, our writing improves. This is the writing process in action as we develop the muscle memory required to flex our writing muscles with the strength and vigor necessary to write cogent, concise, convincing prose. And, also like sport, the more we play with writing, the more we come to appreciate the beauty of writing as a game that, at its best, provides us with endless opportunity to play with our voice; to revise and sharpen our perspectives and to craft logical arguments supported by sound evidence and research. These are the essential technical skills every good writer needs to play their "A game." This reader is intended to give us ample opportunity to develop these skills through the continual practice of reading, writing, and thinking critically about the role sport plays in contemporary society.

A final word about writing and sport: We might also think about writing as a *team sport*. Just as any athlete on a team knows she must perform as an individual, she also understands the indispensable role played by her teammates in achieving victory. So it is with writing. As we practice writing draft after draft, we ask our teammates to peer review our writing to provide constructive critique and feedback that helps us improve our writing. And, just as any good coach serves as both a mentor and teacher, in writing, instructors provide models of the kinds of successful writing "performances" that help students eventually reach their "A game." And, while the "team" is the core of an athlete's experience, they often reach out for extra help from trainers, nutritionists, doctors, and other professionals to help them improve their performance. So it is with writing. While we rely on the mentoring of our writing instructors, and we benefit from the help of teammates, we can also improve our writing by seeking outside assistance from other writing professionals, like writing tutors, often found on campus at writing centers. Here, we can get the one-on-one attention needed to really improve our writing so that we can achieve one writing victory after another as we engage with writing assignments that ask us to think about how the very sporting notions of competition and victory inform our understandings of American culture.

I have taught writing courses on sport, its media, its bodies, its conflicts and its celebrations for the past five years and I am always amazed at how much I learn from students as we work our way through sport and society by way of the writing process. As we work our way through the writing process in this reader, my hope is that we will come to develop an appreciation for both the world of sport and its bodies as much as the kinds of writing, thinking, and researching that help us thoughtfully articulate sport's impact on society in ways that are ultimately as challenging as they are inspiring. Happy practicing!

Works Cited

Hawhee, Debra. "Bodily Pedagogies: Rhetoric, Athletics, and the Sophists' Three R's." *College English* 65.2 (2002): 142-62. Print.

This exercise will help prepare you for Major Assignment #1: The Sports Memoir. Compose a two to three page essay in which you recount a vivid sporting experience and reflect on its significance. Why do you remember the event? What did you learn from the event? What important lesson(s) might you want to teach others about sport as it relates to this event? Remember to use descriptive language and other aspects of memoir and storytelling: setting/scene, moral or "so what," character development, and conflict to help you craft a compelling and coherent reflection. Share your reflections with the class during the next meeting.

In small groups, spend about 15 minutes informally researching one of the topics/themes mentioned in the Reading Selection section of the Introduction. What kind of information do you find about this topic? What prominent and current headlines and textual documents turn up in your search? As a group, brainstorm and collaboratively draft a 250-word journal that outlines your initial findings and asks interesting questions to help further research on the topic. Share your findings with the class. Your instructor might help collate responses to help start the beginning of a "research map" for topics related to readings in this book.

Read one of the selections from the Table of Contents and write a 300-500 word blog post summarizing its major argument and reflecting on its significance as a potential source for a broader research project. What would the project look like? What other kinds of sources might you want to include in the project? How would this source inform the project and serve as a springboard for future research?

What questions do you have about sport and culture and identity after reading the Introduction? Spend about ten minutes reflecting and free writing your reaction to the Introduction. What selections might you be most interested in reading and why? What kinds of research projects do you imagine yourself pursuing in this class concerning sport and how did the Introduction inform this direction? What other areas of sport might you be interested in exploring that were not considered in the Introduction?

Exercise science professor Jeffrey Segrave is also an athletic director at Skidmore College. His research concerns the sociolinguistics of sport, and he teaches courses on sport and social issues, including Olympic Studies. The following article originally appeared in the third volume of Culture, Sport, Society.

THE SPORTS METAPHOR IN AMERICAN CULTURAL DISCOURSE

By Jeffrey O. Segrave

Metaphor is one of the most distinctive and salient features of language. Nietzsche in fact took the metaphor so seriously that he considered it the basic principle of all language: so-called literal talk remained a sort of frozen sediment of metaphor.[1] Ortega y Gasset also valued the metaphor considering it, like Nietzsche, a principle component of reality: far from being the deformation of reality, it was rather its organization.[2] As both Nietzsche and Ortega y Gasset realized, the metaphor is nuclear rather than atomistic, an intellectual device that links rather than isolates the distinctive features of everyday experiences. It is therefore through rhetorical devices like metaphor that we communicate a common set of symbols; language, communication, symbolism and communal life become inseparable and interrelated components of an identifiable cultural perspective. As a result, culture becomes encoded in metaphor.

One of the sources of metaphor, and hence one of the mechanisms by which our communal reality is mediated, is the world of sport. The language of sport—'sportspeak' as Robert Lipsyte[3] once called it—has penetrated our entire national language system. R. Palmatier and H. Ray, in fact, have identified as many as 1700 commonly used sports metaphors, taken from more than 100 games and sports ranging from boxing ('catch someone off guard') to bull-fighting ('take the bull by the horns'), cricket ('shiver my timbers') to rowing ('pull your

1. F. Nietzsche, 'On Truth and Lies in the Nonmoral Sense,' in D. Breazeale (ed.), *Philosophy and Truth: Selections from Nietzsche's Notebooks of the Early 1870s* (Atlantic Highlands, NJ: Humanities Press, 1979), pp. 79–97.
2. J. Lukacs, *Historical Consciousness* (New York: Harper Row, 1968), p. 7.
3. R. Lipsyte, *Sportsworld: An American Dreamland* (New York: Quadrangle Books, 1975), p. 1.

From *Culture, Sport, Society* (2000).

weight'), polo ('come a cropper') to wrestling ('no holds barred').[4] The idea of sport as a metaphor for life ('life is a game') is so common in America and American literature that it has become a part of our conventional wisdom. But as frequently as we use the sports metaphor, often unwittingly, its omnipresence must be qualified by specificity. Metaphors from particular sports predominate in particular cultural discourses. The purpose of this article is to identify and account for the sports metaphors that dominate particular cultural discourses, often noting a change over time. In my analysis, I will uncover patterns of metaphor use and in so doing I will explore the nexus of shared values and assumptions that undergird our collective way of life. The four discourses I am most concerned with are warfare, politics, business and sexual relations, those discourses that have most readily embraced the sports metaphor.

WARFARE

The language of sport has long been incorporated into the language of the military. Shakespeare was one of the first to recognize that natural synergy between sport and war, a synergy grounded in the similarity between the means and ends of both—conquest, glory and victory through courage, aggression, and strength. In what is perhaps the most prominent and well-known example, King Henry, looking for an excuse to attack France, finds one upon receipt of a gift from the Dauphin—a present of 'tennis balls' which serves as an insult to the heroic king, an estimation of Henry's maturity, or lack of it:

> We are glad the Dauphin is so pleasant with us.
> His present and your pains we thank you for.
> When we have matched our rackets to these balls
> We will in France, by God's grace, play a set
> Shall strike his father's crown into the hazard
> Tell him he hath made a match with such a wrangler
> That all the courts of France will be disturbed
> With chaces (1, ii, 258–268)…
> And tell the pleasant Prince this mock of his
> Hath turned his ball into gunstones.[5]

However, while the sport of tennis, a frivolous indulgence among England's aristocratic youth at the time, may well have appealed to Shakespeare's audiences, the modern proclivity has tended toward a more overtly militaristic sport—football. After all, war, as Tom Callahan of the *U.S. News & World Report* has noted with parodic aplomb, is at least 'the moral equivalent of football'.[6] Both football and war share a fundamental structural

---

4. R.A. Palmatier and H.L. Ray, *Sports Talk: A Dictionary of Sports Metaphors* (New York: Greenwood Press, 1989).
5. *King Henry V,* 1, ii, 281–2.
6. Quoted in L. Berkow, 'Once Again, It's the Star-Spangled Super Bowl,' *New York Times*, 27 January 1991, 8.

homology as M. Real's definition of football suggests: 'North American professional football is an aggressive, strictly regulated team game fought between males who use both violence and technology to gain control of property for the economic gain of individuals within a nationalistic entertainment context'.[7]

Conflation of the metaphors and specialized vocabularies of football and war are commonplace. Seeking to disassociate himself from Lyndon Johnson's Vietnam war policy, Presidential hopeful, Hubert Humphrey, once remarked: 'I have not been calling the signals. I have been in the position of a lineman doing some of the downfield blocking'.[8] More recently, General 'Stormin' Norman Schwartzkopf described the final manoeuver in the Gulf War as 'the equivalent of a "Hail Mary" play on a football field[9] and Schwartzkopf, himself, was characterized as having the 'gut of a middle linebacker but a quarterback's brain'.[10] Brian Duffy of the *U.S. News & World Report* wrote that 'a stunning endgame killed Saddam Hussein's army'[11] and one of Schwartzkopf's officers concluded that Operation Desert Storm was 'like the Super Bowl to end Super Bowls'.[12] So prevalent is the football/war metaphor that Fred Mish, editor-in-chief of *Merriam-Webster Dictionary* claimed, in reference to the Gulf War, that George Bush had 'taken football words to war'.[13] Examples of the language of war in the language of football are equally legion: attack, blitz, bombs, ground and air assaults, offence and defence, scouts, and trenches are standard terms in football argot. Football coaches, as Real reminds us, are like 'field marshals directing troops trained in boot camp, aided by scouts, prepared for complex attack and defence maneuvers'.[14]

More recently, and in perfect keeping with the new technological sophistication associated with modern warfare, a new sport metaphor has crept into the national discourse of war—the video game metaphor. Reflecting the pinpoint accuracy and 'info-tech' wizardry of contemporary weaponry, the video game metaphor has appeared most recently in the discourse surrounding Operation Desert Storm. 'We hit the target with video game precision,' George Cheney noted,[15] and the *U.S. News & World Report* described the aerial assault on Baghdad as 'the "Nintendo" videos of bomb attack'.[16]

7. M. Real, 'Super Bowl: Mythic Spectacle,' *Journal of Communications,* 25 (1975), 43.
8. M.D. Tullai, 'Football and Politics,' *Scholastic Coach,* 58 (1989), 34.
9. B. Duffy, 'The 100-Hour War,' *U.S. News & World Report,* 11 March 1986, 14.
10. T. Mathews, C.S. Manegold and T.M. DeFrank, 'A Soldier of Conscious,' *Newsweek,* 11 March 1991, 34.
11. Duffy, 'The 100-Hour War,' 11.
12. Quoted in R. Wilkinson, 'Anatomy of a Cakewalk', *Newsweek,* 11 March 1991, 48.
13. Quoted in M. Capuzzo, *Philadelphia Inquirer,* 19 Jan. 1991, D2.
14. Real, 'Super Bowl: Mythic Spectacle', 36.
15. G. Cheney, '"We're Talking War": Symbols, Strategies, and Images,' in B.S. Greenberg and W. Gantz (eds.), *Desert Storm and the Mass Media* (Cresskill, NJ: Hampton Press, 1993), p. 63.
16. 'The Fury of Desert Storm,' *U.S. News & World Report,* 11 March 1981, 67.

But if, as several commentators have argued, football/war metaphors serve as crucial rhetorical resources for valorizing and rationalizing the ideological hegemony of white, male elites, as well as for desensitizing us to the horrors of war,[17] then the video game metaphor might suggest something new in the American cultural dialogue—the degendering of war and the escalation of public insensitivity to the realities of war. Unlike football, there is nothing inherently gender-specific about video games or increasingly about the demography of the armed forces. Perhaps the video game metaphor represents a shift away from androcentric forms of discourse, signaling less an intensification or renewal of the language, practices and values of male domination, as S. Jansen and D. Sabo[18] suggest, and more an incipient cultural acknowledgement of the diminishing relevance of gender in the conduct of our military agenda.

On the other hand, the video game metaphor would also appear to operate as an increasingly powerful form of cultural anesthetic, numbing us beyond the language of football to the atrocities of war and duping us into the false consciousness that modern warfare is somehow without human cost and suffering. So we mix our play/war metaphors—'the Nintendo War'—as easily as we mix our medical/war metaphors—'surgical strike'. Both sanitize the cruelties of war and both release us from feelings of remorse, guilt, and responsibility.

POLITICS

Not only did Shakespeare recognize the value of a good sports metaphor in the language of war, he also recognized its value in the language of politics. Exhorting his troops before the siege of Harfleur, King Henry V declared: 'I see you stand like greyhounds in the slips, straining upon the start. The game's afoot ...'[19]

The game's been afoot ever since and metaphors drawn from a wide variety of sports have emerged as an indelible feature of the American political landscape. Early metaphors were often taken from the honourable sport of pugilism. Theodore White wrote: 'Like aging prize-fighters, short of wind and stiffening of muscle, the Southerners were left with no reserve but cunning'.[20] But it was another Theodore, Theodore Roosevelt, who truly popularized the boxing metaphor, announcing his willingness to run as the Republican Presidential nominee with the following statement: 'My hat's in the ring. The fight's on,

---

17. S.C. Jansen and D. Sabo, 'The Sport/War Metaphor: Hegemonic Masculinity, the Persian Gulf War, and the New World Order' (hereafter 'The Sport/War Metaphor'), Sociology of Sport Journal, 11 (1994), 1–17; M.J. Shapiro, 'Representing World Politics: The Sport/War Intertext,' in J.D. Derian and M.J. Shapiro (eds.), *International/Intertextual Relations: Postmodern Readers of World Politics* (Lexington, MA: D.C. Heath, 1989), pp. 69–96.
18. Jensen and Sabo, 'The Sport/War Metaphor', 7.
19. King Henry V, 3, i, 31–2.
20. Quoted in W. Safire, *The New Language of Politics: An Anecdotal Dictionary of Catchwords, Slogans, and Political Usage* (New York: Random House, 1968), p. 421.

and I'm stripped to the buff'.[21] The 'hat in the ring' metaphor was to remain both durable and flexible: Harold Ickes once derided young Thomas E. Dewey for 'throwing his diaper in the ring'[22] and in 1967 the *New York Times* noted that Congressional candidate Shirley Temple Black had 'thrown her curls in the ring'.[23]

Over the course of the century the boxing metaphor, reflective in part of the mano-y-mano nature of early political campaigning as well as the ethic of fair play and sportsmanship, has given way to the bombastic football metaphor with its emphasis on teamwork and a win-at-all-cost mentality. Other individual sports metaphors have infiltrated the American political dialogue at one time or another, especially the horse-racing analogy with its references to front-runners and dark horses, long-shots and shoo-ins, also-rans and nose-outs[24]—a metaphor incidentally that reveals the seamier, more disreputable face of politics as well as the affinity of politics to gambling—and other team sports metaphors have proven popular on occasions—FDR, for example, dismissed his failures with 'I have no expectation of making a hit every time I come to bat,'[25] and Sherman Adams discarded the first Soviet sputnik with a refusal to become engaged in 'an outer-space basketball game'[26]—but the football metaphor has emerged as the pre-eminent figure of speech, the root metaphor of American political discourse.

Examples are legion, but just to name a few: John F. Kennedy once told his press secretary, Pierre Salinger, 'politics is like football. If you see daylight, go through it;'[27] former Secretary of State, Dean Acheson, once said that 'when the President fumbles, the whole goal line is open';[28] more recently, reporting on the progress of the campaign, one of George Bush's advisors noted that 'We're moving the ball on the ground just fine. Unless they make us put it in the air, why do it?,'[29] and Presidential hopeful, Pat Robertson, charged George Bush with stealing delegates away from him which was 'like trying to take a touchdown back after the game';[30] even more recently, Bill Clinton included the following remarks about the fragile peace in Bosnia in his 1998 State of the Union Address: 'This is like being ahead in the fourth quarter of a football game. Now is not the time to walk off the field and forfeit the victory'.[31] No one, of course, mixed football and political metaphors more frequently or more manipulatively—'public doublespeak' as F. Hardaway called

21. Ibid., p. 185.
22. Ibid.
23. Ibid.
24. Ibid., p. 101.
25. Ibid., p. 421.
26. Ibid.
27. Tullai, 'Football and Politics', 34.
28. Ibid.
29. Ibid., 35.
30. Ibid.
31. 'President Clinton's State of the Union Address', *New York Times*, 28 Jan. 1998, A19–20.

it[32]—than Richard Nixon, whose 'macho jocko' talk,[33] was as Hugh Rank writes, 'akin to verbal locker room swaggering of muscle-flexing *machismo* at the beach'.[34]

The salience of the football metaphor is partly grounded in the construct of teamwork and the concomitant values of loyalty, co-ordination, and unity, and a pious attitude toward hierarchy and authority, and if Nixon accentuated the aggressive dimension of teamwork with metaphors like 'tough it out,' 'zone defense,' and 'bottom line it,'[35] then Ronald Reagan emphasized the disciplinary aspect of teamwork with his constant, restraining references to his administration as 'team players'.[36] Subsequent to a political rebuff from Reagan after his depiction of the Kemp-Roth bill as a 'Trojan Horse,' controller David Stockman was referred to as 'a chastened team player'.[37] Even a contrite Stockman, himself, during his press conference, stated that 'the President asked me to stay on the team'.[38] To Reagan, to be a 'member of the President's team,' as one of his top officials referred to it,[39] clearly presumed and demanded the sublimation of the individual ego for the sake of the team goal.

But there is something more to the football metaphor than the notion of team unity and purpose. I. Balbus, for example, has argued that football both reflects and popularizes the technocratic model of contemporary politics, a model that asserts the neutral 'scientific' character of state economic decisions, the technical expertise of those who make them, and their overall integration in the form of a plan.[40] Football, like politics, becomes increasingly heroic, the preserve of men of mythic dimensions and capabilities, reducing the rest of the electorate to the role of spectator or fan. The danger is obvious—the ritualization and celebration of both football and politics is entertainment spectacles, and the corresponding exclusion, and ultimately the atrophy, of popular political will; citizenship transformed into acclamation. All of which suggests that the ultimate sports metaphor for the *fin de millinaire*—a metaphor often employed predictably by Reagan— is sadly but accurately the 'Monday-morning quarterback'.

---

32. F. Hardaway, 'Foul Play: Sports Metaphors as Public Doublespeak,' *College English*, 38 (1976), 78–82.

33. Nicholas Von Hoffman quoted in H. Rank (ed.), 'Watergate and Language,' *Language and Public Policy* (Urbana, IL: National Council of Teachers of English, 1974), p. 7.

34. Rank, 'Watergate and Language', p. 7.

35. Ibid.

36. J. Bineham, 'Some Ethical Implications of Team Sports Metaphors in Politics' (hereafter 'Some Ethical Implications'), *Communication Reports*, 4 (1991), 35–42.

37. E. Cowen, 'Chastened Team Player,' *New York Times*, 13 Nov. 1981, 39.

38. Quoted in Bineham, 'Some Ethical Implications,' 39.

39. Ibid., 38.

40. I. Balbus, 'Politics as Sports: The Political Ascendancy of the Sports Metaphor in America,' *Monthly Review*, 26 (1989), 26–39.

BUSINESS

According to J. Clancy[41] in a fascinating study based on an analysis of business speeches of 43 business leaders from the past 200 years, the most prominent metaphor in the discourse of business during the first half of the twentieth century was the metaphor of the journey, a metaphor by Clancy's account that spoke to the heritage of American business as a humanitarian endeavor dedicated to the service of society. 'The business of business,' George Draper-Dayton, the founder of Dayton-Hudson, once wrote in 1932, 'is serving society, not just making money'.[42] The journey metaphor also implied peril and the notion of a mission fraught with danger and potential failure.

The journey metaphor, however, with its altruistic connotations gradually made room for the game metaphor, an analogy that more precisely captured the intricacies and complexities of a burgeoning corporate America at the same time as it encapsulated the emergent ethics of instrumentalism, teamwork, and winning. Serving society, in other words, gave way to making a profit, production for consumption to maximizing shareholder wealth. Consequently, while Henry Ford could once write that 'business as a mere money-making game was not worth giving much thought,'[43] Andrew Carnegie could also proclaim that 'the end was money and yet more money … business is the greatest game in the world'.[44] Walter Winston, once chair of Citicorp, also talked of 'winning the game in the marketplace'[45] and Lee Iacocca, CEO of Chrysler, advocated game principles as directly relevant to business: teach the fundamentals, enforce discipline, and play as a team.[46] In the 1983 study of the top business executives of their day, Donaldson and Lorsch aptly noted that, business leaders 'are fundamentally gamesmen, motivated to win the game they are playing'.[47]

But—and perhaps predictably by now—the generic game metaphor has given way to the more specific, and increasingly ubiquitous football metaphor. 'No figure of speech is as tenth as seductive to the businessman,' writes Whyte.[48] Reflecting a more modern zeitgeist, Ross Perot recently dismissed the 'level playing field' metaphor, attributing US post-war economic domination over Japan rather to American ownership of 'both teams and the stadium'. Perot also advised "blocking and tackling" instead of 'buying

---

41. J.J. Clancy, The Invisible Powers: The Language of Business (hereafter The Invisible Powers) (Lexington, MA: D.C. Heath, 1989).

42. Quoted in J. O'Toole, *Vanguard Management: Redesigning the Corporate Future* (Garden City, NY: Doubleday, 1986), p. 147.

43. H. Ford, *My Life and Works* (New York: Doubleday, 1923), p. 41. .

44. Quoted in J.K. Winkler, *Incredible Carnegie* (New York: Vanguard Press, 1931), p.95.

45. Quoted in H. Levinson and S. Rosenthal, CEO: *Corporate Leadership in Action* (New York: Basic Books, 1984), p. 69.

46. L. Iacocca, *Iacocca* (New York: Bantam Books, 1986).

47. G. Donaldson and J.E. Lorsch, *Decision Making at the Top* (New York: Basic Books, 1983), p. 25.

48. W.H. Whyte, 'The Language of Business,' in H.A. Estrin (ed.), *Technical and Professional Writing: A Practical Anthology* (New York: Harcourt, Brace and World, 1983), p. 82.

new uniforms' in our escalating competition with the Japanese.[49] Not unsurprisingly, the language of business—'reverse gobbledygook' as Whyte calls it[50]—is also more than reminiscent of the rhetoric of Republican Presidents like Nixon and Reagan. Harold Green at ITT, for example, speaks of his associates as 'a team,' with a 'game plan' that frequently 'huddles' and occasionally needs 'new players'.[51]

The success of the football metaphor is predicted, according to Whyte, on 'its adaptability to all sorts of situations'.[52] It is, as Whyte argues, a 'satisfying' analogy because football is 'bounded by two goal lines and is thus finite. There is always a solution'.[53] But it is how the solution is reached that is perhaps most telling. Success in business, like success in football, is predicted on aggression, instrumentalism, regimentation, and the zero-sum game that epitomizes corporate capitalism as an ideology. Both football and business require a highly specialized division of labour which, as Clancy puts it, presumes 'precision, analysis, and optimization of each process and the worker's unthinking performance of regimented tasks…If there is a game, that is not a game, play that is not play, with the focus on regimentation as opposed to spontaneity, it is football'.[54] This is what makes the football analogy so appealing and as Whyte recognizes so 'treacherous';[55] while the lingo of football may serve as a malleable dramaturgical device for motivation and persuasion, it can also serve as a rhetorical subterfuge that falsely clarifies moral complexity with images of ethical simplicity. Human issues are portrayed as strategic dilemmas, moral issues as technical problems.

The truth of the matter of course is that football is not *like* American business; it *is* American business. The metaphor is so complete that it appears incontrovertible, even, ironically, from a feminist perspective. The task of both football and business is unequivocally unimodal, the development of the most efficient means to achieve the predetermined and uncontestable end—success, winning, and making a profit. But football is more than just a caricature of corporate America, it has become a caricature of our entire corporate-military complex, which is why the football metaphor is so commonplace in the languages of war, politics and business, and why it is ultimately so dangerous—'normal problems,' as John Updike so poignantly reminds us, 'have no rules and no end'.[56]

49. Quoted in D.P. Levin and P. Ingrassia, 'New on the Inside: Ross Perot Tells GM and its Rivals How They Must Change,' *Wall Street Journal*, 8 Nov. 1986, 7.
50. Whyte, 'The Language of Business,' p. 82.
51. Quoted in H. Geneen and A. Moscow, *Managing* (Garden City, NY: Doubleday, 1984), p. 99.
52. Whyte, 'The Language of Business,' p. 82.
53. Ibid., p. 83.
54. Clancy, *The Invisible Powers*, p. 47.
55. Whyte, 'The Language of Business,' p. 83.
56. Quoted in J. Reston, 'Sports and Politics in America,' *New York Times*, 12 Sept. 1969, 42.

SEXUAL RELATIONS

As common a rhetorical convention as the sport metaphor is in the language of corporate-*realpolitik*, nowhere do we appear to have developed a more popular affliction for its use than in the language of sexual relations. And, once again, Shakespeare provides us with an historical template; the hunt metaphor, perhaps not surprisingly given Shakespeare's patriarchal and traditional society, is the most prominent metaphor used. Referring to Rosaline, Romeo notes that 'The game was ne'er so fair'.[57] Likewise, Ulysses remarks to Nestor:

> Set them down
> For the sluttish spoils of opportunity
> And daughters of the game.[58]

No doubt in deference to the subtleties and intricacies of romantic interplay, Shakespeare also used the angling metaphor. Having sent Hermione and Polinixes out into the garden alone, Leontes comments: 'I am angling now, Though you perceive me not how I give line'.[59] The often censored French poet, Theophile de Viau also predicted our contemporary proclivity for the sports metaphor when, in 1622, he conscripted the tennis metaphor into service in the infamous lines:

> If you kiss her, count fifteen
> If you touch her buds, thirty...[60]

The hunt and tennis metaphors of medieval and Renaissance Europe, however, have more recently been replaced by a variety of sports metaphors, among the most prominent being 'go all the way,' 'sink the putt,' 'put the puck in the net,' 'get a hole on one,' and 'score'.[61] But of all the language used this way, baseball jargon is by far the most frequently heard. One can, for example, 'get to first, second, or third base,' 'hit a home run,' 'go to extra innings,' or 'strike out'. In my own informal investigation among a sample of 127 undergraduate students, I found that 47 percent of all sports metaphors used in this way were drawn from the sport of baseball. The four most commonly reported metaphors—'get to first, second, or third base,' 'hit a home run,' 'score,' and 'strike out'—accounted for 57 percent of all sports metaphors reported.[62]

The salience of the baseball metaphor may be because it offers the possibilities of gradation of sexual encounter; that is, one can 'get to first, second, or third base,' before

57. *Romeo and Juliet*, 1, iv, 39.
58. *Troilus and Cressida*, 4, vi, 61–3.
59. *The Winter's Tale*, 1, ii, 180.
60. Quoted in Alexander, 'The Birth of Tennis,' *Lingua Franca* (Dec./Jan. 1999), 18–20.
61. J.O. Segrave, 'The Perfect 10: "Sportspeak" in the Language of Sexual Relations,' *Sociology of Sport Journal*, 11 (1994), 95–113.
62. Ibid.

finally 'hitting a home run' or 'striking out'. Here, the sexual interlude is likened to an epic sprint around the bases in which more venturesome levels of physical intimacy are accomplished with every base. Maybe it is simply that 'getting a hit,' especially a 'home run,' is as difficult and as exciting in baseball as it is in sexual relations.

Perhaps, it is that baseball embodies a more primitive, elemental myth, the myth of the man carrying a club. Hercules, the Greek patron of athletics, was often pictured carrying a club, and in Bernard Malamud's *The Natural*,[63] the bat, Roy Hobbs' 'Wonderboy,' the 'foolproof lance,' serves as the archetype symbol of strength and fertility, power and potency, an image reminiscent of Marshall Smelser's description of Babe Ruth as 'the man with the club, primitive but successful, the fundamental man who was victor over everything'.[64]

But perhaps the underlying homology between baseball and sexual relations revolves around the issue of privacy. Baseball is, after all, a more private game than football or field hockey for example. In both football and field hockey, all the players are always visible, on the field or on the bench, under our gaze; in baseball, players are often invisible, in the dugout or in the bullpen, out of sight. Privacy in sport is rare; only in baseball can one find privacy and security of home, as baseball commissioner Bart Giamatti so beautifully reminds us:

> Home plate radiates a force no other spot on the field possesses … even opponents gather at the same curious, unique place called home plate. Catcher and batter, siblings who may see the world differently but share the same sight lines, are backed up and get ruled by the parent figure, the umpire…This tense family clusters at home, facing the world together, each with separate responsibilities and tasks and perspectives, each with different obligations and instruments.[65]

All literary romance begins—as Odysseus so well knew—with a journey of discovery, a separation from home, a tour around the base paths, and it ends with a rejoicing, a reunion at home. Both baseball and sex are ultimately about romance, about union and reunion; both as Giamatti notes are about the 'restoration of the right relations among things—and going home is where that restoration occurs because that is where it matters most'.[66]

Upon deeper reflection, perhaps the language of baseball is most suitably employed metaphorically to represent sexual relations because both sex and baseball so poignantly reflect the problematic nexus of self-interest and social responsibility. No sport more

63. B. Malamud, *The Natural* (New York: Avon Books, 1952).
64. M. Smelser, 'The Babe on Balance,' *American Scholar*, 44 (1975), 301.
65. A.B. Giammati, *Take Time for Paradise: Americans and Their Games* (New York: Summit Books, 1989), pp. 87–8.
66. Ibid., p. 92.

than baseball symbolically enacts the ontological tensions between domestic, private, and individual concerns, on the one hand, and social, public and communal concerns on the other. After all, baseball reflects a recurrent cultural dilemma: how to reconcile communal values with a powerful tradition of heroic individualism and privatism. Although this tension operates on several different levels—from the clash of two teams each demanding intense social loyalties to the mythic clash between pitcher and batter—it is crystallized in the confrontation between the batter at home plate and the opposition arrayed in the field. It is here that the game most vividly and most earnestly seeks to reconcile notions of community and fair play with those of privacy and individual heroism.

Nor, as a matter of fact, is the language of baseball gender specific. It is only by default assumption that we assume it is. The language of baseball is, of course, also the language of softball; there is nothing inherently androcentric about such euphemisms as 'strike out' or 'get to first base'. Given the consensual nature of sexual relations, it is oxymoronic to presuppose that sex is an exclusively male domain, although our default assumption does suggest a cultural perspective that reinforces a traditional masculine sovereignty even in this the most domestic of habits.

The greater danger in all of this parlance is that it functions as a mechanism for transforming a profound and delicate human relations issue into a problem of strategy. It objectifies women linguistically conceiving of them as parts, and it constructs notions of masculine hegemony and hegemonic masculinity, in the end, contributing to a larger cultural discourse through which patterns of empowerment and subordination are socialized into successive generations of men and women. Of all our linguistic proclivities, the athleticization of sexual relations may be our most dangerous, the most threatening to our ongoing sense of humanness—the reduction and transmogrification of the most human of affairs to the level of a game.

CONCLUSION

Once a mere establishment of language, a rhetorical flourish, the metaphor is now recognized not only for its affective and oratorical efficacy but for its cognitive contribution. Its study, according to P. Ricoeur, is less a matter of semantics and more a matter of hermeneutics.[67] Or as Aristotle once wrote: 'Midway between the unintelligible and the common place, it is a metaphor which most produces knowledge'.[68] Consequently, what I have attempted to do in this essay is to demonstrate the ways in which the sports metaphor is, to borrow a phrase from E. Kittay, 'cognitively meaningful,'[69] the site of

---

67. P. Ricouer, 'The Metaphorical Process as Cognition, Imagination, and Feeling,' in S. Sacks (ed.), *On Metaphor* (Chicago: University of Chicago Press, 1979).
68. *Rhetoric*, III, 1410b.
69. E.F. Kittay, *Metaphor: Its Cognitive Force and Linguistic Structure* (Oxford: Claredon Press, 1987), p. 2.

many a deep-seated, often unexamined belief or attitude and so a significant factor in the structure of knowledge and experience.

In so doing, however, I have tended to adopt an accuracy or representationalist perspective, one that suggests that any given metaphor validates some authentic and accessible objective reality. This view presumes the possibility of an epitemic position 'outside' of language and reality, a supposedly neutral position. However, within post-structuralist and anti-representationalist positions, the metaphor is viewed as more than just reflective of reality but actually constitutive of it. Metaphors, as Lakoff and Johnson put it, 'create realities' and therefore serve as 'a guide for future action'.[70] Or to steal a term from Althusser and Marxist cultural studies, the metaphor 'interpellates' its subjects; it beckons subjects to be certain kinds of people.[71] Consequently, as Rorty points out: 'It is useless to ask whether one vocabulary rather than another is close to reality. For different vocabularies serve different purposes, and there is no such thing as a purpose that is closer to reality than another purpose'.[72] The better question to ask about the sports metaphor then becomes not whether any one particular metaphor provides a better picture of a knowable reality than another, but since any way of talking about war, politics, business and sexual relations will inevitably and in fact necessarily elevate one set of human purposes over another, what objectives and whose agenda will be furthered by mediating cultural life through certain sports metaphors rather than others.

Several studies have fruitfully adopted this approach. Jansen and Sabo, for example, have demonstrated that the sport/war metaphors during the Persian Gulf War were used as powerful rhetorical devices for mobilizing the patriarchal values that construct, mediate and maintain hegemonic forms of masculinity.[73] Similarly, S. Walk has shown how Lyndon Johnson and Ronald Reagan differentially employed the footrace metaphor to frame basic assumptions about public policy in keeping with their own party ideologies.[74] Finally, Bineham has argued that the deployment of team sport metaphors in the discourse surrounding David Stockman's offer of resignation as Reagan's Director of the Office of Management and Budget constituted subjects with a particular range of expectations, including the public's orientation to the situation as well as the form of Stockman's response.[75]

As each of these studies suggest, the sports metaphor has so thoroughly colonized our cultural discourse that the guiding logics and ethical dimensions of sports are now

---

70. G. Lakoff and M. Johnson, *Metaphors We Live By* (Chicago: University of Chicago Press), p. 156.
71. L. Althusser, *Lenin and Philosophy* (New York: Basic Books, 1970), pp. 170–7.
72. R. Rorty, Objectivity, Relativism, and Truth: Philosophical Papers Volume 1 (Cambridge: Cambridge University Press, 1990), p. 3.
73. Jansen and Sabo, 'The Sport/War Metaphor'.
74. S.R. Walk, 'The Footrace Metaphor in American Presidential Rhetoric,' *Sociology of Sport Journal*, 12 (1995), 36–55.
75. Bineham, 'Some Ethical Implications'.

routinely employed in the form of language as frames for not only commenting upon and understanding a vast complexity of issues but for interpellating us as cultural beings who are a part of the complexity. Explaining who or what agenda is best served by the deployment of sports metaphors in a wide array of cultural arenas and settings remains the ongoing challenge for future research on the topic.

Invent

More than a decade ago, Segrave notes that there were more than 1,700 commonly used sports metaphors in everyday American discourse. How many can you think of? Spend ten or so minutes quickly jotting down all the sports metaphors that come to mind and, if applicable, arrange by sport.

Collaborate

Segrave argues that the sports metaphor carries important connotations for how we understand culture and society. He focuses in particular on the impact of the sports metaphor in discourse concerned with warfare, business, and sexual relations. In a small group, brainstorm 10-20 sports metaphors and their corresponding sports (or, compare and select from your individual lists from the Invent exercise above) and try to arrange these metaphors according to Segrave's tripartite scheme. After you sort your metaphors, brainstorm possible connotations and cultural values these metaphors carry in these discursive contexts. Are there any other discursive genres to which your metaphors apply that Segrave doesn't mention? What are the gendered implications of sports metaphor? Share and discuss your findings and reflect on how the exercise changes your understanding of the relationship between sports and language.

Explore

What sports metaphors do you regularly use in your own daily language practice? Make a journal log over the next 24-48 hours in which you record all the sports metaphors you observe yourself using in everyday language practice. Then, write an essay in which you reflect on your findings. How do you use sports metaphors in everyday language, and how, given your reading of Segrave, do you understand your own values about warfare, business, sexual relations, etc. given your patterns of sports metaphor usage?

Angelo Bartlett Giamatti was the president of Yale University and the seventh Commissioner of Major League Baseball, during which time he oversaw the "Pete Rose betting scandal."

HYPERBOLE'S CHILD

BY A. BARTLETT GIAMATTI

It suddenly became clear to me, sitting in Madison Square Garden on September 29, watching the preliminary bouts to the Ali-Shavers fight, that the basis of sport is work. Running, jumping, lifting, pushing, bending, pulling, planting the legs and using the back—these exertions are essential to physical labor and to athletic competition. The closeness of a given game to the rituals and efforts of work invests the game with dignity; without that proximity to labor, the game would be merely a release from work instead of a refinement of it. The radical difference between work and game, however, occurs when limits or rules are imposed on this labor, patterns which acknowledge that this new work, this sport, is not a matter of life and death. Whereas that work, the work of your back and arms, in field or mill, on ship or in forest, was crucial to your survival, and to the survival of those dependent on you, this work is different; it is delimited, separate, independent, a refinement of reality but distinct. This work is fully as serious and difficult as real work, but this unreal work is not coextensive with life. This work of sport, usually but not always at some predetermined point, will have an end. It will be over, not to begin again with the sun. This work, unlike that real work, does not sustain life in any immediate and practical way, such as providing food; but this unreal serious work does sustain life in the sense that is makes life bearable. It allows all of us to go back renewed to whatever real work we do, perhaps to go back for a moment redeemed. I have often thought that the world-wide appeal of soccer lies in part in its unabashed emphasis on penetrating the other's territory; partly in its wonderfully seamless and continuous quality, where no quarter is given, no pause taken, but like the tides men come and go; but mostly in its denial of the use of the hands. For the millions who work with their hands, there can be no greater relief than to escape the daily focus on

From *Rules of the Game: The Best Sports Writing from Harper's Magazine* (2010).

those instruments of labor, and no greater confirmation of the centrality of hands to life than their denial in this sport.

These notions formed while I waited for the Ali-Shavers fight. I had been watching the undercard, and admiring the way Alfredo Evangelista of Uruguay would get his back into his punches, like a man digging a hole, and how the sheer expenditure of effort had forced Pedro Soto to fight Evangelista's fight until, in the eighth round, Soto was so badly punished by the patient, awkward digging of Evangelista that the referee stopped the bout. At this moment of victory, which is also a moment of reunion, as the men finish work and leave together, the crowd's attention was diverted from Soto and Evangelista by the presence of Ali, who suddenly appeared in the back of the Garden and roared through the aisles shaking his finger, surrounded by about ten of his entourage. The crowd responded with delight—"A-li, A-li, A-li," they chanted; and when they turned from that spectacle, Evangelista and Soto were gone. If for most athletes and spectators sport is work conceived in some special way as play, for Muhammad Ali sport is work conceived as theater.

Ali has theatricalized his work in that, rather than continuing to serve his work as a worker, or slave, he has made what he does serve him as a setting. Ali has extended himself and boxing, the sport most like work, in the direction of theater by emphasizing the other being that lives beside the worker in every athlete, the actor. In the athlete worker and actor meet, the expenditure of energy and the power to give shape come together. Of course, workers "perform" tasks and actors work hard; the spectrum worker-athlete-actor is not a broad one and the three points are distinguished by emphasis more than anything else. As the athlete resembles the worker in the way he exerts his body, and in the way he catches the deep rhythms in work, so the athlete resembles the actor in the way he uses his body to express what I can only call an inner vision. Both athlete and actor release energy in order to restrain it and in restraining it, to give shape to a new idea. Both are judged effective or ineffective (that is what "good" or "bad" means in these two professions) by how well they execute what is set them; and for both athlete and actor execution depends not on inspiration or luck or the weather, inner or outer, but on coordination, economy of gesture, timing, good coaching.

It is Ali who has brought to the surface the actor in every athlete more successfully and obsessively than anyone else. Ali is in many ways profoundly bored, and he knows only one craft. In order to remain interested in what he must do, Ali has allowed the performer to erupt unchecked, burying the worker in him, the skilled artisan with extraordinary hands and legs and specific, worldly ambitions, under the sulfurous, scalding lava of his improvisations. Improvisation is the only way he has found to order the endless days: the monologizing, poetizing, and prophesying, all that grimacing and exhorting and praying, is the style of a man who is not even sure he knows when his acts are simply acting, but who does know he does not care.

And when the fight is in view, and training is required, a regimen guaranteed to exacerbate boredom with brutal fatigue, Ali goes deeper into his protean reserves and whole dramas emerge. There is often the heroic beast fable—Ali will slay a dragon in the form of a Bear, a Rabbit, a Gorilla, or, lately, an Acorn. As time goes on, other subplots emerge. Howard Cosell once regularly took a part; occasionally whole countries, like Zaire, are cast. In recent years the press has been less and less willing to be the megaphone to this sideshow, but the press has no choice but to be megaphone when the source of news insists on defining himself as a barker. So we are treated to sermons, doggerel, parables, myths, even creations from whole cloth: "Jimmy Ellis, Sparring Partner, Knocks Down Champ Twice Today." That particular story, out of Ali's Pennsylvania training camp some eight days before the bout, is a good example of the problems Ali poses and the problem he has.

Perhaps only a headline announcing the pope's intention to remarry would be as immediately unconvincing as the news that Ellis knocked Ali down twice in one round. The gloves used in sparring sessions weigh sixteen ounces apiece; Billy Carter would have trouble knocking over a schooner of Schlitz with one of those mitts. Then there is the fact that these two know each other well, having met more than twenty years ago in Louisville when they were both young teenagers. Ali and Ellis cannot surprise each other and while Ellis would work for a man he could knock down, Ali would not hire a man who might even try it. Even once. But twice! Such an idea staggers the imagination.

What put out the story then? In part because whereas the rest of us were born under a star, Ali was born under a rhetorical figure, hyperbole, defined by the great Quintilian as "an elegant straining of the truth." Surely Ali was also impelled by a realization that the advance sale for September 29 was slow; that the publicity, at the time of the Lance affair and a hot mayoral primary race in New York, had been soggy; and he was propelled by that instinct of his to hype the gate, to work his own crowd (as he would do as Soto and Evangelista finished work), to shill for himself, to be both the show and the man who hustled them into the tent. If there is one born every minute, Ali wants to be the midwife. But does that deep instinct justify putting out such a palpably transparent story as the one about being knocked down twice? No, that instinct does not justify straining the truth quite so inelegantly. An even deeper need justifies the story, the need to pump up once again the white man's hope to see the black champion beaten.

Here we engage Ali's deepest game, the only work he does with a will. While you are being encouraged to think he can be beaten, you are being allowed to understand that the form the encouragement takes is fraudulent. Your ability to see through the con undermines your belief in his vulnerability (he can't be beaten if he says he can) and reaffirms your faith in his theatrical mastery (knocked down twice, my foot! What a showman). You are now his. Ali has transformed all the potential spectators, the fight crowd, into something far different, an audience; he has enticed the naive, titillated the devoted, amused the jaded, outraged the mass; he has had it out with his opponent now in the press and on television for at least two weeks, his sense of pace impeccable, the whole spectacle building to the grand final number, the climax just before the last curtain, the weigh-in; and, most important, he has managed to legitimize race as an issue in the fight by making it part of the show, or, for those so inclined, the whole show. One so inclined is Ali, and the last scene is played.

At the weigh-in, the state lends whatever moral and legal credibility it has to the ritual of assessing the fighters' weight and physical fitness. They are always found to be fit. Examinations and X rays conducted on September 28 could find no injuries, indeed no trace of trauma, resulting from the two knockdowns suffered by the champion during training. And after the tape and scales, Ali takes over, and tears a passion to tatters, splitting the ears of the groundlings in the press, o'erdoing Termagant and out-heroding Herod, now the player, now the Prince, doing all the parts and, at the weigh-in on September 28, ranting at length about the theatrical nature of his ranting, exposing the structure of his illusion, the old actor getting himself worked up for the part, doing what Elvis Presley could no longer do, getting into the circle, recapturing the energy and interest to go out on stage by pretending to have it—all of this working precisely to the extent that all the hangers-on and reporters and onlookers and cuties and commission people and cameramen and friends and spies and flunkies and acolytes, who have seen it dozens of times, get pulled in, and begin to laugh and nudge and shake their heads and stamp their feet as if it were the first time; and yet, if you listen rather than acquiesce, at the center of this whirlwind of words and gestures and postures and poses the chosen epithet of the chosen opponent is chanted and honed and, finally, hurled like a knife at the man it signifies. The real fight is now almost over, as Ali turns on his opponent all the power of the opponent, turning the man's physical characteristics, his background, his class, his worth as a man against him. Ali deflects the opponent's strength from Ali, and now the opponent is left, in the weeks or hours remaining (for this process does not start at the weigh-in), to fight himself, to fight his ugliness or his awkwardness or his lack of education or, in the most savage blow of all, to fight his race. If the man is white, he is not allowed to be the White Hope. Ali bestows this duty as if it were a dukedom, and then watches while the opponent tries to figure out whether to hoist this load, and, if he will, how to gain a purchase on it, and, once it is up, where to take it. It is too easy.

With black fighters there is more sport, though the press here draws a line and the public does not, evidently, get the full force of Ali's treatment of black opponents. But the technique is clear. In calling Frazier a gorilla, or Shavers "shiftless," Ali simply unleashes the power of traditional racist epithets. He thus sets his black opponent to battling two chimeras, both now identified with himself. The opponent must confront his main sense of himself, his strength, his identity as a black man, as if it were a weakness; he must struggle with, rather than use, the source of his power, because this black champion has turned their race into a vicious insult. Lest the opponent miss the point to the burden that he alone now carries, Ali will during the fight clarify his status for him as he did for Shavers by calling him throughout the fight, according to reports, "nigger." It is a technique as simple, and decent, as rubbing your glove's laces on an opponent's swollen eye.

But while Ali has a black opponent fighting his blackness, he also has the other man fighting his whiteness. Everyone who fights Ali must be the white hope. The gate demands it, and hyperbole's child would have it no other way. Every opponent is the champion of that vast, hostile white mass that, since February 28, 1964, when Ali announced that he had a few months before joining the Nation of Islam, and especially since his refusal in Houston on April 28, 1967, to be inducted into the army, has wanted to see him knocked out. So, at least, Ali believes; and so believed the elegantly dressed, affable black man who sat behind me at the Ali-Shavers bout, and who laughingly insisted for fifteen rounds that I had come to see Ali beaten by my fighter, Shavers. But I believe that the act at Houston and the announcement about the Nation of Islam were themselves not the causes of an attitude, but the results of an even older attitude of Ali's. For those acts of 1967 and 1964 were acts of separation, of secession from black and white America's traditional assumptions about how to behave, and were themselves responses to the conviction, held by the boy who by his account in My Own Story felt a "deep kinship" with Emmett Till, that they wanted him out, and that he would dance inside and sting them before they could put him down and put him out.

Ali's boredom with training and fighting only masks a fear, a fear of being peripheral, a terror of being out, and that fear account for his need to be at the center of something, a stage, a ring, a Nation, a cosmic racial drama. His fear of being marginal accounts for the savagery of his desire to get in, to land the first blow, and for the outlandish intensity of his acting center stage, before the bell has ever rung or the lights have dimmed. Ali's sense of racial antagonism forces him to scorn his black opponents for being black, while at the same time smearing Frazier, Norton, Shavers with whiteface, grotesquely deforming the other's face in every way while trumpeting the beauty of his own, that clean-shaven, smooth, unblemished face so unlike the scarred, roughened laborers' faces his mocks. His is an extraordinary series of performances, culminating in the weigh-in, each scene contributing, as do rounds, to that overall accumulation of episode and pace and shaped energy we call a starring role. He has, particularly in the last year or so as preparation gets more and more difficult, set up the actual fight as an anticlimax to the weeks before it. And certainly the bout on the evening of September 29 was an anti-climax; for, regardless of what you saw on television, where close-ups on intense faces covered a great deal of standing, leaning, peek-a-booing, clowning, missing, waiting, the Shavers-Ali fight was a good fight only once you had accepted how much less good a fighter Ali has become.

The real struggle goes on earlier, when Ali transforms the coming fight into a ghastly minstrel show, he never more black than when the other end man is daubed in white, the other never blacker than when Ali sneers at his color, the races locked together, at one and at odds, the whole a parody of race relations in every city street and union and school and firehouse and subway and unemployed black waking hour in America, the prizefight finally only a skirmish in the larger race war, this little battle masquerading as a show starring Muhammad Ali and a cast of everyone else.

Ali has known from the beginning what every good athlete learns: make him play your game, fight your fight, and you will beat him every time. But Ali has also learned a lesson kept from the most athletes precisely by the pleasure of their work, a pleasure now beneath Ali, a pleasure in work insufficiently exhilarating to one who has the art born in him, the art of filling a scene: and that subtler lesson is that while you can only beat him if he fights your fight, you can destroy him if he acts in your play. If, like Othello, he will accept the role you set for him, you will master him as you master all scenes. And if you can make him play nigger and white racist all at once, surely you are the greatest and he is yours. This is, after all, an old drama and an old style, learned from the white slave-masters; they were the ones who based their play on others' brutal work and who forced the others to enact roles simply to survive. Ali, with his incredible gifts of body and mind, has brought the central drama of his people's history in America to a bright, gaudy life, for everyone to see. He has brought the patterns of work, play, and acting that commingle in slaves and athletes to the surface, and he has refined his techniques for communicating, through the media, what those old patterns mean.

Sitting in Madison Square Garden on September 29, I did not think Ali beat Shavers; even giving Ali all the even rounds, I scored the fight for Shavers, 8–7. I do not think Ali beat Shavers this September any more than many think he beat Ken Norton in September of 1976, or beat Jimmy Young in the spring of 1976. I also do not believe that Ali, at this point, really cares what anyone thinks, or cares what really happened. The fights in the ring, vastly remunerative, full of effort and clowning, are only incidental to the real battle. I believe he will participate in the ring fights longer than he should because he cannot stop until his has fought down the need, compounded of fear and fury, to act out completely what, in his view, it is to be black in America, to be always living at the margin, on the edge, in a position where, despite the pain of your work and the beauty of your play, a man may announce with superb casualness at any given moment that you have been counted out.

"Hyperbole's Child" is considered one of *Harper's Magazine's* best pieces of sportswriting. Why? What makes the piece powerful and evocative? How does the writing style change the way you think of sport? What is the tone and mood of Giamatti's piece? How does he describe the game of boxing? In one column, make a list of all the textual conventions (metaphor, simile, analogy, verb tense, thick description, for example) that strike you as a reader; in a second column, make a list of their effect on you as a reader. For example, how does a particular turn of phrase make you "feel" or "think" about Ali or boxing in a certain way?

Muhammad Ali's career is interesting and rich and riddled with controversial historical anecdotes, including his stance on the Civil Rights Movement and Vietnam War. In small groups, spend five to 10 minutes researching Ali's career and life choices and discuss how this information informs your reading of "Hyperbole's Child." What would an important takeaway from the piece be for today's readers? How should we remember Ali and what makes him so iconic as an athlete?

Write a descriptive essay in which you profile a famous athlete using some of the textual conventions you observed from Giamatti's writing in the Invent exercise. What story do you want to tell? What scene do you set? What message do you want to impart? What mood do you want to convey? Use language to sketch a descriptive portrait of an athlete that connects her or his career to broader socio-historical implications, as Giamatti used Ali's boxing career as an analogy for racial relations in the 1970s.

Hunter S. Thompson has written extensively on sport and its politics, both in literary journals as well as for ESPN's original blog, Page 2. "The Kentucky Derby Is Decadent and Depraved" is considered to have originated gonzo journalism and departs radically from the traditional conventions of sports journalist practices.

THE KENTUCKY DERBY IS DECADENT AND DEPRAVED

By Hunter S. Thompson

I got off the plane around midnight and no one spoke as I crossed the dark runway to the terminal. The air was thick and hot, like wandering into a steam bath. Inside, people hugged each other and shook hands...big grins and a whoop here and there: "By God! You old bastard! Good to see you, boy! Damn good...and I mean it!"

In the air-conditioned lounge I met a man from Houston who said his name was "something or other"—"but just call me Jimbo"—and he was here to get it on. "I'm ready for anything, by God! Anything at all. Yeah, what are you drinkin?" I ordered a Margarita with ice, but he wouldn't hear of it: "Naw, naw...what the hell kind of drink is that for Kentucky Derby time? What's wrong with you, boy?" He grinned and winked at the bartender. "Goddam, we gotta educate this boy. Get him some good whiskey..."

I shrugged. "Okay, a double Old Fitz on ice." Jimbo nodded his approval.

"Look." He tapped me on the arm to make sure I was listening. "I know this Derby crowd, I come here every year, and let me tell you one thing I've learned—this is no town to be giving people the impression you're some kind of faggot. Not in public, anyway. Shit, they'll roll you in a minute, knock you in the head and take every goddam cent you have."

I thanked him and fitted a Marlboro into my cigarette holder. "Say," he said, "you look like you might be in the horse business...am I right?"

"No," I said. "I'm a photographer."

From *Scanlon Monthly* (1970).

"Oh yeah?" He eyed my ragged leather bag with new interest. "Is that what you got there—cameras? Who you work for?"

"*Playboy*," I said.

He laughed. "Well, goddam! What are you gonna take pictures of—nekkid horses? Haw! I guess you'll be workin' pretty hard when they run the Kentucky Oaks. That's a race just for fillies." He was laughing wildly. "Hell yes! And they'll all be nekkid too!"

I shook my head and said nothing; just stared at him for a moment, trying to look grim. "There's going to be trouble," I said. "My assignment is to take pictures of the riot."

"What riot?"

I hesitated, twirling the ice in my drink. "At the track. On Derby Day. The Black Panthers." I stared at him again. "Don't you read the newspapers?"

The grin on his face had collapsed. "What the hell are you talkin' about?"

"Well…maybe I shouldn't be telling you…" I shrugged. "But hell, everybody else seems to know. The cops and the National Guard have been getting ready for six weeks. They have 20,000 troops on alert at Fort Knox. They've warned us—all the press and photographers— to wear helmets and special vests like flak jackets. We were told to expect shooting…"

"No!" he shouted; his hands flew up and hovered momentarily between us, as if to ward off the words he was hearing. Then he whacked his fist on the bar. "Those sons of bitches! God Almighty! The Kentucky Derby!" He kept shaking his head. "No! Jesus! That's almost too bad to believe!" Now he seemed to be sagging on the stool, and when he looked up his eyes were misty. "Why? Why here? Don't they respect anything?"

I shrugged again. "It's not just the Panthers. The FBI says bus loads of white crazies are coming in from all over the country—to mix with the crowd and attack all at once, from every direction. They'll be dressed like everybody else. You know—coats and ties and all that. But when the trouble starts…well, that's why the cops are so worried."

He sat for a moment, looking hurt and confused and not quite able to digest all this terrible news. Then he cried out: "Oh…Jesus! What in the name of God is happening in this country? Where can you get away from it?"

"Not here," I said, picking up my bag. "Thanks for the drink…and good luck."

He grabbed my arm, urging me to have another, but I said I was overdue at the Press Club and hustled off to get my act together for the awful spectacle. At the airport newsstand I picked up a *Courier-Journal* and scanned the front page headlines: "Nixon Sends GI's into Cambodia to Hit Reds"…"B-52's Raid, then 20,000 GI's Advance 20 Miles"…

"4,000 U.S. Troops Deployed Near Yale as Tension Grows Over Panther Protest." At the bottom of the page was a photo of Diane Crump, soon to become the first woman jockey ever to ride in the Kentucky Derby. The photographer had snapped her "stopping in the barn area to fondle her mount, Fathom." The rest of the paper was spotted with ugly war news and stories of "student unrest." There was no mention of any trouble brewing at a university in Ohio called Kent State.

I went to the Hertz desk to pick up my car, but the moon-faced young swinger in charge said they didn't have any. "You can't rent one anywhere," he assured me. "Our Derby reservations have been booked for six weeks." I explained that my agent had confirmed a white Chrysler convertible for me that very afternoon but he shook his head. "Maybe we'll have a cancellation. Where are you staying?"

I shrugged. "Where's the Texas crowd staying? I want to be with my people." He sighed. "My friend, you're in trouble. This town is flat full. Always is, for the Derby." I leaned closer to him, half-whispering: "Look, I'm from *Playboy*. How would you like a job?" He backed off quickly. "What? Come on, now. What kind of a job?"

"Never mind," I said. "You just blew it." I swept my bag off the counter and went to find a cab. The bag is a valuable prop in this kind of work; mine has a lot of baggage tags on it—SF, LA, NY, Lima, Rome, Bangkok, that sort of thing—and the most prominent tag of all is a very official, plastic-coated thing that says "Photog. *Playboy* Mag." I bought it from a pimp in Vail, Colorado, and he told me how to use it. "Never mention *Playboy* until you're sure they've seen this thing first," he said. "Then, when you see them notice it, that's the time to strike. They'll go belly up ever time. This thing is magic, I tell you. Pure magic."

Well…maybe so. I'd used it on the poor geek in the bar, and now humming along in a Yellow Cab toward town, I felt a little guilty about jangling the poor bugger's brains with that evil fantasy. But what the hell? Anybody who wanders around the world saying, "Hell yes, I'm from Texas," deserves whatever happens to him. And he had, after all, come here once again to make a nineteenth-century ass of himself in the midst of some jaded, atavistic freakout with nothing to recommend it except a very saleable "tradition." Early in our chat, Jimbo had told me that he hadn't missed a Derby since 1954. "The little lady won't come anymore," he said. "She grits her teeth and turns me loose for this one. And when I say 'loose' I do mean loose! I toss ten-dollar bills around like they were goin' out of style! Horses, whiskey, women…shit, there's women in this town that'll do anything for money."

Why not? Money is a good thing to have in these twisted times. Even Richard Nixon is hungry for it. Only a few days before the Derby he said, "If I had any money I'd invest it in the stock market." And the market, meanwhile, continued its grim slide.

The next day was heavy. With only thirty hours until post time I had no press credentials and—according to the sports editor of the *Louisville Courier-Journal*—no hope at all of getting any. Worse, I needed two sets: one for myself and another for Ralph Steadman, the English illustrator who was coming from London to do some Derby drawings. All I knew about him was that this was his first visit to the United States. And the more I pondered the fact, the more it gave me fear. How would he bear up under the heinous culture shock of being lifted out of London and plunged into the drunken mob scene at the Kentucky Derby? There was no way of knowing. Hopefully, he would arrive at least a day or so ahead, and give himself time to get acclimated. Maybe a few hours of peaceful sightseeing in the Bluegrass country around Lexington. My plan was to pick him up at the airport in the huge Pontiac Ballbuster I'd rented from a used-car salesman named Colonel Quick, then whisk him off to some peaceful setting that might remind him of England.

Colonel Quick had solved the car problem, and money (four times the normal rate) had bought two rooms in a scumbox on the outskirts of town. The only other kink was the task of convincing the moguls at Churchill Downs that *Scanlan's* was such a prestigious sporting journal that common sense compelled them to give us two sets of the best press tickets. This was not easily done. My first call to the publicity office resulted in total failure. The press handler was shocked at the idea that anyone would be stupid enough to apply for press credentials two days before the Derby. "Hell, you can't be serious," he said. "The deadline was two months ago. The press box is full; there's no more room…and what the hell is *Scanlan's Monthly* anyway?"

I uttered a painful groan. "Didn't the London office call you? They're flying an artist over to do the paintings. Steadman. He's Irish. I think. Very famous over there. Yes. I just got in from the Coast. The San Francisco office told me we were all set."

He seemed interested, and even sympathetic, but there was nothing he could do. I flattered him with more gibberish, and finally he offered a compromise: he could get us two passes to the clubhouse grounds but the clubhouse itself and especially the press box were out of the question.

"That sounds a little weird," I said. "It's unacceptable. We must have access to everything. All of it. The spectacle, the people, the pageantry and certainly the race. You don't think we came all this way to watch the damn thing on television, do you? One way or another we'll get inside. Maybe we'll have to bribe a guard—or even Mace somebody." (I had picked up a spray can of Mace in a downtown drugstore for $5.98 and suddenly, in the midst of that phone talk, I was struck by the hideous possibilities of using it out at the track. Macing ushers at the narrow gates to the clubhouse inner sanctum, then slipping quickly inside, firing a huge load of Mace into the governor's box, just as the race starts. Or Macing helpless drunks in the clubhouse restroom, for their own good…)

By noon on Friday I was still without press credentials and still unable to locate Steadman. For all I knew he'd changed his mind and gone back to London. Finally, after giving up on Steadman and trying unsuccessfully to reach my man in the press office, I decided my only hope for credentials was to go out to the track and confront the man in person, with no warning—demanding only one pass now, instead of two, and talking very fast with a strange lilt in my voice, like a man trying hard to control some inner frenzy. On the way out, I stopped at the motel desk to cash a check. Then, as a useless afterthought, I asked if by any wild chance a Mr. Steadman had checked in.

The lady on the desk was about fifty years old and very peculiar-looking; when I mentioned Steadman's name she nodded, without looking up from whatever she was writing, and said in a low voice, "You bet he did." Then she favored me with a big smile. "Yes, indeed. Mr. Steadman just left for the racetrack. Is he a friend of yours?"

I shook my head. "I'm supposed to be working with him, but I don't even know what he looks like. Now, goddammit, I'll have to find him in the mob at the track."

She chuckled. "You won't have any trouble finding him. You could pick that man out of any crowd."

"Why?" I asked. "What's wrong with him? What does he look like?"

"Well…" she said, still grinning, "he's the funniest looking thing I've seen in a long time. He has this…ah…this growth all over his face. As a matter of fact it's all over his head." She nodded. "You'll know him when you see him; don't worry about that."

Creeping Jesus, I thought. That screws the press credentials. I had a vision of some nerve-rattling geek all covered with matted hair and string-warts showing up in the press office and demanding *Scanlan's* press packet. Well…what the hell? We could always load up on acid and spend the day roaming around the clubhouse grounds with bit sketch pads, laughing hysterically at the natives and swilling mint juleps so the cops wouldn't think we're abnormal. Perhaps even make the act pay; set up an easel with a big sign saying, "Let a Foreign Artist Paint Your Portrait, $10 Each. Do It NOW!"

———————

I took the expressway out to the track, driving very fast and jumping the monster car back and forth between lanes, driving with a beer in one hand and my mind so muddled that I almost crushed a Volkswagen full of nuns when I swerved to catch the right exit. There was a slim chance, I thought, that I might be able to catch the ugly Britisher before he checked in.

But Steadman was already in the press box when I got there, a bearded young Englishman wearing a tweed coat and RAF sunglasses. There was nothing particularly odd about him. No facial veins or clumps of bristly warts. I told him about the motel woman's description and he seemed puzzled. "Don't let it bother you," I said. "Just keep in mind for the next few days that we're in Louisville, Kentucky. Not London. Not even New York. This is a weird place. You're lucky that mental defective at the motel didn't jerk a pistol out of the cash register and blow a big hole in you." I laughed, but he looked worried.

"Just pretend you're visiting a huge outdoor loony bin," I said. "If the inmates get out of control we'll soak them down with Mace." I showed him the can of "Chemical Billy," resisting the urge to fire it across the room at a rat-faced man typing diligently in the Associated Press section. We were standing at the bar, sipping the management's Scotch and congratulating each other on our sudden, unexplained luck in picking up two sets of fine press credentials. The lady at the desk had been very friendly to him, he said. "I just told her my name and she gave me the whole works."

By mid afternoon we had everything under control. We had seats looking down on the finish line, color TV and a free bar in the press room, and a selection of passes that would take us anywhere from the clubhouse roof to the jockey room. The only thing we lacked was unlimited access to the clubhouse inner sanctum in sections "F&G"...and I felt we needed that, to see the whiskey gentry in action. The governor, a swinish neo-Nazi hack named Louis Nunn, would be in "G," along with Barry Goldwater and Colonel Sanders. I felt we'd be legal in a box in "G" where we could rest and sip juleps, soak up a bit of atmosphere and the Derby's special vibrations.

The bars and dining rooms are also in "F&G," and the clubhouse bars on Derby Day are a very special kind of scene. Along with the politicians, society belles and local captains of commerce, every half-mad ding bat who ever had any pretensions to anything at all within five hundred miles of Louisville will show up there to get strutting drunk and slap a lot of backs and generally make himself obvious. The Paddock bar is probably the best place in the track to sit and watch faces. Nobody minds being stared at; that's what they're in there for. Some people spend most of their time in the Paddock; they can hunker down at one of the many wooden tables, lean back in a comfortable chair and watch the ever-changing odds flash up and down on the big tote board outside the window. Black waiters in white serving jackets move through the crowd with trays of drinks, while the experts ponder their racing forms and the hunch bettors pick lucky numbers or scan the lineup for right-sounding names. There is a constant flow of traffic to and from the pari-mutuel windows outside in the wooden corridors. Then, as post time nears, the crowd thins out as people go back to their boxes.

Clearly, we were going to have to figure out some way to spend more time in the clubhouse tomorrow. But the "walk around" press passes to F&G were only good for thirty minutes at a time, presumably to allow the newspaper types to rush in and out for photos or quick interviews, but to prevent drifters like Steadman and me from spending all day in the clubhouse, harassing the gentry and rifling the odd handbag or two while cruising around the boxes. Or Macing the governor. The time limit was no problem on Friday, but on Derby Day the walk around passes would be in heavy demand. And since it took about ten minutes to get from the press box to the Paddock, and ten more minutes to get back, that didn't leave much time for serious people-watching. And unlike most of the others in the press box, we didn't give a hoot in hell what was happening on the track. We had come there to watch the real beasts perform.

Later Friday afternoon, we went out on the balcony of the press box and I tried to describe the difference between what we were seeing today and what would be happening tomorrow. This was the first time I'd been to a Derby in ten years, but before that, when I lived in Louisville, I used to go every year. Now, looking down from the press box, I pointed to the huge grassy meadow enclosed by the track. "That whole thing," I said, "will be jammed with people; fifty thousand or so, and most of them staggering drunk. It's a fantastic scene—thousands of people fainting, crying, copulating, trampling each other and fighting with broken whiskey bottles. We'll have to spend some time out there, but it's hard to move around, too many bodies."

"Is it safe out there? Will we ever come back?"

"Sure," I said. "We'll just have to be careful not to step on anybody's stomach and start a fight." I shrugged. "Hell, this clubhouse scene right below us will be almost as bad as the infield. Thousands of raving, stumbling drunks, getting angrier and angrier as they lose more and more money. By mid afternoon they'll be guzzling mint juleps with both hands and vomiting on each other between races. The whole place will be jammed with bodies, shoulder to shoulder. It's hard to move around. The aisles will be slick with vomit; people falling down and grabbing at your legs to keep from being stomped. Drunks pissing on themselves in the betting lines. Dropping handfuls of money and fighting to stoop over and pick it up."

He looked so nervous that I laughed. "I'm just kidding," I said. "Don't worry. At the first hint of trouble I'll start pumping this 'Chemical Billy' into the crowd."

He had done a few good sketches, but so far we hadn't seen that special kind of face that I felt we would need for a lead drawing. It was a face I'd seen a thousand times at every Derby I'd ever been to. I saw it, in my head, as the mask of the whiskey gentry—a pretentious mix of booze, failed dreams and a terminal identity crisis; the inevitable result of too much inbreeding in a closed and ignorant culture. One of the key genetic rules in breeding dogs, horses or any other kind of thoroughbred is that close inbreeding tends to magnify the weak points in a bloodline as well as the strong points. In horse breeding, for instance, there is a definite risk in breeding two fast horses who are both a little crazy. The offspring will likely be very fast and also very crazy. So the trick in breeding thoroughbreds is to retain the good traits and filter out the bad. But the breeding of humans is not so wisely supervised, particularly in a narrow Southern society where the closest kind of inbreeding is not only stylish and acceptable, but far more convenient—to the parents—than setting their offspring free to find their own mates, for their own reasons and in their own ways. ("Goddam, did you hear about Smitty's daughter? She went crazy in Boston last week and married a nigger!")

So the face I was trying to find in Churchill Downs that weekend was a symbol, in my own mind, of the whole doomed atavistic culture that makes the Kentucky Derby what it is.

On our way back to the motel after Friday's races I warned Steadman about some of the other problems we'd have to cope with. Neither of us had brought any strange illegal drugs, so we would have to get by on booze. "You should keep in mind," I said, "that almost everybody you talk to from now on will be drunk. People who seem very pleasant at first might suddenly swing at you for no reason at all." He nodded, staring straight ahead. He seemed to be getting a little numb and I tried to cheer him up by inviting to dinner that night, with my brother.

Back at the motel we talked for awhile about America, the South, England—just relaxing a bit before dinner. There was no way either of us could have known, at the time, that it would be the last normal conversation we would have. From that point on, the weekend became a vicious, drunken nightmare. We both went completely to pieces. The main problem was my prior attachment to Louisville, which naturally led to meetings with old friends, relatives, etc., many of whom were in the process of falling apart, going mad, plotting divorces, cracking up under the strain of terrible debts or recovering from bad accidents. Right in the middle of the whole frenzied Derby action, a member of my own family had to be institutionalized. This added a certain amount of strain to the situation, and since poor Steadman had no choice but to take whatever came his way, he was subjected to shock after shock.

Another problem was his habit of sketching people he met in the various social situations I dragged him into—then giving them the sketches. The results were always unfortunate. I warned him several times about letting the subjects see his foul renderings, but for some perverse reason he kept doing it. Consequently, he was regarded with fear and loathing by nearly everyone who'd seen or even heard about his work. He couldn't understand it. "It's sort of a joke," he kept saying. "Why, in England it's quite normal. People don't take offense. They understand that I'm just putting them on a bit."

"Fuck England," I said. "This is Middle America. These people regard what you're doing to them as a brutal, bilious insult. Look what happened last night. I thought my brother was going to tear your head off."

Steadman shook his head sadly. "But I liked him. He struck me as a very decent, straightforward sort."

"Look, Ralph," I said. "Let's not kid ourselves. That was a very horrible drawing you gave him. It was the face of a monster. It got on his nerves very badly." I shrugged. "Why in hell do you think we left the restaurant so fast?"

"I thought it was because of the Mace," he said.

"What Mace?" He grinned.

"When you shot it at the headwaiter, don't you remember?"

"Hell, that was nothing," I said. "I missed him…and we were leaving, anyway."

"But it got all over us," he said. "The room was full of that damn gas. Your brother was sneezing and his wife was crying. My eyes hurt for two hours. I couldn't see to draw when we got back to the motel."

"That's right," I said. "The stuff got on her leg, didn't it?" "She was angry," he said.

"Yeah…well, okay…Let's just figure we fucked up about equally on that one," I said. "But from now on let's try to be careful when we're around people I know. You won't sketch them and I won't Mace them. We'll just try to relax and get drunk."

"Right," he said. "We'll go native."

———————

It was Saturday morning, the day of the Big Race, and we were having breakfast in a plastic hamburger palace called the Fish-Meat Village. Our rooms were just across the road in the Brown Suburban Hotel. They had a dining room, but the food was so bad that we couldn't handle it anymore. The waitresses seemed to be suffering from shin splints; they moved around very slowly, moaning and cursing the "darkies" in the kitchen.

Steadman liked the Fish-Meat place because it had fish and chips. I preferred the "French toast," which was really pancake batter, fried to the proper thickness and then chopped out with a sort of cookie cutter to resemble pieces of toast.

Beyond drink and lack of sleep, our only real problem at that point was the question of access to the clubhouse. Finally, we decided to go ahead and steal two passes, if necessary, rather than miss that part of the action. This was the last coherent decision we were able to make for the next forty-eight hours. From that point on—almost from the very moment we started out to the track—we lost all control of events and spent the rest of the weekend churning around in a sea of drunken horrors. My notes and recollections from Derby Day are somewhat scrambled.

But now, looking at the big red notebook I carried all through that scene, I see more or less what happened. The book itself is somewhat mangled and bent; some of the pages are torn, others are shriveled and stained by what appears to be whiskey, but taken as a whole, with sporadic memory flashes, the notes seem to tell the story. To wit:

_____

Rain all night until dawn. No sleep. Christ, here we go, a nightmare of mud and madness... But no. By noon the sun burns through—perfect day, not even humid.

Steadman is now worried about fire. Somebody told him about the clubhouse catching on fire two years ago. Could it happen again? Horrible. Trapped in the press box. Holocaust. A hundred thousand people fighting to get out. Drunks screaming in the flames and the mud, crazed horses running wild. Blind in the smoke. Grandstand collapsing into the flames with us on the roof. Poor Ralph is about to crack. Drinking heavily, into the Haig & Haig.

Out to the track in a cab, avoid that terrible parking in people's front yards, $25 each, toothless old men on the street with big signs: PARK HERE, flagging cars in the yard.

"That's fine, boy, never mind the tulips." Wild hair on his head, straight up like a clump of reeds.

Sidewalks full of people all moving in the same direction, towards Churchill Downs. Kids hauling coolers and blankets, teenyboppers in tight pink shorts, many blacks...black dudes in white felt hats with leopard-skin bands, cops waving traffic along.

The mob was thick for many blocks around the track; very slow going in the crowd, very hot. On the way to the press box elevator, just inside the clubhouse, we came on a row of soldiers all carrying long white riot sticks. About two platoons, with helmets. A man walking next to us said they were waiting for the governor and his party. Steadman eyed them nervously. "Why do they have those clubs?"

"Black Panthers," I said. Then I remembered good old "Jimbo" at the airport and I wondered what he was thinking right now. Probably very nervous; the place was teeming with cops and soldiers. We pressed on through the crowd, through many gates, past the paddock where the jockeys bring the horses out and parade around for a while before each race so the bettors can get a good look. Five million dollars will be bet today. Many winners, more losers. What the hell. The press gate was jammed up with people trying to get in, shouting at the guards, waving strange press badges: Chicago Sporting Times, Pittsburgh Police Athletic League...they were all turned away. "Move on, fella, make way for the working press." We shoved through the crowd and into the elevator, then quickly up to the free bar. Why not? Get it on. Very hot today, not feeling well, must be this rotten climate. The press box was cool and airy, plenty of room to walk around and balcony seats for watching the race or looking down at the crowd. We got a betting sheet and went outside.

———

Pink faces with a stylish Southern sag, old Ivy styles, seersucker coats and button down collars. "Mayblossom Senility" (Steadman's phrase)...burnt out early or maybe just not much to burn in the first place. Not much energy in the faces, not much curiosity. Suffering in silence, nowhere to go after thirty in this life, just hang on and humor the children. Let the young enjoy themselves while they can. Why not?

The grim reaper comes early in this league...banshees on the lawn at night, screaming out there beside that little iron nigger in jockey clothes. Maybe he's the one who's screaming. Bad DT's and too many snarls at the bridge club. Going down with the stock market. Oh Jesus, the kid has wrecked the new car, wrapped it around the big stone pillar at the bottom of the driveway. Broken leg? Twisted eye? Send him off to Yale, they can cure anything up there.

Yale? Did you see today's paper? New Haven is under siege. Yale is swarming with Black Panthers...I tell you, Colonel, the world has gone mad, stone mad. Why, they tell me a goddam woman jockey might ride in the Derby today.

I left Steadman sketching in the Paddock bar and went off to place our bets on the fourth race. When I came back he was staring intently at a group of young men around a table not far away. "Jesus, look at the corruption in that face!" he whispered. "Look at the madness, the fear, the greed!" I looked, then quickly turned my back on the table he was sketching.

The face he'd picked out to draw was the face of an old friend of mine, a prep school football star in the good old days with a sleek red Chevy convertible and a very quick hand, it was said, with the snaps of a 32 B brassiere. They called him "Cat Man."

But now, a dozen years later, I wouldn't have recognized him anywhere but here, where I should have expected to find him, in the Paddock bar on Derby Day...fat slanted eyes and a pimp's smile, blue silk suit and his friends looking like crooked bank tellers on a binge...

Steadman wanted to see some Kentucky Colonels, but he wasn't sure what they looked like. I told him to go back to the clubhouse men's rooms and look for men in white linen suits vomiting in the urinals. "They'll usually have large brown whiskey stains on the front of their suits," I said. "But watch the shoes, that's the tip-off. Most of them manage to avoid vomiting on their own clothes, but they never miss their shoes."

In a box not far from ours was Colonel Anna Friedman Goldman, Chairman and Keeper of the Great Seal of the Honorable Order of Kentucky Colonels. Not all the 76 million or so Kentucky Colonels could make it to the Derby this year, but many had kept the faith, and several days prior to the Derby they gathered for their annual dinner at the Seelbach Hotel.

The Derby, the actual race, was scheduled for late afternoon, and as the magic hour approached I suggested to Steadman that we should probably spend some time in the infield, that boiling sea of people across the track from the clubhouse. He seemed a little nervous about it, but since none of the awful things I'd warned him about had happened so far—no race riots, fire storms or savage drunken attacks—he shrugged and said, "Right, let's do it."

To get there we had to pass through many gates, each one a step down in status, then through a tunnel under the track. Emerging from the tunnel was such a culture shock that it took us a while to adjust. "God almighty!" Steadman muttered. "This is a…Jesus!" He plunged ahead with his tiny camera, stepping over bodies, and I followed, trying to take notes.

———

Total chaos, no way to see the race, not even the track…nobody cares. Big lines at the outdoor betting windows, then stand back to watch winning numbers flash on the big board, like a giant bingo game.

Old blacks arguing about bets; "Hold on there, I'll handle this" (waving pint of whiskey, fistful of dollar bills); girl riding piggyback, T-shirt says, "Stolen from Fort Lauderdale Jail." Thousands of teenagers, group singing "Let the Sun Shine In," ten soldiers guarding the American flag and a huge fat drunk wearing a blue football jersey (No. 80) reeling around with quart of beer in hand.

No booze sold out here, too dangerous…no bathrooms either. Muscle Beach… Woodstock…many cops with riot sticks, but no sign of a riot. Far across the track the clubhouse looks like a postcard from the Kentucky Derby.

———

We went back to the clubhouse to watch the big race. When the crowd stood to face the flag and sing "My Old Kentucky Home," Steadman faced the crowd and sketched frantically. Somewhere up in the boxes a voice screeched, "Turn around, you hairy freak!" The race itself was only two minutes long, and even from our super-status seats and using 12-power glasses, there was no way to see what really happened to our horses. Holy Land, Ralph's choice, stumbled and lost his jockey in the final turn. Mine, Silent Screen, had the lead coming into the stretch but faded to fifth at the finish. The winner was a 16-1 shot named Dust Commander.

Moments after the race was over, the crowd surged wildly for the exits, rushing for cabs and busses. The next day's *Courier* told of violence in the parking lot; people were punched and trampled, pockets were picked, children lost, bottles hurled. But we missed all this, having retired to the press box for a bit of post-race drinking. By this time we were both half-crazy from too much whiskey, sun fatigue, culture shock, lack of sleep and general dissolution. We hung around the press box long enough to watch a mass interview with the winning owner, a dapper little man named Lehmann who said he had just flown into Louisville that morning from Nepal, where he'd "bagged a record tiger." The sportswriters murmured their admiration and a waiter filled Lehmann's glass with Chivas Regal. He had just won $127,000 with a horse that cost him $6,500 two years ago. His occupation, he said, was "retired contractor." And then he added, with a big grin, "I just retired."

The rest of the day blurs into madness. The rest of that night too. And all the next day and night. Such horrible things occurred that I can't bring myself even to think about them now, much less put them down in print. I was lucky to get out at all. One of my clearest memories of that vicious time is Ralph being attacked by one of my old friends in the billiard room of the Pendennis Club in downtown Louisville on Saturday night. The man had ripped his own shirt open to the waist before deciding that Ralph was after his wife. No blows were struck, but the emotional effects were massive. Then, as a sort of final horror, Steadman put his fiendish pen to work and tried to patch things up by doing a little sketch of the girl he'd been accused of hustling. That finished us in the Pedennis.

Sometime around ten-thirty Monday morning I was awakened by a scratching sound at my door. I leaned out of bed and pulled the curtain back just far enough to see Steadman outside. "What the fuck do you want?" I shouted.

"What about having breakfast?" he said.

I lunged out of bed and tried to open the door, but it caught on the night-chain and banged shut again. I couldn't cope with the chain! The thing wouldn't come out of the track—so I ripped it out of the wall with a vicious jerk on the door. Ralph didn't blink. "Bad luck," he muttered.

I could barely see him. My eyes were swollen almost shut and the sudden burst of sunlight through the door left me stunned and helpless like a sick mole. Steadman was mumbling about sickness and terrible heat; I fell back on the bed and tried to focus on him as he moved around the room in a very distracted way for a few moments, then suddenly darted over to the beer bucket and seized a Colt .45. "Christ," I said. "You're getting out of control."

He nodded and ripped the cap off, taking a long drink. "You know, this is really awful," he said finally. "I must get out of this place…" he shook his head nervously. "The plane leaves at three-thirty, but I don't know if I'll make it."

I barely heard him. My eyes had finally opened enough for me to focus on the mirror across the room and I was stunned at the shock of recognition. For a confused instant I thought that Ralph had brought somebody with him—a model for that one special face we'd been looking for. There he was, by God—a puffy, drink-ravaged, disease-ridden caricature…like an awful cartoon version of an old snapshot in some once-proud mother's family photo album. It was the face we'd been looking for—and it was, of course, my own. Horrible, horrible…

"Maybe I should sleep a while longer," I said. "Why don't you go on over to the Fish-Meat place and eat some of those rotten fish and chips? Then come back and get me around noon. I feel too near death to hit the streets at this hour."

He shook his head. "No…no…I think I'll go back upstairs and work on those drawings for a while." He leaned down to fetch two more cans out of the beer bucket. "I tried to work earlier," he said, "but my hands kept trembling…It's teddible, teddible."

"You've got to stop this drinking," I said.

He nodded. "I know. This is no good, no good at all. But for some reason it makes me feel better…"

"Not for long," I said. "You'll probably collapse into some kind of hysterical DT's tonight—probably just about the time you get off the plane at Kennedy. They'll zip you up in a straightjacket and drag you down to the Tombs, then beat you on the kidneys with big sticks until you straighten out."

He shrugged and wandered out, pulling the door shut behind him. I went back to bed for another hour or so, and later—after the daily grapefruit juice run to the Nite Owl Food Mart—we had our last meal at Fish-Meat Village: a fine lunch of dough and butcher's offal, fried in heavy grease.

By this time Ralph wouldn't order coffee; he kept asking for more water. "It's the only thing they have that's fit for human consumption," he explained. Then, with an hour or so to kill before he had to catch the plane, we spread his drawings out on the table and pondered them for a while, wondering if he'd caught the proper spirit of the thing…but we couldn't make up our minds. His hands were shaking so badly that he had trouble holding the paper, and my vision was so blurred that I could barely see what he'd drawn. "Shit," I said. "We both look worse than anything you've drawn here."

He smiled. "You know—I've been thinking about that," he said. "We came down here to see this teddible scene: people all pissed out of their minds and vomiting on themselves and all that…and now, you know what? It's us…"

————————

Huge Pontiac Ballbuster blowing through traffic on the expressway.

A radio news bulletin says the National Guard is massacring students at Kent State and Nixon is still bombing Cambodia. The journalist is driving, ignoring his passenger who is now nearly naked after taking off most of his clothing, which he holds out the window, trying to wind-wash the Mace out of it. His eyes are bright red and his face and chest are soaked with beer he's been using to rinse the awful chemical off his flesh. The front of his woolen trousers is soaked with vomit; his body is racked with fits of coughing and wild chocking sobs. The journalist rams the big car through traffic and into a spot in front of the terminal, then he reaches over to open the door on the passenger's side and shoves the Englishman out, snarling: "Bug off, you worthless faggot! You twisted pigfucker! [Crazed laughter.] If I weren't sick I'd kick your ass all the way to Bowling Green—you scum sucking foreign geek. Mace is too good for you…We can do without your kind in Kentucky."

Thompson's "The Kentucky Derby Is Decadent and Depraved" is often credited as the birth of a new genre known as gonzo journalism, which favors aesthetics over objectivity and tends toward the gritty, often featuring the author as a primary character. Take a moment and reflect on the textual devices and strategies used by Thompson that seem particularly apt of the "gonzo style." What particular turns of phrase, literary devices, choices of scene and content stand out to you? How does the piece feel different from other sports journalism you've read?

For the piece, Thompson collaborated with British cartoonist R. Steadman, whose visual style is considered a complement to Thompson's gonzo's aesthetic. You can view Steadman's famous portrait of the Derby that was featured alongside Thompson's *Scanlon's Monthly* article here: http://www.npr.org/2013/05/04/180907071/a-decadent-and-depraved-derby-with-hunter-s-thompson. In small groups, identify and share which aesthetic qualities in the cartoon complement Thompson's portrayal of the Derby and why. What makes Steadman's style a visual medium of "gonzoism"?

Attend a local or school sporting event. Then, write an essay in which you recount the sports event in Thompson's gonzo literary style. What characters, scenes, moments do you capture and why? What is the overall tone and message of the piece? How are you working to tell a story? How might you introduce yourself as one of the characters in the piece?

William Carlos Williams was a pediatrician and noted American modernist poet renown for his stylistic experimentation with triadic line poetry and interest in the everyday. In "The Crowd at the Ball Game," Williams reflects on the sublime beauty of the baseball crowd at a time when the game represented one of the largest forms of American entertainment.

THE CROWD AT THE BALL GAME

By William Carlos Williams

The crowd at the ball game
is moved uniformly

by a spirit of uselessness
which delights them—

all the exciting detail
of the chase

and the escape, the error
the flash of genius—

all to no end save beauty
the eternal—

So in detail they, the crowd,
are beautiful

for this
to be warned against

From *The Collected Poems of William Carlos Williams, Volume 1*, 1909-1939.

saluted and defied—
It is alive, venomous

it smiles grimly
its words cut—

The flashy female with her
mother, gets it—

The Jew gets it straight—it
is deadly, terrifying—

It is the Inquisition, the
Revolution

It is beauty itself
that lives

day by day in them
idly—

This is
the power of their faces

It is summer, it is the solstice
the crowd is

cheering, the crowd is laughing
in detail

permanently, seriously
without thought

Invent What is Williams's view of baseball in the 1920s? How does he capture the function of baseball in American culture in his poem? What poetic strategies does he use to convey his opinion of baseball and its crowd (run-ons, enjambment lines, rhyme, meter, metaphor, imagery, alliteration)? Take a few minutes and jot down your observations about how Williams uses poetic devices to create his ode to baseball.

Explore Using archival library databases, find five to six newspaper articles from the 1920s that help put Williams's poem in context with the broader culture of the time. What were the 1920s like? What role did baseball play in the 1920s and why? How do these articles inform your understanding of Williams's poem and its major argument? Write a 500-word journal response noting your findings and synthesizing key points from the archival newspaper articles with lines from Williams's poem.

Collaborate In his reverie to the growing popularity of baseball in the 1920s, Williams writes, "So in detail, they, the crowd, are beautiful." How do you feel about sports fandom? Is is beautiful as Williams writes, or tragic and empty as Halberstam argues? Why? In what way? What experiences do you have as part of a crowd at a sporting event and how does Williams capture that feeling and experience in his poem or not capture it?

Compose Compose a poem that plays with Williams's triadic-line form in which you reflect on your understandings and memories of sports fandom. What makes it beautiful or tragic? What moments are worth capturing? Which kinds of personas and what details of the physical space? What metaphors adequately capture the essence of being a sports fan? If you have never attended a major sports event, perhaps write a poem in which you imagine yourself at one.

Michael Serazio is an assistant professor of communication at Fairfield University. In the following feature story for The Atlantic, Serazio reflects on the rituals of sports fandom and their religious-like associations.

JUST HOW MUCH IS SPORTS FANDOM LIKE RELIGION?

By Michael Serazio

Pro sports teams are like what religion and sociology scholars call "totems"—symbols of greater entities that communities gather around for identity and unity.

The Super Bowl, professional sports' highest holy day, is again upon us. As fans paint their faces and torsos, pile on licensed apparel, and quixotically arrange beer cans in the shape of team logos, the question must, again, be asked: Why exactly do we do this for our teams?

Why, in my own case, do I feel the need to sport a Chargers cap on fall Sundays sitting in front of the television when decades of futility, not to mention common sense, suggests it has little effect on outcome?

The answer—and the secret of fandom—might just be found in a context far removed from professional football.

RELATED STORY

The Psychology of Rooting for the Guy With the (Fake) Dead Girlfriend

Almost precisely a century ago, Emile Durkheim pondered along similar lines. Durkheim, a pioneering sociologist, began digging through accounts of "primitive" cultures like the Arunta tribe of Australia, hoping to excavate the ancient source of ties that bind. His conclusion—as revealed in The Elementary Forms of the Religious Life—remains as profound and relevant today as it is elegantly simple: Whenever a society (or, here, sports subculture) worships a divine form, it is, in fact, also simultaneously worshipping itself.

From *The Atlantic* (2013).

For Durkheim, this all hinged on what he called "the totem." As he wrote, "On the one hand, [the totem] is the external and tangible form of what we have called the…god. But on the other, it is the symbol of that particular society we call the clan. It is its flag; it is the sign by which each clan distinguishes itself from others, the visible mark of its personality."

In other words, our religious totems, while "officially" symbolizing deities, also implicitly offer vessels for fellowship; licenses to congregate together. As social creatures, there is something universal—and still enduring—in that tribal yearning. Yet community is often more abstract and imagined than concrete and identifiable.

The totem, then, gives believers a physical representation of that need for identity and unity: a Star of David hung from the neck; a Ganesh figurine placed on the dashboard; a St. Christopher medal tucked in the wallet. Theological justifications are really just incidental; what matters is that through our faith in these common artifacts, community is forged.

Alas, formal, organized religion in America today seems but a shell of its former self. A recent Pew study noted that the percentage of the U.S. public declaring themselves religiously "unaffiliated" had grown to one-fifth, including one-third of those under 30— the highest figures in the poll's history. Faith in other institutions—family, one's employer, political entities—is equally dwindling, though such institutions once also rooted the individual in something larger.

What totems, therefore, still survive in this culture of ours? The Red Sox. The Packers. The Lakers. And so on. The notion that sports remain our civic religion is truer than we often let on: In fandom, as in religious worship, our social connections are brought to life, in the stands as in the pews. It serves as a reminder of our interconnectedness and dependency; it materially indexes belonging. Like others, I indulge the royal "we" when speaking of my team, though there is little evidence they need me much beyond ticket sales, merchandise, and advertising impressions. Nonetheless, as Durkheim long ago noticed, "Members of each clan try to give themselves the external appearance of their totem…When the totem is a bird, the individuals wear feathers on their heads." Ravens fans surely understand this.

In short, if you look hard at sports, you can't help but see contours of religion.

Others have gestured to these parallels over the years. Some have highlighted how both preserve revered spaces (e.g., Sistine Chapel, Wrigley Field) and observe seasonal rhythms and orderly ceremonial frameworks. Elsewhere, it has been claimed that with its religious metaphors, regular invocations of good and evil, and sacred vestments (The Shroud of Schilling!), sports channel a natural religious impulse—driving one, somehow, "Godward."

The notion that sports remain our civic religion is truer than we often let on: In fandom, as in religious worship, our social connections are brought to life, in the stands as in the pews.

Writing about British soccer fans, one sociologist observed that: "Just as Durkheim suggested aboriginal tribes worship their society through the totem, so do the lads reaffirm their relations with other lads through the love of the team."

The sports totem therefore gives me reason to strike up a conversation with a stranger; better still, it offers phone fodder for calls to Grandpa. We routinely speak of being "born" into a particular fandom and treat those who change allegiances to rival teams with the same alienation familiar to heretics and apostates.

And should the Chargers ever reward my faith with a Super Bowl win—and, having lived through the Ryan Leaf years, I'm not holding my breath here—I'll finally have recourse to revel riotously, just as we'll see for one lucky, exhilarated fan base in a few days' time.

Durkheim had a name for this, too. He called it "collective effervescence," that social "electricity" that gets generated when groups gather to exalt in epic rituals. In that, the post-game celebration and day-after parades, with its feverish outpouring of emotion— all that hugging and high-fiving, those deafening howls and blubbery weeping—might look like chaotic disorder but it is actually a rare moment of social order: a glimpse of spontaneous solidarity, an interlude of uninhibited integration. This is not to excuse the excess of vandalism or violence that often accompanies the effervescence; the same social norms that maintain chilly anonymity in day-to-day modern life also serve to uphold law and decorum.

Yet that anonymity can inevitably be an unsettling thing; just ask anyone who's ever moved far from home. It doesn't really matter whether our teams win or lose on the field. As long as the totem survives, so do we. Turns out, that's what I'm really rooting for and why I'm still wearing that Chargers cap every Sunday afternoon.

What arguments does Serazio make for understanding sports fandom as a religion? Make a list of each of his central claims. Then note your reaction: Do you agree or disagree with these claims? Can you think of counterexamples that complicate Serazio's reasoning?

In small groups, share your own experiences with sports fandom. Do you have similar rituals associated with your fan identities? Do you feel similarly or differently about sports fandom? Share your findings and make a list about the possible positive and negative outcomes of a strong sports fandom identity.

This exercise will prepare you for Major Assignment #1: The Sports Memoir and/or Major Assignment #4: Sports Media and Identity. Write a short essay (two to three pages) in which you reflect on your own relationship to and experiences with sports fandom. Do you identity as a sports fan? Why or why not? Do you have a particular team you follow? Do you have any sacred rituals associated with your fandom identity? How do you understand sports fandom shaping your broader identity? If you do not identify with sports fandom, reflect why that is and create a compelling argument for how sports fandom has not appealed to you over the years and what concerns you about sports fandom.

Known for his involvement in the 1968 Olympic Boycotts, John Carlos is part of one of the most iconic sports moments of the twentieth century, the 1968 Olympics black power salute. In his excerpt from his memoir, Carlos recounts the events leading up to that memorable moment, including how Dr. Martin Luther King, Jr. and Muhammad Ali came to be supporters of the Olympic Project for Human Rights.

THE JOHN CARLOS STORY

BY JOHN CARLOS WITH DAVE ZIRIN

We went back to New York City to touch ground and try to develop some kind of strategy as to what the next move in our lives would be. Kim wanted me to find a job and work. I wanted to stay in shape by running in amateur individuals and hustle money on the side. But the Lord had other plans for me. When we moved back to the big city, a gentleman by the name of Dr. Harry Edwards happened to be visiting at the same time. Harry, as I mentioned, was the lead organizer for this floating idea of an African American boycott of the 1968 Olympics. He was a very charismatic professor and public speaker. He was a former athlete, standing six foot eight inches tall, muscle-bound, decked out in leather and shades, with a motor that just wouldn't quit. Harry was from the tough streets of East St. Louis, and had used his athletic abilities to leverage a doctorate from Cornell. He was still just twenty-six at this time, a peer and a leader.

Harry tracked me down at my mother's house, where I was helping her with some painting, and said that there was a meeting that night and people were asking if I could attend. The story of supporting the boycott at East Texas State had made its way to Harry's ears and he wanted me involved in the planning. Hearing that there was some actual organizing, that I would be breaking out of my isolation on these issues, was music to my ears. I didn't have to think twice that this was where I needed to be. It was clear to me by that time that Harry was more than someone with style and the power to shock the press. He was a very committed individual who understood and was able to articulate the way racism and athletics mixed.

From *The John Carlos Story* (2011).

Harry had a great deal of courage, in my eyes, to even consider an attempt to challenge racism in society from within the world of sports. This was not exactly friendly territory. I felt in my heart that at that moment in history, he was an essential person and he was without fear. If you showed Harry any system, any government, or any status quo, he made it his business to get in its face. He also had picked the perfect tactic: the boycott.

The word of the day was boycott and anyone who was either a black athlete or sympathetic to the cause of black athletes was well versed in the arguments on both sides. And it was clear that you couldn't be a bystander in this struggle: Black, white, or brown, we needed to know which side you were on. When it came time to lend support, the color of your skin didn't matter. And as I learned in East Texas, this was a struggle that was really far more generational than it was racial.

You had a lot of the elder African American "statesmen" and mainstream civil rights leaders hating this kind of plan. You had the older athlete, like Jesse Owens, shocked that we would even consider such a thing. You also had young Caucasian individuals like the rowers from Harvard University lending us some serious support. The movement had gained steam because in February 1968 the president of the IOC, Avery Brundage, the man who delivered the 1936 Olympics to Hitler's Germany, readmitted apartheid South Africa to the Olympics community—as if that racist state had somehow reformed. It gave us focus, energy, and a very clear demand to put on the table: if South Africa was in, we were out. This was the movement, as I knew from the pages of *Track and Field News*. This was what I wanted to be a part of. And this was why I was thrilled when the telephone rang in my mother's apartment, and it was Harry Edwards extending an invite.

Harry told me over the phone that the meeting was taking place downtown at the Americano Hotel. It doesn't even exist anymore, but back then the Americano Hotel used to be right across from the old Madison Square Garden. I would have run out of the door and just left my dust behind, but I did at least have the manners to turn to my mother and ask her if she needed me to finish this paint job or if I could go. She looked at me, saw the fever in my eyes, and told me to just get my behind out of the house.

I recall going down to the Americano that evening, walking into the lobby and being just overwhelmed by the size of it all. I had never really made time in the downtown hotels and my eyes almost popped out of my head. It looked like a movie set, with 50-foot-high ceilings, gaudy chandeliers, and the kind of deep, smoky woodwork that looked like it had been carved and sanded for kings. Honestly, I thought I'd turn the corner and bump into John Dillinger. I gathered myself and I went up to the room where the meeting was to take place.

When I entered that room, I had no expectations whatsoever as to who might be at the meeting or anything of the sort. I just knew it would be the place to be to talk boycott.

Other than Harry Edwards, I had no idea who would be there or why. When I walked in, I was immediately shocked to see some of the social-movement political giants that I had seen on television—Andrew Young for one, and Ralph Abernathy, the number two man of the Southern Christian Leadership Conference (SCLS). I was thinking to myself that I couldn't possibly get in trouble with my parents for walking out on that paint job because the SCLS could do no wrong in our household. I was already feeling like gold and awestruck around Abernathy and Young. But not in my wildest imagination was I ready for the next individual to walk into the room: Dr. Martin Luther King Jr. When he walked into our meeting, for the first time in my life I was absolutely and completely tongue-tied. All I could do at that precise moment was think about my mother. My momma admired Dr. King so much, she could talk about him and tears would pool in the corners of her eyes. She felt like Dr. King was the first lieutenant to God, sent to this planet to heal the sins of this nation. At that moment, all I could think was, "Wow! I wish that my Mom could be a rock in my pocket or a bug on my lapel and just be here to take in this moment." I was in awe. I know I probably looked completely unnerved, but Dr. King had this way of putting the people around him at ease. He came out with such a warm manner—you could say an almost comedic style—and it relaxed all the young athletes who might have been star-struck in his presence.

If Dr. King had been born in another life and another skin, and didn't get involved in religion and the civil rights movement, he could have made a Brinks truck worth of money as a stand-up comic because he was so funny and charismatic, cracking jokes before the meeting, putting everyone in stitches and making us all comfortable. Then, with Dr. King present and accounted for, the meeting started in earnest. Dr. King made it clear from the beginning that he wasn't just there to lend moral support. He wanted to help us hammer out a plan and he made it clear that he would be a public supporter of the Olympic boycott. He also stated that while we had public support, he wouldn't and couldn't be the lead man at the front of the march and in front of the cameras. He said that it would do the movement no favors. He wanted Harry Edwards to be the lead man, and said he would be very happy taking marching orders from Harry on this. Dr. King felt the boycott was a very worthy project and could prove to be a mighty platform to make clear the need to establish justice and equality for all men and women on this planet. He said that our strongest leverage was that an Olympic boycott could have a global reach. We could shock the world and we could do it by also adhering to the principles of nonviolence that he held so dear. We could bring attention to the problems of society, but we did not have to throw a rock or burn a building in order to do so.

This was Dr. King's methodology. He understood that militancy didn't mean violence. He understood that courage did not mean throwing punches. Sometimes it meant just the opposite. He also told us that if we wanted to go down and hold a demonstration during the Olympics in Mexico City, he would join us and bring the civil rights marches people knew from Selma and Montgomery right to the Mexican capital. I still remember him saying that he would get to work on that right after he saw through this garbage strike he was working on supporting in Memphis, Tennessee.

At the end of the meeting, I finally found my voice and was able to ask two questions of Dr. King. The first question I asked him, very respectfully, was why this idea of an Olympic boycott was attractive to him. He expressed to me that the concept and visual power of an Olympic boycott would be like a ripple in the water spreading throughout the world to let people know that the people of color of this earth were very disenchanted about their treatment and we could aspire to something better as a human race. He said that the visual power was in the void it would create: an Olympics without black athletes. He said that the process would be like black soldiers stepping back from the military. "We're not saying 'burn it down,'" he said. "We're just merely saying we don't care to participate and see how you feel without us as a part of the show." I totally agreed. We weren't throwing any fire. We were just saying that we choose not to go. We felt like we had to step up because as I remember someone saying at the meeting, "If not us, who?" How do you become a "leader"? Well it helps if you decide that you are going to lead.

My second question to Dr. King was something a lot of people in the room were wondering and it had nothing to do with anything that had to do with the Olympics. We wanted to know, "Why are you going back to Memphis when they are threatening your life?" Remember, Dr. King had been back and forth to Memphis where he was supporting a sanitation strike that had gotten so violent it became an article of faith that Dr. King had been marked for death. We all knew it. We knew that if someone had a clear shot at this great man, the trigger would be squeezed. He was addressing not just racism at home, but also standing up against the war in Vietnam. He was just becoming too dangerous to too many people. At the moment Dr. King made a very positive statement directly to me. He said, "John, I had to go back and stand for those that won't stand for themselves, and I have to go back for those that can't stand for themselves." The way he said it was very distinct and very precise. Once again, he said he had to "stand for those who won't stand for themselves, and stand for those who can't stand for themselves." Won't and can't: he had enough room in his heart for both.

When Dr. King said that, it made my life more certain. Maybe this is just the way I remember it more than forty years later, but that moment gave me direction. Until then I was kind of a rebel without a cause, like Brando when they said, "What are you rebelling against?" and he replied, "What have you got?" I never had any kind of a game plan or formula for what I was going to do in my life. I didn't have a compass. I would improvise and speak out against injustice as I saw it arise. But when Dr. King said those words to me, it was like he joined my mind and my heart and guided them toward one direction. This is when I became a heart and soul member of what we called the Olympic Project for Human Rights.

As we discussed that night, our demands as the OPHR had to go beyond just getting apartheid South Africa disinvited from the games. The fact that they had been readmitted in the first place spoke to how deep racism festered in the heart of the IOC. That was why one of the critical demands of OPHR was to remove Avery Brundage as head of the IOC. Now, I had never met Avery Brundage. I'd seen his rants on television, but that was about the extent of it. My impression was that Avery Brundage was very comfortable standing to the right of all things right wing. He came off like someone with money and power who couldn't or wouldn't hear what we were trying to say. I also felt like he was a puppet for other darker, even more reactionary, forces. He might've been the face of the IOC, but I think there were a lot of very powerful forces pushing him out front to be the tip of the spear. In other words, he had a lot of serious support behind the things he was saying. But as their figurehead, he hurt a great many people. He was the voice for apartheid South Africa and what was then known as Rhodesia. He was the voice saying that our concerns regarding having more African American coaches were irrelevant. He wasn't an honest broker for any nation of the global South. He had to go.

TOMMY AND LEE

By this time, I had also cemented my relationship with the gifted young men who would be seen as the leaders of the OPHR, Lee Evans and Tommie Smith. I had met them before, but that was always in the heat of competition. I had gone west to San Jose State when we went to the national in 1965. To be honest with you, coming out of New York, I felt like they were country boys. I used to always bust their chops, saying to them, "Man, it's like you guys are still putting caps on your sneakers and wearing suspenders." But even then, as much as I called them "country," it was obvious that they had the highest abilities in the sport. I had nothing but respect and admiration for them and the talents that they brought to the track for each and every race.

Tommie in particular was someone I paid close attention to because we both ran the 200 meters and Tommie was the acknowledged number one runner of that race in the world. He was also the type of guy who would not race against the best competition, like myself, unless it was absolutely necessary. I understood why he had this approach to racing, but it still got under my skin. I respected Tommie and his abilities, but I also felt like our skills were commensurate. We should have been like Ali and Frazier in the lead-up to the 1968 Olympics, racing against each other every few months. But he avoided me like I had smallpox and we only ran head to head maybe five times over the course of my entire career.

I think the first time I ran against Tommie was in 1967 at the Los Angeles Coliseum. I was running in a relay with the great Jimmy Hines and some other guys from Houston. We called ourselves the Houston Striders and we formed a team to come out west to California, to run at the Coliseum. Tommie Smith was running the anchor leg in the mile relay, and so was I and I ran him down and we got kind of tangled up a little bit coming off that last turn. He kind of bumped me and got away from me, and I kind of ran back on him again, and he won the race, and I remember I was a little disturbed because I felt like we took second and it was okay, but then I found out later they weren't giving out second place prizes, which made it all worse.

I think he was a little scared of me. I had already run 9.2 in the 100-yard dash and 20.2 in the 200. He and everyone had gotten word of this wild Mexican runner named Juan Carlos. There isn't a drop of Mexican blood in my body, but to this day, people call me Juan Carlos mistakenly. In California, with its large Mexican population, I had my own fan base waiting for me. The press asked me questions about my Mexican upbringing and I just never said a thing. I never said a word and let them think what they wanted to think. The *Los Angeles Times* even put my name out there as "Juan Carlos, the Mexican from Texas!" The *Times* also messed up my age and came up with a story of a twenty-seven-year-old Mexican freshman Juan Carlos running those times. But soon people knew I was just John Carlos from Harlem. When it came to Tommie, I had a chip on my shoulder. But when we started linking arms and making our case with the OPHR, that changed. Tommie stopped looking at me like a threat and I stopped looking at him like someone I was constantly trying to catch. From that time on, we were brothers in the struggle to build a boycott groundswell for the 1968 games.

In those early days of 1968, we really felt like we could make it happen. We had Dr. King on our side. We also happened to have the biggest, baddest athletes on earth on our side. We had the legendary Jackie Robinson, who broke baseball's color line in 1947, on our side. I have to say that I laugh when coaches and media talkers make the case that if an athlete is political, it somehow distracts from team concepts and winning. Four of the greatest winners in the history of sports were with us all the way: In the world of pro sports, we had Bill Russell and Jim Brown square in our corner. Bill Russell, the great Boston Celtics center, was in the midst of a run of winning eleven championships in thirteen years. He also was an outspoken opponent of racism and injustice in his adopted hometown of Boston. As for Jim Brown, he was pro football's all-time leading rusher and he led the Cleveland Browns to the 1964 NFL title. That's still the last title Cleveland has won in any sport. Russell and Brown supported us in the most helpful possible way. They were public. They showed up on all the talk shows and defended our efforts. But they also told us, "We will do whatever we can do to lend you support. But this is your ball of wax. Y'all are going to run this show. All we are going to do is be there to support you and do what you request of us." We asked them to go out and make the case for what we were doing and they did not disappoint. We also had Lew Alcindor, who of course would go on to change his name to Kareem Abdul Jabbar. Alcindor was in the middle of winning three straight NCAA titles at UCLA and he was militant. Hardly poisoning his team, that's for sure. Young Alcindor was public about how if there was a boycott, he would proudly adhere to it. Then there was the champion boxer Muhammad Ali. Restoring Ali's title was one of our central planks and it made me proud that he supported us and we supported him. Ali was young, gifted, and black. And he was proud of all three of those attributes. He was a gift from God to this society. And he protected the gift that God gave him. And then, once he converted to Islam and engaged with the Nation of Islam, he began to become educated. Ali, like me, had some learning disorders. But he was very sure of himself in terms of what knowledge he did have, and how he could use his knowledge and his fame for the greater good.

Ali represented black people. Ali represented his race. At the same time, there weren't a whole bunch of people jumping out there to support him, black or white. First of all, Ali didn't do anything to justify taking away his title. What they were doing to Ali, or attempting to do to Ali, was the same thing they were attempting to do to us in trying to take our medals away. We were going to be punished for standing up for what we believed in. Ali was being punished for standing up for what he believed in. He said he was against the war in Vietnam. And he had a right to be against the war in Vietnam. Nobody really explained to the public why we should fight this war. When we were going through so much sinister stuff here in the United States, merely for the color of our skin, he made a very poignant statement when he said these people [the Vietnamese] have never done anything to us. And at the same time he was making that statement, I was making the statement that if the Vietnamese ever come across the Harlem River Bridge, I'll be the first one to pick up arms against them. But for us to go far away to a foreign land that most of us hadn't heard of, it's difficult for clear-thinking individuals to stand up and say, I'm going to go fight a war even though I know nothing about it. So, quite naturally, you want to support the individual that stands up for his own rights and for human rights generally.

I also like Ali because I came from a military family. Two of my brothers were in the military. One was in the army and the other was in the air force. And I remember they used to tell me, "Johnny, it's your patriotic duty to go in the army, to join the war." And I said, for what? Those people ain't done nothing to me. My other brother stared at me and said, "If nothing else, Johnny, we get a chance to see the world." I laughed and put my arms around his shoulder and said, "My brother, there has to be a better way to see the world."

CHALLENGES

This was the apex of our struggle, getting this kind of high-profile support. The low point of our situation was when we would have to argue with other young athletes about the need for them to support the boycott. They would look at us like they understood and agreed with us, but had no choice but to take a pass. It felt like they were saying to me, "Man, this is just the way life is. There's no changing anything. We can do it on the field and that needs to be good enough." It was almost like these guys were in quicksand, they could feel themselves sinking, and here we were trying to throw them a lifeline, but they were afraid to accept it.

We were taking our leadership from people like Bill Russell and Jim Brown, but the young runners resistant to the boycott had leaders and men of respect on their side as well. For instance, all of us looked up to the great Olympic runner Ralph Boston. Ralph was the predominant competitive elder in our sport. He also was born in Mississippi. When Ralph was asked by the media about whether he felt the need to say something about racism in the United States during the Olympics, he said that he wouldn't know what to say because he had never experienced any kind of prejudice or racism in Mississippi when he was coming up as a youngster. This was a terrible untruth that he told to the media. He had certainly said otherwise when we were all together in the training room. So I was simply shocked to hear him say such a thing publicly, and I wasn't alone. There were several of us together at that time when we heard him make this statement, and our jaws just hit the floor. Ralph certainly wasn't alone in opposing the boycott or trying to put a smiley face on what it meant to be black in America at that time. The general assumption was that anyone who tried to mix sports and the politics of resistance would pay a terrible price. But by the end of the Olympics, Ralph was singing a very different tune. Like Harry Edwards wrote, by the time the Olympics were done Ralph came back capital-B "Black."

But the story had yet to be written and Ralph was hardly alone in his misguidedness. In those early months of 1968, it was a sad situation to see my teammates, my comrades in athletic competition, pretending that they didn't know their history or how life was for themselves and their ancestors. Maybe they truly didn't know the blood and bondage that defined our history and our present. But I just found that impossible to believe. Far more likely, they were blinded by the glitter of a medal, or they just didn't care to see or understand what was happening right in front of their faces. Those of us who identified ourselves as part of the OPHR could only tell them that we couldn't make them accept the boycott. We weren't trying to coerce anyone to agree with us. We couldn't make them give up their Olympic dreams. No pressure. All we could do is put our ideas and demands on the table and hope that they could embrace them for themselves. But the desire for that medal had at this point become the great motivator in their lives. Actually, it was more than a motivator. It was their compass. It was like they'd been taken over by gold, silver, and bronze. They couldn't get around those medals and face the reality of life head-on.

Then two events occurred in April of 1968 that took the wind out of our sails. The first and most devastating was the assassination of Dr. King in Memphis. The loss of his presence, leadership, and moral authority was difficult enough. Seeing cities around the country burn as the man who epitomized nonviolence was gunned down tore us up.

And most practically, we lost the vision of Dr. King joining us in Mexico City to protest outside the gates of the Olympic stadium. It was like we'd been kicked in the chest. The second event that took place later in the month was the re-banning of apartheid South Africa from the Olympics. Our pressure, at least on that front, had worked. But it also served to make a lot of our allies say, "Well, we accomplished that. So let's line up and go for the gold!"

There came a point after the events in April when people like Dr. Harry Edwards, Tommie Smith, Lee Evans, and I looked at each other and realized, "We don't really have the forces to pull this off." This happened at our last organized meeting before we had to start either packing our bags for Mexico City or announce that we were staying home. We had to try and come to some sort of understanding of what we were going to do collectively and when we did a head count of who was in and who was out, it was obvious that there were too many people saying, "I am not willing or able or ready to sacrifice my opportunities in the Olympic Games for the sake of the boycott." The counterargument we made was "Your life is going to go on a lot longer after your Olympic medal moments and what standard of living do you expect to have? We have a chance to make a difference right here, right now." We were very lonely at this point in standing for the boycott. It's funny because today, you see many individuals trying to rewrite that history and make it seem like back then they were standing with us every step of the way. But what they were saying in reality was, "I understand what you are coming for, I just don't want to hear it, not when there is a medal to be won." I think of Charlie Green, Ralph Boston, Bob Beamon. Before the games, all these guys wanted the taste of Olympic glory more than they wanted a life as a three-dimensional man. They wanted to be princes of their sport even if it meant being a pauper when the uniform came off.

At the time, I thought their heads were in the past and Harry, Tommy, Lee, and I were the voices of the future. But in many ways, these guys who opposed the boycott and saw their individual achievement above all else tragically had a better handle on where the world was going. Getting yours, the hell with everybody else, forgetting about your sisters and brothers: this has defined our modern era, and it defined these hardheaded teammates of ours. I remember getting heated, saying, "Man, what we are talking about ain't sports. It's life! Who cares if you go through life without a medal? So what? Everyone can't be an Olympic champion, but by staying home you could represent so many individuals who would never come close to the Olympic Games. By going, you are representing yourself and you are selling an image of this country to the world that just ain't the truth. By boycotting, you are with everyone."

But we couldn't pull it off. After Dr. King was murdered and the IOC folded on South Africa, the other athletes just weren't hearing what we were trying to say. People were carrying themselves differently. You could see it in their faces, their shoulders, and their attitudes. They were done with this boycott talk.

Now it was down to just a few of us and the question was right there on the table for all the OPHR diehards: were we all actually going to go to the Olympic Games or would we do an entirely symbolic, ineffective boycott made up of people you could count on one hand? We had taken so much heat in the media for the boycott call, and heat from the coaches, from the track federations, from the IOC, and we were ready to stand up to all of it. But we weren't prepared to shovel sand in the ocean. We weren't prepared to look weak. We had no choice but to fold our tent. At this time, we had no thoughts of symbolic protest at the games themselves. We were dissatisfied that our teammates didn't have heart enough to stand with us. I was ticked off, and Harry and Tommy and Lee were just disenchanted.

After we decided to shut it down, the biggest thing I had to decipher in my mind and heart was whether I would just stay at home anyway. I was just so angry at everybody and everything, I wasn't sure if I'd have the stomach for any of it. I remember I had a discussion with Kareem. Kareem was saying that he still didn't want to go. I said to him, "Man, let me tell you something, you're going to be the heart of the NBA. You will be getting paid to play basketball for years to come whether you go or not. If you choose not to go and say you want to stay home to pursue your studies, who is going to argue with you?" That's exactly what he did.

I wanted to stay home as well, but after much deliberation, I decided that I simply couldn't. I felt if I stayed home that someone would win a medal and get on the podium—and be standing where I was meant to stand. I just felt they were not going to represent what I wanted and needed to be represented at that medal moment. It was imperative that I make the team now. It was imperative to me that I win a medal because if I wasn't staying home, I wanted to be in Mexico City to express my feelings. I wasn't sure what I was going to do, but something had to be done, and I was going to do it.

Invent

This exercise will prepare you for Major Assignment #1: The Sports Memoir. Make a list of all the textual strategies, tone, mood, descriptive writing, character development, plot, and narrative arc, you see Carlos employing in his memoir to craft an impressionable moment. Next to these conventions provide clear examples from the excerpt that seem particularly compelling.

Collaborate

Carlos is part of one of the most iconic moments in sports history. Yet, as this selection demonstrates, Carlos's involvement with the Olympic Project for Human Rights is intimately tied up to broader struggles for civil rights in the 1960s. In his path to activism, Carlos is inspired by Malcolm X, Dr. Martin Luther King, Dr. Harry Edwards, and Muhammad Ali. In small groups, research one of these prominent figures. How does the information you discover about these prominent figures change your understanding of Carlos's story and of the Olympic Project for Human Rights?

Compose

This exercise will prepare you for Major Assignment #1: The Sports Memoir. Write a short essay in which you reflect on a prominent sports memory from your childhood. Try to adapt some of the conventions of memoir used by Carlos in this selection to create a memorable impression for your reader. What message do you want to convey? How can you use descriptive language to impart meaning to your memory?

Gold medallist Tommie Smith and bronze medallist John Carlos showing the raised fist on the podium after the 200m in the 1968 Summer Olympics wearing Olympic Project for Human Rights badges. The athletes raised their fists during the playing of the National Anthem in what was originally viewed as a symbol of protest. Smith later stated in his autobiography, Silent Gesture, that the gesture was a "human rights salute." The third athlete is silver medalist Peter Norman from Australia wearing an OPHR, Olympic Project for Human Rights, badge to show his support for the two Americans.

1968 OLYMPICS BLACK POWER SALUTE

John Dominis/Getty Images

"The Black Power Salute" is perhaps one of the most iconographic images of twentieth century sports history. What images, associations, or feelings arise from this image? Take five minutes to freewrite about whatever impressions the image evokes in you as a viewer.

In an essay, explore under what conditions as an athlete you would feel inspired to use sports for activism, and for what cause. If you have never played sports before, write an essay in which you explore how you feel about athletes and activism, using examples like Carlos and Smith from which to draw your argument.

With a group of your classmates, quickly search the web for images and articles pertaining to athletes and activism. What issues, which athletes, and what historical periods come up in your search? Which activist approaches seem the most important to you as a group, and why? Make and title a collage of your favorite activist images and articles to share with the class.

Visit Wikipedia's web page dedicated to the Olympic Back Power Salute (http://en.wikipedia.org/wiki/1968_Olympics_Black_Power_salute) to learn more about the cultural context in which this iconic sports image of American track and field athletes Smith and Carlos occured. Then visit: http://www.theguardian.com/sport/blog/2008/oct/14/olympicsandthemedia-athletics and explore the British newspaper's retrospective on its own coverage of the historic moment. After reading, reflect on how you feel about Smith and Carlos's actions to use sport as a platform for activism. Given *The Guardian's* coverage of the moment, how do you perceive the impact of Carlos and Smith's activism on an international stage? How do you feel about Australian Peter Norman's decision to stand in solidarity with Smith and Carlos? What would you have done if you were in Norman's position? Why?

In 2012, in response to the death of Trayvon Martin in Florida, Miami Heat basketball members Dwyane Wade and LeBron James used social media to create a viral public argument about the connections between xenophobia and black urban culture, in particular the association of wearing a hoody with "thugism." Among some of the hashtags LeBron circulated with the following photo of his Miami Heat team in their hoodies were *#WeAreTrayvonMartin* and *#WeWantJustice*.

#WEARETRAYVONMARTIN

BY @KINGJAMES (LEBRON JAMES)

From *@KingJames (James, LeBron)*. *"#WeAreTrayvonMartin."* Twitter Image (March 23, 2012).

What argument are LeBron and his Miami Heat teammates making in this photo? What textual evidence can you make in support of this argument? Why the decision to wear the hoods up? Why the purposeful decision to have all players looking down? In what ways does the image resonate with you? Do you agree or disagree with its statement? Why or why not?

What connections can you make between the Miami Heat's use of Twitter as a platform for activism in today's times and John Carlos's use of the Olympics as a platform for activism in the 1960s? Do you think one is more effective than the other? What strengths and weaknesses to each approach do you see? How do these two instances of activism shape your understanding of the role of athletes in social justice and activist movements?

In small groups, read and discuss the following ESPN.com article about the Miami Heat's decision to make the public statement about Trayvon Martin here: http://espn.go.com/nba/truehoop/miamiheat/story/_/id/7728618/miami-heat-don-hoodies-response-death-teen-trayvon-martin. Do you think the Heat's strategy was effective or not? Do you agree or disagree with their statement? How does the Heat's involvement with the Trayvon Martin case shape your understanding of the commonplace attitude that "sports and politics don't mix"? Share your findings with the class.

This exercise will prepare you for Major Assignment #5: The Persuasive Research Paper. The Trayvon Martin case is just one of several examples in recent history in which athletes have used their celebrity status as a platform to speak out on controversial issues. For example, in 2010, the Phoenix Suns wore "Los Suns" jerseys during Western Conference playoffs in response to the controversial state legislation SB1070: http://www.azcentral.com/sports/suns/articles/2010/05/04/20100504phoenix-suns-los-suns-jerseys.html. Write a short essay in which you reflect on the your thoughts and feelings about athletes and activism, using the linked readings in this section and excerpts from Carlos's chapter, "1968," to support your thinking. Do you think athletes have a responsibility to be social role models? Why or why not? Do you think they are effective as activists and if so, why? How do you understand Carlos's decision in the 1960s to take a stand for human rights in relationship to contemporary athletes' approaches to activism?

Taylor Branch is the Pulitzer Prize winning author of a three-volume civil rights movement history, America in the King Years. *In his contribution to the "Pay for Play" debate, Branch explores the ethical dimensions around race, sport, and economics in this widely circulated Atlantic essay.*

COLLEGE LEAGUE

THE SHAME OF COLLEGE SPORTS

BY TAYLOR BRANCH

"I'm not hiding," Sonny Vaccaro told a closed hearing at the Willard Hotel in Washington, D.C., in 2001. "We want to put our materials on the bodies of your athletes, and the best way to do that is buy your school. Or buy your coach."

Vaccaro's audience, the members of the Knight Commission on Intercollegiate Athletics, bristled. These were eminent reformers—among them the president of the National Collegiate Athletic Association, two former heads of the U.S. Olympic Committee, and several university presidents and chancellors. The Knight Foundation, a nonprofit that takes an interest in college athletics as part of its concern with civic life, had tasked them with saving college sports from runaway commercialism as embodied by the likes of Vaccaro, who, since signing his pioneering shoe contract with Michael Jordan in 1984, had built sponsorship empires successively at Nike, Adidas, and Reebok. Not all the members could hide their scorn for the "sneaker pimp" of schoolyard hustle, who boasted of writing checks for millions to everybody in higher education.

"Why," asked Bryce Jordan, the president emeritus of Penn State, "should a university be an advertising medium for your industry?"

Vaccaro did not blink. "They shouldn't, sir," he replied. "You sold your souls, and you're going to continue selling them. You can be very moral and righteous in asking me that question, sir," Vaccaro added with irrepressible good cheer, "but there's not one of you in this room that's going to turn down any of our money. You're going to take it. I can only offer it."

From *The Atlantic* (2011).

William Friday, a former president of North Carolina's university system, still winces at the memory. "Boy, the silence that fell in that room," he recalled recently. "I never will forget it." Friday, who founded and co-chaired two of the three Knight Foundation sports initiatives over the past 20 years, called Vaccaro "the worst of all" the witnesses ever to come before the panel.

But what Vaccaro said in 2001 was true then, and it's true now: corporations offer money so they can profit from the glory of college athletes, and the universities grab it. In 2010, despite the faltering economy, a single college athletic league, the football-crazed Southeastern Conference (SEC), became the first to crack the billion-dollar barrier in athletic receipts. The Big Ten pursued closely at $905 million. That money comes from a combination of ticket sales, concession sales, merchandise, licensing fees, and other sources—but the great bulk of it comes from television contracts.

Educators are in thrall to their athletic departments because of these television riches and because they respect the political furies that can burst from a locker room. "There's fear," Friday told me when I visited him on the University of North Carolina campus in Chapel Hill last fall. As we spoke, two giant construction cranes towered nearby over the university's Kenan Stadium, working on the latest $77 million renovation. (The University of Michigan spent almost four times that much to expand its Big House.) Friday insisted that for the networks, paying huge sums to universities was a bargain. "We do every little thing for them," he said. "We furnish the theater, the actors, the lights, the music, and the audience for a drama measured neatly in time slots. They bring the camera and turn it on." Friday, a weathered idealist at 91, laments the control universities have ceded in pursuit of this money. If television wants to broadcast football from here on a Thursday night, he said, "we shut down the university at 3 o'clock to accommodate the crowds." He longed for a campus identity more centered in an academic mission.

The United States is the only country in the world that hosts big-time sports at institutions of higher learning. This should not, in and of itself, be controversial. College athletics are rooted in the classical ideal of *Mens sana in corpore sano*—a sound mind in a sound body— and who would argue with that? College sports are deeply inscribed in the culture of our nation. Half a million young men and women play competitive intercollegiate sports each year. Millions of spectators flock into football stadiums each Saturday in the fall, and tens of millions more watch on television. The March Madness basketball tournament each spring has become a major national event, with upwards of 80 million watching it on television and talking about the games around the office water cooler. ESPN has spawned ESPNU, a channel dedicated to college sports, and Fox Sports and other cable outlets are developing channels exclusively to cover sports from specific regions or divisions.

With so many people paying for tickets and watching on television, college sports has become Very Big Business. According to various reports, the football teams at Texas,

Florida, Georgia, Michigan, and Penn State—to name just a few big-revenue football schools—each earn between $40 million and $80 million in profits a year, even after paying coaches multimillion-dollar salaries. When you combine so much money with such high, almost tribal, stakes—football boosters are famously rabid in their zeal to have their alma mater win—corruption is likely to follow.

Scandal after scandal has rocked college sports. In 2010, the NCAA sanctioned the University of Southern California after determining that star running back Reggie Bush and his family had received "improper benefits" while he played for the Trojans. (Among other charges, Bush and members of his family were alleged to have received free airfare and limousine rides, a car, and a rent-free home in San Diego, from sports agents who wanted Bush as a client.) The Bowl Championship Series stripped USC of its 2004 national title, and Bush returned the Heisman Trophy he had won in 2005. Last fall, as Auburn University football stormed its way to an undefeated season and a national championship, the team's star quarterback, Cam Newton, was dogged by allegations that his father had used a recruiter to solicit up to $180,000 from Mississippi State in exchange for his son's matriculation there after junior college in 2010. Jim Tressel, the highly successful head football coach of the Ohio State Buckeyes, resigned last spring after the NCAA alleged he had feigned ignorance of rules violations by players on his team. At least 28 players over the course of the previous nine seasons, according to *Sports Illustrated,* had traded autographs, jerseys, and other team memorabilia in exchange for tattoos or cash at a tattoo parlor in Columbus, in violation of NCAA rules. Late this summer, Yahoo Sports reported that the NCAA was investigating allegations that a University of Miami booster had given millions of dollars in illicit cash and services to more than 70 Hurricanes football players over eight years.

The list of scandals goes on. With each revelation, there is much wringing of hands. Critics scold schools for breaking faith with their educational mission, and for failing to enforce the sanctity of "amateurism." Sportswriters denounce the NCAA for both tyranny and impotence in its quest to "clean up" college sports. Observers on all sides express jumbled emotions about youth and innocence, venting against professional mores or greedy amateurs.

For all the outrage, the real scandal is not that students are getting illegally paid or recruited, it's that two of the noble principles on which the NCAA justifies its existence— "amateurism" and the "student-athlete"—are cynical hoaxes, legalistic confections propagated by the universities so they can exploit the skills and fame of young athletes. The tragedy at the heart of college sports is not that some college athletes are getting paid, but that more of them are not.

Don Curtis, a UNC trustee, told me that impoverished football players cannot afford movie tickets or bus fare home. Curtis is a rarity among those in higher education today, in that he dares to violate the signal taboo: "I think we should pay these guys something."

Fans and educators alike recoil from this proposal as though from original sin. Amateurism is the whole point, they say. Paid athletes would destroy the integrity and appeal of college sports. Many former college athletes object that money would have spoiled the sanctity of the bond they enjoyed with their teammates. I, too, once shuddered instinctively at the notion of paid college athletes.

But after an inquiry that took me into locker rooms and ivory towers across the country, I have come to believe that sentiment blinds us to what's before our eyes. Big-time college sports are fully commercialized. Billions of dollars flow through them each year. The NCAA makes money, and enables universities and corporations to make money, from the unpaid labor of young athletes.

Slavery analogies should be used carefully. College athletes are not slaves. Yet to survey the scene—corporations and universities enriching themselves on the backs of uncompensated young men, whose status as "student-athletes" deprives them of the right to due process guaranteed by the Constitution—is to catch an unmistakable whiff of the plantation. Perhaps a more apt metaphor is colonialism: college sports, as overseen by the NCAA, is a system imposed by well-meaning paternalists and rationalized with hoary sentiments about caring for the well-being of the colonized. But it is, nonetheless, unjust. The NCAA, in its zealous defense of bogus principles, sometimes destroys the dreams of innocent young athletes.

The NCAA today is in many ways a classic cartel. Efforts to reform it—most notably by the three Knight Commissions over the course of 20 years—have, while making changes around the edges, been largely fruitless. The time has come for a major overhaul. And whether the powers that be like it or not, big changes are coming. Threats loom on multiple fronts: in Congress, the courts, breakaway athletic conferences, student rebellion, and public disgust. Swaddled in gauzy clichés, the NCAA presides over a vast, teetering glory.

FOUNDING MYTHS

From the start, amateurism in college sports has been honored more often in principle than in fact; the NCAA was built of a mixture of noble and venal impulses. In the late nineteenth century, intellectuals believed that the sporting arena simulated an impending age of Darwinian struggle. Because the United States did not hold a global empire like England's, leaders warned of national softness once railroads conquered the last continental frontier. As though heeding this warning, ingenious students turned variations on rugby into a toughening agent. Today a plaque in New Brunswick, New Jersey, commemorates the first college game, on November 6, 1869, when Rutgers beat Princeton 6–4.

Walter Camp graduated from Yale in 1880 so intoxicated by the sport that he devoted his life to it without pay, becoming "the father of American football." He persuaded other schools to reduce the chaos on the field by trimming each side from 15 players to 11, and it was his idea to paint measuring lines on the field. He conceived functional designations for players, coining terms such as quarterback. His game remained violent by design. Crawlers could push the ball forward beneath piles of flying elbows without pause until they cried "Down!" in submission.

In an 1892 game against its arch rival, Yale, the Harvard football team was the first to deploy a "flying wedge," based on Napoleon's surprise concentrations of military force. In an editorial calling for the abolition of the play, *The New York Times* described it as "half a ton of bone and muscle coming into collision with a man weighing 160 or 170 pounds," noting that surgeons often had to be called onto the field. Three years later, the continuing mayhem prompted the Harvard faculty to take the first of two votes to abolish football. Charles Eliot, the university's president, brought up other concerns. "Deaths and injuries are not the strongest argument against football," declared Eliot. "That cheating and brutality are profitable is the main evil." Still, Harvard football persisted. In 1903, fervent alumni built Harvard Stadium with zero college funds. The team's first paid head coach, Bill Reid, started in 1905 at nearly twice the average salary for a full professor.

A newspaper story from that year, illustrated with the Grim Reaper laughing on a goalpost, counted 25 college players killed during football season. A fairy-tale version of the founding of the NCAA holds that President Theodore Roosevelt, upset by a photograph of a bloodied Swarthmore College player, vowed to civilize or destroy football. The real story is that Roosevelt maneuvered shrewdly to preserve the sport—and give a boost to his beloved Harvard. After *McClure's* magazine published a story on corrupt teams with phantom students, a muckraker exposed Walter Camp's $100,000 slush fund at Yale. In response to mounting outrage, Roosevelt summoned leaders from Harvard, Princeton, and Yale to the White House, where Camp parried mounting criticism and conceded nothing irresponsible in the college football rules he'd established. At Roosevelt's behest, the three schools issued a public statement that college sports must reform to survive, and representatives from 68 colleges founded a new organization that would soon be called the National Collegiate Athletic Association. A Haverford College official was confirmed as secretary but then promptly resigned in favor of Bill Reid, the new Harvard coach, who instituted new rules that benefited Harvard's playing style at the expense of Yale's. At a stroke, Roosevelt saved football and dethroned Yale.

For nearly 50 years, the NCAA, with no real authority and no staff to speak of, enshrined amateur ideals that it was helpless to enforce. (Not until 1939 did it gain the power even to mandate helmets.) In 1929, the Carnegie Foundation made headlines with a report, "American College Athletics," which concluded that the scramble for players had "reached the proportions of nationwide commerce." Of the 112 schools surveyed,

81 flouted NCAA recommendations with inducements to students ranging from open payrolls and disguised booster funds to no-show jobs at movie studios. Fans ignored the uproar, and two-thirds of the colleges mentioned told *The New York Times* that they planned no changes. In 1939, freshman players at the University of Pittsburgh went on strike because they were getting paid less than their upperclassman teammates.

Embarrassed, the NCAA in 1948 enacted a "Sanity Code," which was supposed to prohibit all concealed and indirect benefits for college athletes; any money for athletes was to be limited to transparent scholarships awarded solely on financial need. Schools that violated this code would be expelled from NCAA membership and thus exiled from competitive sports.

This bold effort flopped. Colleges balked at imposing such a drastic penalty on each other, and the Sanity Code was repealed within a few years. The University of Virginia went so far as to call a press conference to say that if its athletes were ever accused of being paid, they should be forgiven, because their studies at Thomas Jefferson's university were so rigorous.

THE BIG BLUFF

In 1951, the NCAA seized upon a serendipitous set of events to gain control of intercollegiate sports. First, the organization hired a young college dropout named Walter Byers as executive director. A journalist who was not yet 30 years old, he was an appropriately inauspicious choice for the vaguely defined new post. He wore cowboy boots and a toupee. He shunned personal contact, obsessed over details, and proved himself a bureaucratic master of pervasive, anonymous intimidation. Although discharged from the Army during World War II for defective vision, Byers was able to see an opportunity in two contemporaneous scandals. In one, the tiny College of William and Mary, aspiring to challenge football powers Oklahoma and Ohio State, was found to be counterfeiting grades to keep conspicuously pampered players eligible. In the other, a basketball point-shaving conspiracy (in which gamblers paid players to perform poorly) had spread from five New York colleges to the University of Kentucky, the reigning national champion, generating tabloid "perp" photos of gangsters and handcuffed basketball players. The scandals posed a crisis of credibility for collegiate athletics, and nothing in the NCAA's feeble record would have led anyone to expect real reform.

But Byers managed to impanel a small infractions board to set penalties without waiting for a full convention of NCAA schools, which would have been inclined toward forgiveness. Then he lobbied a University of Kentucky dean—A. D. Kirwan, a former football coach and future university president—not to contest the NCAA's dubious legal position (the association had no actual authority to penalize the university), pleading that college sports must do something to restore public support. His gambit succeeded when

Kirwan reluctantly accepted a landmark precedent: the Kentucky basketball team would be suspended for the entire 1952–53 season. Its legendary coach, Adolph Rupp, fumed for a year in limbo.

The Kentucky case created an aura of centralized command for an NCAA office that barely existed. At the same time, a colossal misperception gave Byers leverage to mine gold. Amazingly in retrospect, most colleges and marketing experts considered the advent of television a dire threat to sports. Studies found that broadcasts reduced live attendance, and therefore gate receipts, because some customers preferred to watch at home for free. Nobody could yet imagine the revenue bonanza that television represented. With clunky new TV sets proliferating, the 1951 NCAA convention voted 161–7 to outlaw televised games except for a specific few licensed by the NCAA staff.

All but two schools quickly complied. The University of Pennsylvania and Notre Dame protested the order to break contracts for home-game television broadcasts, claiming the right to make their own decisions. Byers objected that such exceptions would invite disaster. The conflict escalated. Byers brandished penalties for games televised without approval. Penn contemplated seeking antitrust protection through the courts. Byers issued a contamination notice, informing any opponent scheduled to play Penn that it would be punished for showing up to compete. In effect, Byers mobilized the college world to isolate the two holdouts in what one sportswriter later called "the Big Bluff."

Byers won. Penn folded in part because its president, the perennial White House contender Harold Stassen, wanted to mend relations with fellow schools in the emerging Ivy League, which would be formalized in 1954. When Notre Dame also surrendered, Byers conducted exclusive negotiations with the new television networks on behalf of every college team. Joe Rauh Jr., a prominent civil-rights attorney, helped him devise a rationing system to permit only 11 broadcasts a year—the fabled Game of the Week. Byers and Rauh selected a few teams for television exposure, excluding the rest. On June 6, 1952, NBC signed a one-year deal to pay the NCAA $1.14 million for a carefully restricted football package. Byers routed all contractual proceeds through his office. He floated the idea that, to fund an NCAA infrastructure, his organization should take a 60 percent cut; he accepted 12 percent that season. (For later contracts, as the size of television revenues grew exponentially, he backed down to 5 percent.) Proceeds from the first NBC contract were enough to rent an NCAA headquarters, in Kansas City.

Only one year into his job, Byers had secured enough power and money to regulate all of college sports. Over the next decade, the NCAA's power grew along with television revenues. Through the efforts of Byers's deputy and chief lobbyist, Chuck Neinas, the NCAA won an important concession in the Sports Broadcasting Act of 1961, in which Congress made its granting of a precious antitrust exemption to the National Football League contingent upon the blackout of professional football on Saturdays. Deftly, without even mentioning the NCAA, a rider on the bill carved each weekend into protected broadcast markets: Saturday for college, Sunday for the NFL. The NFL got its antitrust exemption. Byers, having negotiated the NCAA's television package up to $3.1 million per football season—which was higher than the NFL's figure in those early years—had made the NCAA into a spectacularly profitable cartel.

[...]

THE MYTH OF THE "STUDENT-ATHLETE"

Today, much of the NCAA's moral authority—indeed much of the justification for its existence—is vested in its claim to protect what it calls the "student-athlete." The term is meant to conjure the nobility of amateurism, and the precedence of scholarship over athletic endeavor. But the origins of the "student-athlete" lie not in a disinterested ideal but in a sophistic formulation designed, as the sports economist Andrew Zimbalist has written, to help the NCAA in its "fight against workmen's compensation insurance claims for injured football players."

"We crafted the term student-athlete," Walter Byers himself wrote, "and soon it was embedded in all NCAA rules and interpretations." The term came into play in the 1950s, when the widow of Ray Dennison, who had died from a head injury received while playing football in Colorado for the Fort Lewis A&M Aggies, filed for workmen's-compensation death benefits. Did his football scholarship make the fatal collision a "work-related" accident? Was he a school employee, like his peers who worked part-time as teaching assistants and bookstore cashiers? Or was he a fluke victim of extracurricular pursuits? Given the hundreds of incapacitating injuries to college athletes each year, the answers to these questions had enormous consequences. The Colorado Supreme Court ultimately agreed with the school's contention that he was not eligible for benefits, since the college was "not in the football business."

The term *student-athlete* was deliberately ambiguous. College players were not students at play (which might understate their athletic obligations), nor were they just athletes in college (which might imply they were professionals). That they were high-performance athletes meant they could be forgiven for not meeting the academic standards of their peers; that they were students meant they did not have to be compensated, ever, for anything more than the cost of their studies. *Student-athlete* became the NCAA's signature term, repeated constantly in and out of courtrooms.

Using the "student-athlete" defense, colleges have compiled a string of victories in liability cases. On the afternoon of October 26, 1974, the Texas Christian University Horned Frogs were playing the Alabama Crimson Tide in Birmingham, Alabama. Kent Waldrep, a TCU running back, carried the ball on a "Red Right 28" sweep toward the Crimson Tide's sideline, where he was met by a swarm of tacklers. When Waldrep regained consciousness, Bear Bryant, the storied Crimson Tide coach, was standing over his hospital bed. "It was like talking to God, if you're a young football player," Waldrep recalled.

Waldrep was paralyzed: he had lost all movement and feeling below his neck. After nine months of paying his medical bills, Texas Christian refused to pay any more, so the Waldrep family coped for years on dwindling charity.

Through the 1990s, from his wheelchair, Waldrep pressed a lawsuit for workers' compensation. (He also, through heroic rehabilitation efforts, recovered feeling in his arms, and eventually learned to drive a specially rigged van. "I can brush my teeth," he told me last year, "but I still need help to bathe and dress.") His attorneys haggled with TCU and the state worker-compensation fund over what constituted employment. Clearly, TCU had provided football players with equipment for the job, as a typical employer would—but did the university pay wages, withhold income taxes on his financial aid, or control work conditions and performance? The appeals court finally rejected Waldrep's claim in June of 2000, ruling that he was not an employee because he had not paid taxes on financial aid that he could have kept even if he quit football. (Waldrep told me school officials "said they recruited me as a student, not an athlete," which he says was absurd.)

The long saga vindicated the power of the NCAA's "student-athlete" formulation as a shield, and the organization continues to invoke it as both a legalistic defense and a noble ideal. Indeed, such is the term's rhetorical power that it is increasingly used as a sort of reflexive mantra against charges of rabid hypocrisy.

Last Thanksgiving weekend, with both the FBI and the NCAA investigating whether Cam Newton had been lured onto his team with illegal payments, Newton's Auburn Tigers and the Alabama Crimson Tide came together for their annual game, known as the Iron Bowl, before 101,821 fans at Bryant-Denny Stadium. This game is always a highlight of the football season because of the historic rivalry between the two schools, and the 2010 edition had enormous significance, pitting the defending national champion Crimson Tide against the undefeated Tigers, who were aiming for their first championship since 1957. I expected excited fans; what I encountered was the throbbing heart of college sports. As I drove before daybreak toward the stadium, a sleepless caller babbled over WJOX, the local fan radio station, that he "couldn't stop thinking about the coin toss." In the parking lot, ticketless fans were puzzled that anyone need ask why they had tailgated for days just to watch their satellite-fed flat screens within earshot of the roar. All that morning, pilgrims packed the Bear Bryant museum, where displays elaborated the misery of Alabama's 4–24 run before the glorious Bryant era dawned in 1958.

Finally, as Auburn took the field for warm-ups, one of Alabama's public-address-system operators played "Take the Money and Run" (an act for which he would be fired). A sea of signs reading $CAM taunted Newton. The game, perhaps the most exciting of the season, was unbearably tense, with Auburn coming from way behind to win 28–27, all but assuring that it would go on to play for the national championship. Days later, Auburn suspended Newton after the NCAA found that a rules violation had occurred: his father was alleged to have marketed his son in a pay-for-play scheme; a day after that, the NCAA reinstated Newton's eligibility because investigators had not found evidence that Newton or Auburn officials had known of his father's actions. This left Newton conveniently eligible for the Southeastern Conference championship game and for the postseason BCS championship bowl. For the NCAA, prudence meant honoring public demand.

"Our championships," NCAA President Mark Emmert has declared, "are one of the primary tools we have to enhance the student-athlete experience."

[…]

"THE PLANTATION MENTALITY"

"Ninety percent of the NCAA revenue is produced by 1 percent of the athletes," Sonny Vaccaro says. "Go to the skill positions"—the stars. "Ninety percent African Americans." The NCAA made its money off those kids, and so did he. They were not all bad people, the NCAA officials, but they were blind, Vaccaro believes. "Their organization is a fraud."

Vaccaro retired from Reebok in 2007 to make a clean break for a crusade. "The kids and their parents gave me a good life," he says in his peppery staccato. "I want to give something back." Call it redemption, he told me. Call it education or a good cause. "Here's what I preach," said Vaccaro. "This goes beyond race, to human rights. The least educated are the most exploited. I'm probably closer to the kids than anyone else, and I'm 71 years old."

Vaccaro is officially an unpaid consultant to the plaintiffs in *O'Bannon v. NCAA*. He connected Ed O'Bannon with the attorneys who now represent him, and he talked to some of the additional co-plaintiffs who have joined the suit, among them Oscar Robertson, a basketball Hall of Famer who was incensed that the NCAA was still selling his image on playing cards 50 years after he left the University of Cincinnati.

Jon King, an antitrust lawyer at Hausfeld LLP in San Francisco, told me that Vaccaro "opened our eyes to massive revenue streams hidden in college sports." King and his colleagues have drawn on Vaccaro's vast knowledge of athletic-department finances, which include off-budget accounts for shoe contracts. Sonny Vaccaro and his wife, Pam, "had a mountain of documents," he said. The outcome of the 1984 Regents decision validated an antitrust approach for O'Bannon, King argues, as well as for Joseph Agnew in his continuing case against the one-year scholarship rule. Lawyers for Sam Keller—a former quarterback for the University of Nebraska who is featured in video games—are pursuing a parallel "right of publicity" track based on the First Amendment. Still other lawyers could revive Rick Johnson's case against NCAA bylaws on a larger scale, and King thinks claims for the rights of college players may be viable also under laws pertaining to contracts, employment, and civil rights.

Vaccaro had sought a law firm for O'Bannon with pockets deep enough to withstand an expensive war of attrition, fearing that NCAA officials would fight discovery to the end. So far, though, they have been forthcoming. "The numbers are off the wall," Vaccaro says. "The public will see for the first time how all the money is distributed."

Vaccaro has been traveling the after-dinner circuit, proselytizing against what he sees as the NCAA's exploitation of young athletes. Late in 2008, someone who heard his stump speech at Howard University mentioned it to Michael Hausfeld, a prominent antitrust and human-rights lawyer, whose firm had won suits against Exxon for Native Alaskans and against Union Bank of Switzerland for Holocaust victims' families. Someone tracked down Vaccaro on vacation in Athens, Greece, and he flew back directly to meet Hausfeld. The shoe salesman and the white-shoe lawyer made common cause.

Hausfeld LLP has offices in San Francisco, Philadelphia, and London. Its headquarters are on K Street in Washington, D.C., about three blocks from the White House. When I talked with Hausfeld there not long ago, he sat in a cavernous conference room, tidy in pinstripes, hands folded on a spotless table that reflected the skyline. He spoke softly, without pause, condensing the complex fugue of antitrust litigation into simple sentences. "Let's start with the basic question," he said, noting that the NCAA claims that student-athletes have no property rights in their own athletic accomplishments. Yet, in order to be eligible to play, college athletes have to waive their rights to proceeds from any sales based on their athletic performance.

"What right is it that they're waiving?," Hausfeld asked. "You can't waive something you don't have. So they had a right that they gave up in consideration to the principle of amateurism, if there be such." (At an April hearing in a U.S. District Court in California, Gregory Curtner, a representative for the NCAA, stunned O'Bannon's lawyers by saying: "There is no document, there is no substance, that the NCAA ever takes from the student-athletes their rights of publicity or their rights of likeness. They are at all times owned by the student-athlete." Jon King says this is "like telling someone they have the winning lottery ticket, but by the way, it can only be cashed in on Mars." The court denied for a second time an NCAA motion to dismiss the O'Bannon complaint.)

The waiver clause is nestled among the paragraphs of the "Student-Athlete Statement" that NCAA rules require be collected yearly from every college athlete. In signing the statement, the athletes attest that they have amateur status, that their stated SAT scores are valid, that they are willing to disclose any educational documents requested, and so forth. Already, Hausfeld said, the defendants in the Ed O'Bannon case have said in court filings that college athletes thereby transferred their promotional rights forever. He paused. "That's ludicrous," he said. "Nobody assigns rights like that. Nobody can assert rights like that." He said the pattern demonstrated clear abuse by the collective power of the schools and all their conferences under the NCAA umbrella—"a most effective cartel."

The faux ideal of amateurism is "the elephant in the room," Hausfeld said, sending for a book. "You can't get to the bottom of our case without exposing the hypocrisy of amateurism, and Walter Byers says it eloquently." An assistant brought in Byers's memoir. It looked garish on the shiny table because dozens of pink Post-its protruded from the text. Hausfeld read to me from page 390:

> The college player cannot sell his own feet (the coach does that) nor can he sell his own name (the college will do that). This is the plantation mentality resurrected and blessed by today's campus executives.

He looked up. "That wasn't me," he said. "That was the NCAA's architect." He found a key recommendation on page 388:

> Prosecutors and the courts, with the support of the public, should use antitrust laws to break up the collegiate cartel—not just in athletics but possibly in other aspects of collegiate life as well.

Could the book become evidence? Might the aged Byers testify? (He is now 89.) Was that part of the plaintiffs' strategy for the O'Bannon trial? Hausfeld smiled faintly. "I'd rather the NCAA lawyers not fully understand the strategy," he said.

He put the spiny book away and previewed what lies ahead. The court soon would qualify his clients as a class. Then the Sherman Antitrust Act would provide for thorough discovery to break down exactly what the NCAA receives on everything from video clips to jerseys, contract by contract. "And we want to know what they're carrying on their books as the value of their archival footage," he concluded. "They say it's a lot of money. We agree. How much?"

The work will be hard, but Hausfeld said he will win in the courts, unless the NCAA folds first. "Why?" Hausfeld asked rhetorically. "We know our clients are foreclosed: neither the NCAA nor its members will permit them to participate in any of that licensing revenue. Under the law, it's up to them [the defendants] to give a pro-competitive justification. They can't. End of story."

In 2010 the third Knight Commission, complementing a previous commission's recommendation for published reports on academic progress, called for the finances of college sports to be made transparent and public—television contracts, conference budgets, shoe deals, coaches' salaries, stadium bonds, everything. The recommendation was based on the worthy truism that sunlight is a proven disinfectant. But in practice, it has not been applied at all. Conferences, coaches, and other stakeholders resisted disclosure; college players still have no way of determining their value to the university.

"Money surrounds college sports," says Domonique Foxworth, who is a cornerback for the NFL's Baltimore Ravens and an executive-committee member for the NFL Players Association, and played for the University of Maryland. "And every player knows those millions are floating around only because of the 18-to-22-year-olds." Yes, he told me, even the second-string punter believes a miracle might lift him into the NFL, and why not? In all the many pages of the three voluminous Knight Commission reports, there is but one paragraph that addresses the real-life choices for college athletes. "Approximately 1 percent of NCAA men's basketball players and 2 percent of NCAA football players are drafted by NBA or NFL teams," stated the 2001 report, basing its figures on a review of the previous 10 years, "and just being drafted is no assurance of a successful professional career." Warning that the odds against professional athletic success are "astronomically high," the Knight Commission counsels college athletes to avoid a "rude surprise" and to stick to regular studies. This is sound advice as far as it goes, but it's a bromide that pinches off discussion. Nothing in the typical college curriculum teaches a sweat-stained guard at Clemson or Purdue what his monetary value to the university is. Nothing prods students to think independently about amateurism—because the universities themselves have too much invested in its preservation. Stifling thought, the universities, in league with the NCAA, have failed their own primary mission by providing an empty, cynical education on college sports.

The most basic reform would treat the students as what they are—adults, with rights and reason of their own—and grant them a meaningful voice in NCAA deliberations. A restoration of full citizenship to "student-athletes" would facilitate open governance, making it possible to enforce pledges of transparency in both academic standards and athletic finances. Without that, the NCAA has no effective checks and balances, no way for the students to provide informed consent regarding the way they are governed. A thousand questions lie willfully silenced because the NCAA is naturally afraid of giving "student-athletes" a true voice. Would college players be content with the augmented scholarship or allowance now requested by the National College Players Association? If a player's worth to the university is greater than the value of his scholarship (as it clearly is in some cases), should he be paid a salary? If so, would teammates in revenue sports want to be paid equally, or in salaries stratified according to talent or value on the field? What would the athletes want in Division III, where athletic budgets keep rising without scholarships or substantial sports revenue? Would athletes seek more or less variance in admissions standards? Should non-athletes also have a voice, especially where involuntary student fees support more and more of college sports? Might some schools choose to specialize, paying players only in elite leagues for football, or lacrosse? In athletic councils, how much would high-revenue athletes value a simple thank you from the tennis or field-hockey players for the newly specified subsidies to their facilities?

University administrators, already besieged from all sides, do not want to even think about such questions. Most cringe at the thought of bargaining with athletes as a general manager does in professional sports, with untold effects on the budgets for coaches and every other sports item. "I would not want to be part of it," North Carolina Athletic Director Dick Baddour told me flatly. After 44 years at UNC, he could scarcely contemplate a world without amateur rules. "We would have to think long and hard," Baddour added gravely, "about whether this university would continue those sports at all."

I, too, once reflexively recoiled at the idea of paying college athletes and treating them like employees or professionals. It feels abhorrent—but for reasons having to do more with sentiment than with practicality or law. Not just fans and university presidents but judges have often found cursory, non-statutory excuses to leave amateur traditions intact. "Even in the increasingly commercial modern world," said a federal-court judge in *Gaines v. NCAA* in 1990, "this Court believes there is still validity to the Athenian concept of a complete education derived from fostering the full growth of both mind and body." The fact that "the NCAA has not distilled amateurism to its purest form," said the Fifth Circuit Court of Appeals in 1988, "does not mean its attempts to maintain a mixture containing some amateur elements are unreasonable."

But one way or another, the smokescreen of amateurism may soon be swept away. For one thing, a victory by the plaintiffs in O'Bannon's case would radically transform college sports. Colleges would likely have to either stop profiting from students or start paying them. The NCAA could also be forced to pay tens, if not hundreds, of millions of dollars in damages. If O'Bannon and Vaccaro and company win, "it will turn college sports on its ear," said Richard Lapchick, the president of the National Consortium for Academics and Sports, in a recent interview with *The New York Times*.

Though the O'Bannon case may take several years yet to reach resolution, developments on other fronts are chipping away at amateurism, and at the NCAA. This past summer, *Sports Illustrated* editorialized in favor of allowing college athletes to be paid by non-university sources without jeopardizing their eligibility. At a press conference last June, Steve Spurrier, the coach of the South Carolina Gamecocks football team (and the winner of the 1966 Heisman Trophy as a Florida Gator), proposed that coaches start paying players $300 a game out of their own pockets. The coaches at six other SEC schools (Alabama, Florida, Ole Miss, Mississippi State, LSU, and Tennessee) all endorsed

Spurrier's proposal. And Mark Emmert, the NCAA president, recently conceded that big changes must come. "The integrity of collegiate athletics is seriously challenged today by rapidly growing pressures coming from many directions," Emmert said in July. "We have reached a point where incremental change is not sufficient to meet these challenges. I want us to act more aggressively and in a more comprehensive way than we have in the past. A few new tweaks of the rules won't get the job done."

Threats to NCAA dominion also percolate in Congress. Aggrieved legislators have sponsored numerous bills. Senator Orrin Hatch, citing mistreatment of his Utah Utes, has called witnesses to discuss possible antitrust remedies for the Bowl Championship Series. Congressional committees have already held hearings critical of the NCAA's refusal to follow due process in disciplinary matters; other committees have explored a rise in football concussions. Last January, calls went up to investigate "informal" football workouts at the University of Iowa just after the season-ending bowl games— workouts so grueling that 41 of the 56 amateur student-athletes collapsed, and 13 were hospitalized with rhabdomyolysis, a life-threatening kidney condition often caused by excessive exercise.

The greatest threat to the viability of the NCAA may come from its member universities. Many experts believe that the churning instability within college football will drive the next major change. President Obama himself has endorsed the drumbeat cry for a national playoff in college football. This past spring, the Justice Department questioned the BCS about its adherence to antitrust standards. Jim Delany, the commissioner of the Big Ten, has estimated that a national playoff system could produce three or four times as much money as the existing bowl system does. If a significant band of football schools were to demonstrate that they could orchestrate a true national playoff, without the NCAA's assistance, the association would be terrified—and with good reason. Because if the big sports colleges don't need the NCAA to administer a national playoff in football, then they don't need it to do so in basketball. In which case, they could cut out the middleman in March Madness and run the tournament themselves. Which would deprive the NCAA of close to $1 billion a year, more than 95 percent of its revenue. The organization would be reduced to a rule book without money—an organization aspiring to enforce its rules but without the financial authority to enforce anything.

Thus the playoff dreamed of and hankered for by millions of football fans haunts the NCAA. "There will be some kind of playoff in college football, and it will not be run by the NCAA," says Todd Turner, a former athletic director in four conferences (Big East, ACC, SEC, and Pac-10). "If I'm at the NCAA, I have to worry that the playoff group can get basketball to break away, too."

This danger helps explain why the NCAA steps gingerly in enforcements against powerful colleges. To alienate member colleges would be to jeopardize its own existence.

Long gone are television bans and the "death penalty" sentences (commanding season-long shutdowns of offending teams) once meted out to Kentucky (1952), Southwestern Louisiana (1973), and Southern Methodist University (1987). Institutions receive mostly symbolic slaps nowadays. Real punishments fall heavily on players and on scapegoats like literacy tutors.

A deeper reason explains why, in its predicament, the NCAA has no recourse to any principle or law that can justify amateurism. There is no such thing. Scholars and sportswriters yearn for grand juries to ferret out every forbidden bauble that reaches a college athlete, but the NCAA's ersatz courts can only masquerade as public authority. How could any statute impose amateur status on college athletes, or on anyone else? No legal definition of amateur exists, and any attempt to create one in enforceable law would expose its repulsive and unconstitutional nature—a bill of attainder, stripping from college athletes the rights of American citizenship.

For all our queasiness about what would happen if some athletes were to get paid, there is a successful precedent for the professionalization of an amateur sports system: the Olympics. For years, Walter Byers waged war with the NCAA's older and more powerful nemesis, the Amateur Athletic Union, which since 1894 had overseen U.S. Olympic athletes. Run in high-handed fashion, the AAU had infamously banned Jesse Owens for life in 1936—weeks after his four heroic gold medals punctured the Nazi claim of Aryan supremacy—because instead of using his sudden fame to tour and make money for the AAU at track meets across Europe, he came home early. In the early 1960s, the fights between the NCAA and the AAU over who should manage Olympic athletes became so bitter that President Kennedy called in General Douglas MacArthur to try to mediate a truce before the Tokyo Olympic Games.

Ultimately, Byers prevailed and effectively neutered the AAU. In November 1978, President Jimmy Carter signed the bipartisan Amateur Sports Act. Amateurism in the Olympics soon dissolved—and the world did not end. Athletes, granted a 20 percent voting stake on every Olympic sport's governing body, tipped balances in the United States and then inexorably around the world. First in marathon races, then in tennis tournaments, players soon were allowed to accept prize money and keep their Olympic eligibility. Athletes profited from sponsorships and endorsements. The International Olympic Committee expunged the word amateur from its charter in 1986. Olympic officials, who had once disdained the NCAA for offering scholarships in exchange for athletic performance, came to welcome millionaire athletes from every quarter, while the NCAA still refused to let the pro Olympian Michael Phelps swim for his college team at Michigan.

This sweeping shift left the Olympic reputation intact, and perhaps improved. Only hardened romantics mourned the amateur code. "Hey, come on," said Anne Audain, a track-and-field star who once held the world record for the 5,000 meters. "It's like losing your virginity. You're a little misty for awhile, but then you realize, Wow, there's a whole new world out there!"

Without logic or practicality or fairness to support amateurism, the NCAA's final retreat is to sentiment. The Knight Commission endorsed its heartfelt cry that to pay college athletes would be "an unacceptable surrender to despair." Many of the people I spoke with while reporting this article felt the same way. "I don't want to pay college players," said Wade Smith, a tough criminal lawyer and former star running back at North Carolina. "I just don't want to do it. We'd lose something precious."

"Scholarship athletes are already paid," declared the Knight Commission members, "in the most meaningful way possible: with a free education." This evasion by prominent educators severed my last reluctant, emotional tie with imposed amateurism. I found it worse than self-serving. It echoes masters who once claimed that heavenly salvation would outweigh earthly injustice to slaves. In the era when our college sports first arose, colonial powers were turning the whole world upside down to define their own interests as all-inclusive and benevolent. Just so, the NCAA calls it heinous exploitation to pay college athletes a fair portion of what they earn.

How does Branch's argument affect you as a reader? What evidence do you find most persuasive in his argument and why? What word choice and other stylistic devices do you find effective in Branch's writing?

Branch's essay was widely circulated and debated in social media. At the time of writing this book, his article had already been shared more than 33,000 on Facebook and around 3,000 on Twitter. Visit his original article online: www.theatlantic.com/magazine/archive/2011/10/the-shame-of-college-sports/308643/ and click on the accompanying social media hyperlinks. Take five minutes or so exploring audiences' reactions to Branch across the two platforms. How are people responding to the argument? Do they agree or not? What language do they use in support or refutation of Branch? How does this exercise inform your understanding of the role of social media in debating public issues like "Pay for Play"?

Write an essay to your school's athletic director in which you argue for or against "Pay for Play," providing necessary claims and evidence. What tone do you take? What evidence do you use? How will you convince the athletic director of your argument and why should he or she take your letter seriously?

As a class, share your essays from the Compose exercise. How many students were in favor of "Pay for Play"? How many are against it? Why? What evidence is most effective in each case? Consider this: If you could get your school's athletic director to read the essays, what side of the argument do you think she or he would take and why?

At the time of this article, Pat Forde had been a senior writer for ESPN before joining Yahoo! Sports as a columnist ("Forde Yard Dash" and "Forde Minutes"). He is respected as one of the premier college sports journalists. In the following article, Forde weighs in on the growing "Pay for Play" debate, taking a slightly different if controversial view on the professionalization of college sports.

MYTH OF EXPLOITED, IMPOVERISHED ATHLETES

By Pat Forde

For everyone shouting about the desperate need to pay the poor, exploited, impoverished, trod-up college athletes, I present Allan Guei.

Cal State Northridge coach Bobby Braswell's recruit Allan Guei knows the value of a scholarship.

He is going to be a freshman at Cal State Northridge, and you might have heard of him. Recently, Guei relinquished $40,000 in prize money he won in a free throw shooting contest at Compton (California) High School, where he graduated. Under NCAA rules, Guei could have kept most of it, but instead he gave the money to the seven runners-up in the free throw shooting competition.

Why?

Because he had earned a full scholarship to play basketball at Northridge.

"I feel like I was well taken care of to go to school and play the game I love for free," Guei said. "The position I was in was different from a lot of good kids who needed it more than I did."

Imagine that—an athlete who doesn't think he's being treated like a sweatshop employee. A scholarship athlete who actually feels fortunate to have a scholarship.

From *ESPN.com* (2011).

It's true that Northridge basketball is not exactly Kentucky or North Carolina when it comes to producing revenue and exposure for the school. But it's also true that those bluebloods are in the extreme minority. Most revenue-producing football and basketball programs are largely populated with guys like Guei—guys who are unlikely to make a long-term living playing professional sports and understand the value of a cost-free education.

Guei's remarkable gesture runs counter to the mythology that has taken hold with increasing fervor in the past 20 years. The basic gist is that college athletes are the most mistreated individuals on campus, worked like dogs and barely scraping by while the adults who coach them get rich. There is some truth to that, of course, but for the most part it is a gross exaggeration—if not an outright deception.

I date the increased popularity of this narrative to the early 1990s, when Fab Fiver Chris Webber whined to author Mitch Albom about not having enough money for a cheeseburger while the school was selling his jersey for a handsome profit. That got a lot of play as a prime example of The Hypocrisy of College Athletics.

The part Webber left out was that he was on the take at that time for thousands of dollars from booster Ed Martin. Oops.

Despite the audacity of that lie, the idea took root: Overworked athletes can barely afford to survive. "Can't afford a cheeseburger" or "Can't afford to go to the movies" became accepted truths instead of wild exaggerations. "Can't afford Dr. Dre headphones" or "Can't afford the latest 4G iPhone" might be a more realistic lament—although I see plenty of college athletes who can indeed afford those.

For those who feel compelled to monetize everything in college athletics, don't forget to factor in the cost of four years of schooling. At a lot of places, that will run about $200,000. Most students emerge from college saddled with debt that will take years to pay off, but scholarship athletes are exempt from that burden.

What never is factored in anymore is what an athlete can do with four years of free schooling once he is finished—the knowledge and background to earn a living for a lifetime. If they don't take advantage of that incredible opportunity to earn a degree—made all the more attainable by the extensive academic support systems created to serve them at most schools—shame on them.

Even that reckoning still ignores the nonmonetized benefits of college—maturation, socialization, enculturation, life lessons, friendships made, spouses met, and an allegiance to a place that can last a lifetime. Find a few former college athletes in their 30s or 40s and ask them about their experience. How many say they had a lousy time?

And don't forget this: Most college sports fans identify more with the school than the players. They root for the place they attended, or grew up with—the old front-of-the-jersey cliché. If that weren't the case, minor league football and basketball would be more popular.

"Why do we like them or cheer for them?" NCAA president Mark Emmert asked rhetorically in May. The answer, of course, is because of allegiance to the colleges. It has far less to do with the players in the jerseys than the jerseys themselves.

If playing for room, board and books were such a colossal injustice, there is a readily available alternative for basketball players intent on a professional career: the NBA Developmental League. Yet almost none of them choose it, despite the fact that the players are paid and there is no academic requirement at all.

Why? Because they know they've got a better gig as a poor, exploited, unpaid serf in college. They've got access to top-flight coaching, top-flight facilities, medical professionals, a strength and conditioning staff, maximum exposure and all the adulation they can handle. The alternative is earning more spending money in a minor league system playing games in second-rate arenas in front of nobody, with older teammates and less-proven coaches.

College football offers the same: palatial facilities, excellent coaching and the chance to showcase your skills on national television to those who do the hiring (NFL teams, companies looking for endorsers). Compare the benefits to being a low-level college intern at a huge company, where the CEO makes tens of millions. It's really not as bad a gig as it's often made out to be.

What might be the most problematic aspect of paying the players is the risk of further separating the athletic experience from the college experience. It would widen the gap between the athlete and the regular students who cheer them on—and then come back as adults to donate money and build even nicer facilities for the next generation of young studs. And if college is not part of college sports, then move the enterprise off campus and create semipro teams: the Ann Arbor Angels, Tuscaloosa Titans and Norman Conquests. See how that goes over.

It would go over about as well as any plan that calls for paying the football and men's basketball players but stiffing the nonrevenue athletes. If Title IX doesn't squash that notion, campus politics and simple fairness would. And then there is the question of exactly how many universities could balance the books while committing to a significant payment structure for all athletes.

Better to commit to providing a real educational opportunity to incoming athletes. Most of whom are like myth buster Allan Guei—holding out hope for a pro career, but well aware that a college education is a priceless gift.

"I'm probably not the smartest kid, but I'm going to do what I have to do to graduate," Guei said. "If my basketball doesn't earn me a living, I'm going to fall back on that degree."

"Pay for Play" has been well covered in the media by sports journalists and academics alike, often focusing on similar points of argument. In this exercise we will examine how evidence can be mobilized for different arguments and effect. For example, compare and contrast Forde's argument with that of Branch's argument (pp. 75-105). Or, compare Forde to Associate Law Professor Marc Edelman's *U.S. News* opinion editorial: "The Case for Paying College Athletes" (http://www.usnews.com/opinion/articles/2014/01/06/ncaa-college-athletes-should-be-paid). Do both authors cover the issue in the same way? How do Forde and Edelman use similar or dissimilar tone, emphasis of evidence, and other stylistic devices to arrive at different conclusions about "Pay for Play"?

In 2014, *NPR*'s "All Things Considered" picked up the "Pay for Play" debate and did a feature story. Listen to the podcast here: http://www.npr.org/2014/04/03/298763594/should-the-ncaa-change-its-rules-to-pay-for-play and read the corresponding feature story by *NPR* staff. What arguments for or against pay for play are offered in the story, by whom, and how are these arguments framed for the listener? Afterwards, reflect on the "Pay for Play" controversy: How do you feel about "Pay for Play" and why? What evidence seems most convincing in supporting your stance?

In a small group of classmates discuss the following: Should athletes be "paid for play"? What about Title IX and NCAA compliance? What about tuition remission and other "benefits" athletes receive that regular students may not? Who would be responsible for compensating athletes, and what would compensation look like—money, material benefits, sponsorship? What about nonrevenue generating athletes and their rights to compensation? How does "Pay for Play" align or not with the spirit of amateurism on which college athletics was originally based? What values are at the heart of the "Pay for Play" practice?

Often visuals can make powerful pithy arguments. For this exercise, consider the ways you might represent the various aspects of the "Pay for Play" debate visually in the format of an editorial cartoon. Then, draw your own editorial cartoon depicting your perspective on the debate and write a cover memo outlining the strategies and intentions behind your compositional choices.

Blackademics.org is an online forum for young black thinkers interested in relevant issues to the black community and was developed as an extension of Pierce Freelon's internationally acclaimed Blackadamics hip-hop oriented curriculum.

Annie Leibovitz is an acclaimed American portraitist. Among her noted works include her controversial 1981 Rolling Stone cover of John Lennon and Yoko Ono and her 1991 Vanity Fair cover More Demi Moore. She is the second living portraitist and first woman to present her work at the National Portrait Gallery (1991).

FIRST BLACK MALE EVER TO GRACE THE COVER OF *VOGUE*...LE' BRAWN JAMES

By Blackademics Blog (Deen Freelon)

The popular fashion magazine *Vogue* made history this month, placing an African American male on its cover for the first time of its illustrious 116 years of publication. The cover of *Vogue's* annual "Shape" issue features basketball all-star, LeBron James alongside the beautiful Gisele Bündchen. At first glance I was comfortable with this photo, probably because I am used to seeing images of black males portrayed in this manner. Pick up any Basketball or Hip-Hop magazine, *SLAM, XXL, Scratch*—they often display images of Black males that exude energy, swagger, anger, even violence, as this photo does. However, this does not seem to be the standard with *Vogue*. Particularly unnerving in this photo is the drastic stereotypical contrast between the physically dominating, roaring James and the delicate, quaint Gisele—enter the King Kong comparison. This photo resurrects the centuries-old "Birth of a Nation" stereotype

Vogue Magazine/Annie Leibovitz

Article from *Blackademics.org* (2008). Image from *Vogue* (2008).

of an animalistic dark male and his lilly white female interest. I'm surprised none of the editors at *Vogue* raised the red flag on this one. They could have done something a little more tasteful, for their first cover featuring an African American male, ever. You don't open up the league then put Jackie Robinson in a minstrel suit! You might think we're over analyzing this, but Jemele Hill over at ESPN.com makes a great point, "it's hard to believe *Vogue* would have made Brett Favre, Steve Nash or even David Beckham strike his best beast pose."

Can I get an Amen!? Inside the Shape Issue, *Vogue* also featured snowboarder Shawn White, speed skater Apolo Anton Ohno and swimmer Michael Phelps, all reserved and looking very stylish despite their professional outfits. Ain't that some bull?

 Collaborate As the first black male to appear on the cover of *Vogue*, many critics have called this cover photo racially insensitive, including Freelon's blog included herein. As a class, consider Freelon's critique of *Vogue's* cover image. In what ways does Freelon suggest this photo is racially insensitive? Do you agree or disagree? Why? What evidence can you supply in defense of your argument? What argument can you craft to support the significance of discussing why LeBron's portrayal is controversial or not?

 Explore This is an excellent follow up to the previous activity. Do any cultural and or historical referents come to mind when looking at this image? As an individual or in small groups, search for "U.S. WWI Germany recruitment poster" in Google Images. Note the similarities between the *Vogue* cover photo and the war propaganda, which predates the *King Kong* movie poster by more than a decade. How does the *Vogue* cover photo reproduce the visual rhetoric of the U.S. World War I recruitment poster, and how does this impact your understanding of LeBron's character? Does it amplify or minimize Freelon's claims about the racial insensitivity of the cover photo? Why? Share your findings with the class.

Laura Pappano is an award winning journalist currently leading the Women's Sports Leadership Project at Wellesley College. Eileen McDonagh is a professor of political science at Northeastern University who has published extensively on politics and gender. Together, they are co-authors of the acclaimed Playing with the Boys: Why Separate Is Not Equal in Sports, *from which this piece for* The Christian Monitor *was inspired.*

WOMEN AND MEN IN SPORTS: SEPARATE IS NOT EQUAL

By Laura Pappano and Eileen McDonagh

BOSTON—Thirty-three weeks pregnant with twins, yet determined to lead her talented University of Maryland women's basketball team into the national championships, coach Brenda Frese—known for energetically pacing the sideline—found a novel way to relieve her aching lower back during a home game this month: She had an office chair rolled onto the gym floor.

The result, amplified by a giant color photo in *USA Today* of a seated, beach-ball-bellied Ms. Frese thrusting her fist into the air, was a powerful visual metaphor for women in the world of sports.

Frese's example, like Paula Radcliffe training through pregnancy and winning the 2007 New York City Marathon, doesn't camouflage—but actually flaunts—the fact that women are physically different than men.

It also challenges an assumption that still dogs women today: The female body is athletically inferior to a male body.

WOMEN AND MEN IN SPORTS: SEPARATE IS NOT EQUAL

For all the progress women have made—in government, business, and the military—the shadow of female frailty still shapes the environment of sports.

From *The Christian Science Monitor* (2008).

To study the structure of organized athletics today—from youth leagues to the Olympics—is to see a system that feeds the faulty belief that females can't play as long, as well, or as hard as males.

The strict gender segregation of almost all sports is considered normal, even progressive. But separate, it turns out, is not equal.

No, this is not just about athletics. It's about how we view and value one another. That's why it's critical that we create a sports culture that is truly co-ed.

HISTORICAL PREJUDICE

To be sure, this effort runs counter to centuries of prejudice. Credit Aristotle for locating female inferiority precisely in the body part men lack: the uterus.

The Victorians perfected this argument, as a cadre of nineteenth-century physicians and craniologists laid down the "science" explaining the female's natural weakness. Of course, it was rooted in the reproductive role and occasioned all manner of "protections," restrictions, and rest.

Ads for Nike and Gatorade may feature well-muscled, sweat-drenched women athletes pushing personal boundaries, but institutional boundaries remain rigid.

Consider:

- Men's pro tennis players play five sets. Women play three (a holdover from 1902, when the US Lawn Tennis Association cut women's play, fearing over-exertion).

- A 12-year-old girl who enters a local tournament sanctioned by US Kids Golf plays just nine holes; a boy her age in the same tournament plays 18—regardless of their relative skill or experience.

- Co-ed adult sports leagues are rife with special "gender rules" to accommodate the supposedly weaker female sex. In some basketball leagues, women get two points for every basket; the men get just one. In touch football, a female touchdown is worth seven points; a male TD earns six. A 24-year-old who plays on a co-ed softball team recently shared with us her annoyance at rules (no more than two men bat in a row, men hit larger balls, etc...) which presume that any male player is better than every female player. Her beef? She played Division I college softball.

Of course, there are physical differences between men as a group and women as a group. That would support different rules for super-physical sports such as boxing and tackle football. But how does that account for the disparities in billiards and bridge?! Indeed, given that females are physiologically suited for ultra-endurance events, why are women's Olympic events slightly shorter than men's?

The answer to all these questions, in some form, is that sport is not merely about the game. It is, rather, about the identities of those who play and watch the game. It's about what gets established and reinforced every time sex-segregated formulas cast males as categorically superior to females.

Sports matter—and probably far more than they should. Many more people tune into the Super Bowl than the president's State of the Union address.

When we invest in sports as fans, parents, and recreational players, whether we know it or not, we become complicit in a deeply gendered institution in which male superiority and female inferiority are played out as clearly as HDTV.

Ironically, though, we've come to accept this differential treatment of males and females as "normal." It appears to be all right to charge $4 to see the Rutgers women's soccer team play and $7 to see the men's team play, for example.

Likewise, it seems that no one complained (or hardly noticed) when a Massachusetts youth soccer league put a warning in a bold-framed box at the top of the online registration page for Spring 2008. Local officials were no doubt trying to be helpful—but also reflecting a norm played out in communities across the country. It read, "Note: If you are attempting to register a daughter, please be aware that Newton Youth Soccer is co-ed, but primarily boys."

Replace gender descriptors with words reflecting race or religion, and the problem becomes appalling. Be aware that Jews are welcome, but the league is mostly gentiles? Be aware that blacks are allowed, but the program is primarily white? No way.

Sports are a path to social, economic, and political success. It is not enough to permit girls to play with boys; girls playing equally with boys should be the model. Individual ability—not gender—should be the first line drawn when organizing play, especially when sex-based athletic differences are trivial.

Title IX did open doors to girls and women to play sports on a broad scale. But it never demanded equality. Passed at a time when few could imagine the impressive, talented female athletes we have today, the law has codified a sex-separate athletic system in which men's sports are at the center and women's at the periphery. It's an insult in a non-revenue setting to charge unequal ticket prices. And for marquee sports such as college men's and women's basketball, there should be equal promotion at those institutions receiving federal funds.

Some argue that because the men "play above the rim" it's a more exciting game. Ridiculous. "Exciting" is about talent in the face of talent: competition. The Women's Final Four in recent years has been every bit as nail-biting as the men's NCAA playoff. Differences in style of play certainly don't keep fans from tuning into college football just because of the NFL.

MEN AND WOMEN, PLAYING TOGETHER

Some worry that having males and females take the field or court together would be a disaster for women's sports. It may be true that the top male players in the most competitive athletic events outperform the top female players. But look at the larger pool and you see vast overlap in the athletic performance of males and females.

Plus, "having game" is not just about raw speed or strength. If that were the case, NFL scouts who clock college players in the 40-yard dash and note how much they bench press would have a simple job on draft day. They don't.

Because females have historically faced athletic disadvantages, they should be able to play on all-female teams if they choose. But they shouldn't be barred from playing on traditionally male teams.

It's in our collective interest to create a playing structure that encourages men and women—at whatever level they can compete—to pass the ball to one another. Professional golf shows us multiple ways to create compelling competition. Stroke play, match play, partner play, skins. Why not pair Tiger Woods and Annika Sorenstam against Phil Mickelson and Lauren Ochoa? Who wouldn't watch?

The road to coed play—like the road to the Final Four—goes through many venues. Let's recognize that creating such opportunities is not only possible, but critical. Because sports—however much we may wish it were just play—carries wider social and political implications. So credit Maryland coach Brenda Frese for showing off her reproductive power and her coaching power in a single, provocative vision.

And know that one who dared register for that "primarily boys" soccer league (and try out for Little League) is a 9-year-old girl who intuitively "gets" the athletic power axis. She wears her hair short, wears boy's clothes, and will only play on teams with boys. Her mom told us why: "She wants to be taken seriously."

Invent

Opinion editorials are generally written by reputable writers, scholars, activists, and other figures with relevant experience on the issue. The objective of the genre is to convince the readers of a particular publication to take their stance on a given issue, usually controversial in nature. In this piece, although Pappano and McDonagh have co-authored a much longer book on the issue of gender segregation in sports., they must trim down their argument to a few specific claims to convince the readers of *The Christian Science Monitor*. What specific strategies do you notice Pappano and McDonagh using in this piece—what tone, organization, claims, and evidence do they use to convince their readers of their argument? How do these strategies fit with the expectations of *The Christian Science Monitor's* audience (you may have to dig around on the website to discover this answer). Make a list of these strategies and begin identifying the conventions of an "Opinion Editorial."

Collaborate

In small groups discuss Pappano and McDonagh's argument. Do you agree that separate is not equal? Why or why not? Did you grow up playing coed sports and, if so, what were your experiences like? How do you feel about Pappano and McDonagh's vision for a future of coed sports?

Explore

Read four reviews of Pappano and McDonagh's book, *Playing with the Boys* (two book reviews published by scholars in peer-reviewed journals, one consumer review published on a site like Amazon.com, and one journalism review of the book). What are points of agreement and disagreement with Pappano and McDonagh across the reviews? What evidence and claims are consistently cited across the reviews in support of the reviewer's interpretation of the argument?

Compose

Identify two publications that would be interested in the issue of "separate is not equal." Do a little background research on the audience profile and general reader interests of the publication. You may also want to review a few pieces from the Opinion section to get a feel for the overall "slant" of the publication. Then write a letter to the editor in which you argue for the importance of including a piece on "separate is not equal" to the magazine and its significance for the magazine's readership.

Draft two different opinion editorials on the issue of "separate is not equal" in which you try to convince readers in the first piece that "separate is equal" and in the second piece that "separate is not equal." In a cover letter, note the different strategies in tone, evidence, and claims you have to use in the two pieces to try to convince your audience of your stance.

English professor Leslie Heywood is a former collegiate track athlete and bodybuilder. She has published writings extensively on women and sport. In the following excerpt from her memoir, Pretty Good for a Girl: An Athlete's Story, *Heywood reflects on some of the challenges of being a competitive female athlete in a post-Title IX world.*

ONE OF THE GUYS

By Leslie Heywood

"Amphi's Heywood one of the guys." Leslie Heywood is just "one of the guys" as far as Amphi High School cross-country team is concerned. The pretty blond, blue-eyed junior is the best runner on the girls' team, but she regularly works out with the boys' team.... "I want her to stop thinking like a girl runner," Panther coach Ray Estes said. "Not that I want her to stop being a girl, but because I want her to work and think like an athlete. Right now she's just one of the guys." That doesn't seem to bother Leslie. "They [the boys on the team] help me out a lot," she said. "They always push me." And she pushes the guys, too, says girls' coach Tim Barton. "There's a lot of mutual benefit. If she beats one of the JV runners, then we can rib them and they'll work a little harder." The only place either of the coaches sees a problem is in what Barton calls the team concept. He says that without Heywood working with the girls' team, the other girls don't think they can compete with her....

We get up at four in the morning, that hour like a held breath just before the densest blackness starts to shift, just before the mourning doves take over that brief space of cool hanging in front of the sun, before it starts burning so tight you can't breathe. It's two hours by pickup to Peña Blanca Lake, somewhere south of Tucson, with those open dirt roads either climbing or swallowed by sand. It's the weekly Saturday morning workout of the 1,000 mile club: me and eight of the cross-country guys, stuffed in the back of an old green truck.

The club is summer habit: starting in June, we log in our miles for a hundred days, ten miles a day until mid-September. Every week we turn in our mileage sheets, trying to peer over each other's shoulders without being seen. How many miles for Victor? And what about

From *Pretty Good For a Girl: An Athlete's Story* (1999).

Ray? Looks like Mike was slacking off a little bit last week.... Whoever has the most miles by September is officially "the man," officially most tough. It is a distinction I covet with the fierceness of a thousand saguaros, with just as many prickling spines.

So at four in the morning I get out of bed and drag up my father, who, it must be said, does support me, his four-thirty stagger jumbled by too much night-before beer, the frantic grog for coffee and ten miles in the white Toyota pickup the last thing he would have chosen to do had I not given him something on the level of the high-achieving son, the one who does his old man proud, shining him up in deflected glory in a way that the morning teapot did not. It is this, I am sure, that gets him up, sets the teakettle boiling its whistling stove to bubble through Maxwell House instant coffee, enough caffeine for the miles logged in before the radio is anything but static. (*We want to congratulate Leslie Heywood, ASDM Director of Development John Heywood's fifteen-year-old daughter, on her first-place finish last week in the 8.3 mile Saguaro National Monument Run. John must be very proud of her....*) He's a track dad, you know, the one who always buys me the newest model of Nike or Saucony shoes even when Mother protests, track dad at a time when Nike Air wasn't there and the Pegasus was nowhere near a hundred dollars. So instead it is he who gives me my Adi-Star spikes by Adidas, size six, two sizes too small, the size I insist on so my feet will look like what I think are girl's feet, two sizes too small and close to a hundred dollars, reflecting my status on the track.

But that's by day. He's also the track dad who gets drunk at nights and at these times is certain I'm just some whore, prowling the cactuside with too many hills and too many young studs who are boyfriends, yelling at me, telling me this, but really he hasn't hit me for years. The track dad who by day takes me to practice, even those four-thirty miserable stints, who is at every meet with that same camera that takes the same shot from too far away so I am just an empty figure running around and around the same space in the same way forever and ever and ever. Track dad who wants me to be a boy more than he wants to live. My mother tells him I train too hard and I hate her for this. My dad asks me what year I'll shoot for the Olympics, probably '84, and no one is more certain that I'll make it.

Well, I'd disappoint him, but that was later on. In that summer of 1980, that first wonderful summer of Peña Blanca Lake, I'm hell-bent to beat anything that stands in my way, especially "the guys." There is never a time that I'm not at war, and this Saturday morning is it, all out, for blood and guts and glory, my legs hitting the ground like steel pistons, so hard, so fast, the rushing of blood that rises to my face brightly red. The road is old, riveted by rain run and sand but I fly so fast I hardly touch it. Whatever saguaros fly past by my side, what water-starved ocotillos, looking so dead but so strangely alive, I don't notice. I'm too busy holding my place. I am carving it out, running myself from shadow to guts with every carnivorous stride. I am someone you just have to see, not some soft frill girl invisible from the street. I have muscle, God damn it, have legs, and they are going to have to take notice. Those hunched backs before me, male runners in my way, in front of me wiping me out, turning me to smiles and dust. From silhouette to speed, from speed to a certain sense of place, a sense of my muscle so hard I am sure I am there. Certain; not like all those times I'm not, those times I'm invisible, disappeared from space.

July the 4th, a picnic, my father turning the meat on the grill, my mother serving garbanzos and peas on the redwood table under the birches. A sticky calm, glint of fireflies, hint of the frogs warming up. Then the turn like a yawning mouth had swallowed table, hot dogs, our fingers and toes. My father, a focused blankness all through his face, a resurrection, the picnic table on its end. Dogs drawing away before their ribs were kicked, the slink of their backs, pressed ears. Catsup soaring red arcs through mosquito-thick space, the charcoal making light, still burning before it hit the ground. My mother's face, a handprint as big as a burn.

There is no way I'm going to get burned. I've proved it already, too much before, I'm not the one they can char up. I'm going for them, heading in for the kill, my nostrils curled for it, my lips pulled back in a gasp and a snarl. There is no way they're going to get me, they are mine, their legs like so many matchstick backs, their lungs collapsing as I blow on by, burning myself through the ozone with the fierceness of cigarette-holes.

I mark them, fiercely, one by one. A group of them are gone at the beginning, the more casual guys who get through the run by enduring and just kicking back. Not me. This is life, and death, and everything in between. Not for a minute will I let them forget, not for a minute will they fail to see me. We've been out five miles, maybe halfway through. Four of them straggle on behind, three up ahead: is it Mike? Victor? Possibly Joe? It is Ray I catch first; he is smaller, determined but happy to take what he gets—no problem. I open my legs up a little, pump my arms up, breathe deeper down into my lungs. Not just a girl I'm all tough joints with legs and lungs like pumps of lead. The girl who's one of the guys always wins. She's got to win.

A "girl": small, quiet, discreet. Mild and meek. Who smiles, who smiles, who smiles, who smiles. *(Leslie [Airhead], Good luck in your meet today, I hope that you're not in a bad mood. Smile, you're very pretty when you smile. Love, Armando).* Delicate. Effeminate. Weak. No way. I'll be a monster any day. One of the guys. Invincible. Tough. Like last year: *Yesterday's hot weather got the blame for some closer than expected results in high school cross-country meets....However, the heat didn't seem to bother Amphi's Leslie Heywood. She broke Lisa Otte's course record and became the first runner under fifteen minutes on Saguaro's 2.25 mile course at Pantano Stables. Heywood was timed at 14:51, knocking thirteen seconds off Otte's record. Otte was almost a minute behind Heywood in third place....*

I say nothing as I fly by Ray, feeling larger, more solid at every turn. Victor next. Some practices, not many, I can get him. He is tough. I can only get him when he doesn't really try, but I always mark him. It is a matter of pride. I fix my eyes on his shoulders, a little tight. He isn't running loose today, says he hasn't had very much sleep. Why not, I wonder, as I take in the way his hamstrings angle the ground, too tight, his back too rigid, stiff. Today, he is mine, I can't let him off the hook. I'll wait for a hill, my strength. On the straight stretches I'm a little flat, the power in my legs not much to my advantage. It's on the hills that I can kill, my pistons, steel. I work on these in the weight room, ten sets of knee extensions every day. Every day. My legs are big in the world. When I punch them they don't give. And when I urge them on, like now, heading into that hill, they respond. Big bites, big bites, tearing the road, swallowing the distance between me and Victor like a string.

A string of steel stretched between our shoulders, relentless, pull up, pull tight; devouring the ground, I'm closing in, my lungs raspy as a cactus and twice as barbed. *If I had a woman's body, I'd be afraid to hit. Afraid to move around, lash out. Eyes would slide over me, seeing nothing except maybe sex. When I spoke I wouldn't draw myself up. I'd never stride through any space like it was mine. I'd sit quite still, and I wouldn't say no. A body has to* be *before it can* refuse, *you've got to be joined to it.* I'm not going to let anyone forget what I am, someone you don't mess with.

I'm gaining. He hears my footsteps leaving that black map that might just ride him over. He moves his head slightly, a downward tip of the left ear, an acknowledgement that he has heard. He lifts his shoulders, straightens out his stride: the battle lines are drawn. Too bad for him we're heading for a hill. And there is nobody, nothing, that can stop me then. He tries. But his strides are like a spinning top: I breeze by. I am enormous, all open space and closed-out lines, some perfect, flawless, inevitable thing, silent, silent, whisper-thin as I charge into the morning sun with no male backs before me, and six or seven twisted, chastened, diminished forms left struggling for breath in my wake.

Later, though, when the miles have been run, when we pull up dusty, thirsty, tired, ready for food and Gatorade and paddleboats on Peña Blanca Lake, my solid steel has softened. I've picked a new swimsuit just for this, a day in the sun with the all-male team. Now, my hill-domination firmly in place, I can be a girl, maybe it is evened out. If I beat them, they can't erase me. Will pay attention to me, what else—my body is steel but it's pretty, I know from all those guys who keep telling me to smile and following me around. So I play those smiles, muscular fierce in one minute, Barbie blond in the next, my swimsuit black laced with rusty musk and turquoise blue. I get up on the high rock to practice diving, standing just long enough so everyone can look, profile knife-clean to the sky, hair tied back like Bo Derek's.

I hope my waterproof mascara and water shining on my cheekbones will hold, my tanned skin dripping wet. I shine my attention on my fellow runners one at a time, and each basks in that sun until I switch to the next. The others smile together, shout "das!" their code word for disappearance. My body, face, a perplexing, intoxicating miracle: I can make them disappear like I've been disappeared myself. This is another way I can *be*, test my bite, feel alive.

Still, it makes me jittery. Running, you did it; when you won then you won. This is different. I'm playing around—just what is it? How do you win? Smile, well, you have to smile. And giggle, too, like you've not much to say, fluffed like your hair, hot-rollered high. Curled so tight it survives practice, the suicide sweat of mile eight. I guess I do it all right. They say I do, but something is off, a bit out of kilter, too much *(You can be very sweet sometimes but most of the time you can be a real tiger.....Hank Floyd—Yo, Les, one foxy chick, that's also a darn good runner.....Keep out of trouble, Anthony Perez—You're very pretty and you should be proud of it. I really enjoyed knowing you and especially having a locker next to Leslie Heywood the track star.....Love, Troy—I'm going to write something different because I'm not going to write the same thing everyone else did. You are so lucky to be going with such a swell guy. Not really. I'm just kidding. Vince is OK but you're the best and will always be. I hope you train well and come back as next year's state champion because that's what I'm going to try to be. When you do become state champ I won't be surprised. Since you're such a sweet and attractive superstar...do well and stay out of trouble. Love, Kenny Smith).* The pretty track star, smiling and staying out of trouble. Next year's state champ. A real tiger. I was a big girl, a Barbie with a bite.

Invent What writing techniques do you notice Heywood using to recount her experiences? Which turns of phrase are particularly compelling to you as a reader and why? How does Heywood's style affect you as a reader? How does she use setting and character development to enhance her story?

Compose This assignment will prepare you for Major Assignment #1: The Sports Memoir. Reflect on a particularly hard or challenging sports moment in your life and write a short essay in which you use descriptive writing and narrative techniques, like Heywood's excerpt, to teach your readers the significance of this event in your life and how it has changed your understanding of sport and culture.

Collaborate In small groups, share your memoirs. What similar challenging experiences have you shared in sports? How has listening to other students present their essays continued to evolve your thinking about sports and your relationship to them? What writing techniques did you find particularly effective in other students' essays and how could you use these to improve your own essay?

In what is possibly one of the most iconic images in women's sport in the twentieth century, U.S. Women's Soccer player Brandi Chastain celebrates her victory penalty kick against China in the 1999 FIFA World Cup finals at the Rose Bowl in Pasadena, CA.

GIRLS RULE!

From *Newsweek* (1999).

This assignment will help you prepare for Major Assignment #3: Analyzing Sports Media. What is the overall tone and mood of this image? How does the headline, "Girls Rule," affect your understanding of the meaning of the image? What other textual strategies (color, framing, arrangement, angles, lighting, etc.) do you understand contributing to the overall message and tone of this image?

Although renown, this image of Chastain is perhaps one of the more controversial in U.S. women's sports history as critics feel it contributes to a historical problem with the media's sexualization of female athleticism. In a small group discuss the following: Do you agree or disagree the photo sexualizes female athleticism? Why or why not? In what ways might this photo contribute to the infantilizing of women's athleticism via sexualization? In what ways do you think the image contradicts this criticism?

Sports scholars have long been interested in how the media represents female athletes. Often, the news is not good. Scholars find two main devices used by media to discredit female athleticism: gender-marking (referring to female sports as "women's soccer," for example, as opposed to just soccer, which denotes the male game) and sexual imagery (which detracts from the athlete's sporting ability by focusing on her presumably straight sexuality). How do you understand these concepts working here in this image? Is the "Girls Rule!" tag a gender mark. Why or why not? What about the framing of Chastain herself? Is she being sexualized in a way that detracts from her athleticism?

While majoring in psychology at Stanford University, Mariah Burton Nelson was also a member of Stanford's women's basketball team. She has also played professional ball overseas in Europe before going on to write more than five books on gender and sport, including The Stronger Women Get, The More Men Like Football, *from which the following excerpt is taken.*

STRONGER WOMEN

BY MARIAH BURTON NELSON

Boy, don't you men wish you could hit a ball like that!
- Babe Didrikson Zaharias

The way many women gain strength, and keep gaining strength, is through sports. Women can become strong in other ways, without being athletes, but athletic strength holds particular meaning in this culture. It's tangible, visible, measurable. It has a history of symbolic importance. Joe Louis, Jackie Robinson, Jesse Owens, Billie Jean King: Their athletic feats have represented to many Americans key victories over racism and sexism, key "wins" in a game that has historically been dominated by white men.

Sports have particular salience for men, who share childhood memories of having their masculinity confirmed or questioned because of their athletic ability or inability. Along with money and sex, sports in this culture define men to men. Sports embody a language men understand.

Women also understand sports—their power, their allure—but historically, most women were limited to a spectator's perspective. When a woman steps out of the bleachers or slips off her cheerleader's costume and becomes an athlete herself, she implicitly challenges the association between masculinity and sports. She refutes the traditional feminine role (primarily for white women) of passivity, frailty, subservience. If a woman can play a sport—especially if she can play it better than many men—then that sport can no longer be used as

From *Equal Play: Title IX and Social Change* (2007).

a yardstick of masculinity. The more women play a variety of sports, the more the entire notion of masculine and feminine roles—or any roles at all assigned by gender—becomes as ludicrous as the notion of roles assigned by race. Female athletes provide obvious, confrontational evidence—"in your face" evidence, some might say—of women's physical prowess, tangible examples of just what women can achieve.

The athlete's feminism begins with the fact that her sports participation is a declaration of independence. Female athletes don't necessarily see it this way. They don't necessarily call themselves feminists. They cycle or swim or surf because it's fun and challenging, because it feels good, because they like the way it makes them look, because it allows them to eat more without gaining weight, because it gives them energy and confidence and time spent with friends, female or male. Many are ignorant about the women's rights movement. I've heard college students confuse feminism with feminine hygiene.

In fact, female athletes have a long tradition of dissociating themselves from feminism. Their desire to be accepted or to acquire or keep a boyfriend or a job has often equaled their passion for sports. Thus athletes have taken great pains—and it can hurt—to send reassuring signals to those who would oppose their play: "Don't worry, we're not feminists. We're not dykes, we're not aggressive, we're not muscular, we're not a threat to you. We just want to play ball." It has been a survival strategy.

It's time to tell the truth. Our behavior is feminist.[1] Some of us—including some pioneers who lobbied for Title IX, some coaches who volunteered to teach girls, and some athletes who competed in the first pro-baseball and -basketball leagues—are lesbians. Some of us are aggressive. Some of us are muscular. All of us, collectively, are a threat—not to men, exactly, but to male privilege and to masculinity as defined through manly sports. By reserving time each day for basketball dribbling, or for runs or rides or rows, women are changing themselves and society. Feminism is rarely an individual's motivating force but always the result: A woman's athletic training, regardless of the factors that lead to her involvement, implicitly challenges patriarchal constraints on her behavior. We take care of ourselves. For a group of people who have historically been defined by our ability to nurture others, the commitment to nurture ourselves is radical. Sport for women changes the woman's experience of herself and others' experience of her. It is feminist: It alters the balance of power between the sexes. It is daring. It is life changing. It is happening every day.

Several writers have used sports as a metaphor, depicting women emancipated by the process of building muscle and endurance. In Alice Adams's short story "A Public

---

1. Susan Greendorfer, "Making Connections: Women's Sport Participation as a Political Act" (paper presented at the National Girls and Women in Sports Symposium, Slippery Rock State University, Slippery Rock, Pennsylvania, February 13, 1993). Susan Greendorfer, professor of kinesiology at the University of Illinois, Urbana-Champaign, was the first or one of the first to assert that women's sports are inherently a political act.

Pool," a shy, anxious, unemployed woman feels too tall and too fat. She lives with her depressed mother. By swimming laps, she is slowly and subtly transformed. As first she feels embarrassed to appear, even in the locker room, in her bathing suit. Swimming twenty-six laps, a half-mile, seems a struggle. She feels flattered by attention from a blond, bearded swimmer not because he is kind of interesting—in fact he cuts rudely through the water with a "violent crawl"—but because he is male.

By the end of the story, she becomes "aware of a long strong body (mine) pulling through the water, of marvelous muscles, a strong back, and long, long legs." She applies for a job she'll probably get and looks forward to moving out of her mother's house. When she happens upon "Blond Beard" outside a café, she realizes that he is a gum-chewing, spiffily dressed jerk. The story ends with his inviting her to join him for coffee, and her declining. "I leave him standing there. I swim away."[2]

Feminism is about bodies: birth control, sexual harassment, child sexual abuse, pornography, rape, date rape, battering, breast cancer, breast enlargement, dieting, Liposuction, abortion, anorexia, bulimia, sexuality.

And then there is sports.

"The repossession by women of our bodies," wrote the poet and author Adrienne Rich in *Of Woman Born*, "will bring far more essential change to human society than the seizing of the means of production by workers."

As athletes, we repossess our bodies. Told that we're weak, we develop our strengths. Told that certain sports are wrong for women, we decide what feels right. Told that our bodies are too dark, big, old, flabby, or wrinkly to be attractive to men, we look at naked women in locker rooms and discover for ourselves the beauty of actual women's bodies in all their colors, shapes, and sizes. Told that certain sports make women look "like men," we notice the truth: Working out doesn't make us look like men, it makes us look happy. It makes us smile. More important, it makes us healthy and powerful. It makes us feel good.

The National Center for Health Statistics reports that physical fitness is linked to a general sense of well-being, a positive mood, and lower levels of anxiety and depression, especially among women. The athlete is more likely than her nonathletic sisters to have self-confidence.[3]

Women who exercise weigh less than non-athletes, and have lower blood pressure and lower levels of cholesterol and triglycerides. They miss fewer days of work.[4]

---

2. Alice Adams, "A Public Pool," Mother Jones, November 1984, 38.
3. Physician and Sportsmedicine 26, no. 5 (May 1998), 86–97; cited by Women's Sports Foundation, 2004.
4. American Journal of Health Promotion 10 (1996), 171–174; cited by "Women's Sports and Fitness Facts and Statistics," Women's Sports Foundation, June 1, 2004.

Female student-athletes in college are more likely to graduate than their nonathletic peers. White female athletes have a graduation rate of 72 percent, compared to 64 percent of white women in the general student body. African American female athletes have a graduation rate of 62 percent, compared to only 46 percent of black women in the general student body.[5]

A Harvard study of more than 72,000 nurses found that the more a woman exercises, the less likely she is to suffer a stroke.[6] A Penn State study found that exercise may be even more important than calcium consumption to ensure bone health.[7]

Exercise reduces an older woman's chances of developing osteoporosis. Postmenopausal women who start exercising report improved health status and fewer chronic disease than their peers who do not exercise.[8] Pregnant athletes report a lower incidence of back pain, easier labor and delivery, fewer stress-related complaints, and less postpartum depression than women who don't exercise.

According to research by the Women's Sports Foundation, female high school athletes are more likely than non-athletes to do well in high school and college, to feel popular, to be involved in extracurricular activities, to stay involved in sport as adults, and to aspire to community leadership. Female high school athletes are less likely to get involved with marijuana, cocaine, PCP, and other drugs;[9] less likely to get pregnant;[10] less likely to have sexual intercourse in high school;[11] and three times more likely than their nonathletic peers to graduate from high school.[12]

And the effects of exercise persist throughout a lifetime. As little as one to three hours of weekly exercise can lower a teenage girl's lifelong risk of breast cancer by 20 or 30 percent. Four hours of weekly exercise can reduce the risk by almost 60 percent. Women who were athletic as children report having greater confidence, self-esteem, and pride in their physical and social selves than those who were sedentary as children. If, as a society, we are interested in the health and welfare of women, we should encourage and enable them to play sports.

In a country where male politicians and judges make key decisions about our bodies and all of us are vulnerable to random attacks of male violence, the simple act of taking control of our own bodies—including their health, their pleasure, and their power—is radical. In

5. NCAA News, September 1, 2003; cited by *Women's Sports Foundation*, 2004.
6. *Journal of the American Medical Association* (June 2000); cited by Women's Sports Foundation, 2004.
7. *Pediatrics Fitness Bulletin* 23, no. 8 (August 2000), 2; cited by Women's Sports Foundation, 2004.
8. *Archives of Internal Medicine* 158, no. 15 (August 10–24, 1998), 1695–1701; cited by Women's Sports Foundation, 2004.
9. The Women's Sport Foundation Report: Health Risks and the Female Athlete, 2001.
10. The Women's Sport Foundation Report: Sport and Teen Pregnancy, 1998.
11. Ibid.
12. The Women's Sport Foundation Report, 2001.

a society in which real female bodies (as opposed to media image of female bodies) are unappreciated at best, the act of enjoying one's own female body is radical. It contradicts all feminine training to move, to extend our arms, to claim public space as our own, to use our bodes aggressively, instrumentally, to make rough contact with other bodes. Temple University doctoral student Frances Johnston interviewed dozens of female ice hockey and rugby players and found that "physicality" was one of the most appealing aspects of the games. "They enjoyed the tackling, the checking, the falling down and getting up, the discovery that they had 'survived' another hard hit or rough game." Besides body contact, they enjoyed "kicking the ball, getting rid of the ball right before a tackle, the power of a well-hit slap shot."[13]

Lunging for a soccer ball, we do not worry if our hair looks attractive. Leaping over a high bar, we do not wish we had bigger breasts. Strapped snugly into a race car, roaring around a track at 220 miles per hour, we do not smile or wave. While playing sports, our bodies are ours to do with as we please. If in that process our bodies look unfeminine—if they become bruised or bloody or simply unattractive—that seems irrelevant. Our bodies are ours. We own them. While running to catch a ball, we remember that.

I have coached recreational, AAU, junior high, and high school basketball. My players have been girls (nine through twelve), teenagers (fifteen through eighteen) and grown women (twenty through forty). Most of these players had trouble with the defensive stance, and with "being big."

The defensive stance requires a player to squat, low to the ground, her legs wide. Her knees should gape open, farther apart than her shoulders, her hands ready to deflect passes or shots. From this position she can react quickly to any moved an offensive player makes.

Why is this difficult for girls and women to learn? It's the leg spread. It's unladylike to yawn one's legs wide open. Even little girls growing up today are receiving this message. I can tell because I tease them, imitating the way they try to squat without separating their legs. "It's okay," I say. "No one's going to look up your skirt." They laugh and I know I've hit the mark. Most little girls don't even wear skirts to school anymore. But their foremothers did, and some of their big sisters in high school do. This concept of "skirt," with its implicit vulnerability, still haunts them, even on the basketball court.

My players are haunted, too, by size taboos. They don't like to feel tall, to seem wide, to make loud noises. They don't feel comfortable inhabiting a big space. Even many young ones talk quietly and act timid. In basketball, you need to snatch a rebound as if you own

13. Frances Johnson, "Life on the Fringe: The Experience of Rugby and Ice Hockey Playing Women" (paper presented at the annual meeting of the North American Society for the Sociology of Sport, Toledo, Ohio, November 5, 1992).

the ball, as if you're starving and it's the last coconut on the tree. You have to protect the ball, elbows pointed outward like daggers, lest others try to grab it. You have to decide where you want to be, then get there, refusing to let anyone push you out of the way. You have to shout, loudly, to let your teammates know who's cutting through the lane or who's open for a shot. Basketball teaches women and girls to renounce the suffocating vestiges of ladylike behavior and act instead like assertive, honest, forthright human beings. It's about unlearning femininity.

Simone de Beauvoir wrote in *The Second Sex* that the athlete receives from sports a sense of authority and an ability to influence others. "To climb higher than a playmate, to force an arm to yield and bend, is to assert one's sovereignty over the world in general." By contrast, the woman deprived of sports "has no faith in a force she has not experienced in her body; she does not dare to be enterprising, to revolt, to invent; doomed to docility, to resignation . . . she regards the existing state of affairs as something fixed."[14]

Thus the very desire to change the conditions of our lives—to demand the equal rights that are a cornerstone of feminism—may be traceable to our own sense of our physical power. This is supported by "tomboy" studies: Female politicians, business leaders, and other successful women often started out as athletes.

Several pro athletes in the post–Billie Jean King generations have become outspoken advocates for women. Golfer Carol Mann, race car driver Lyn St. James, Olympic swimmers Nancy Hogshead and Donna de Varona, basketball pioneer Nancy Lieberman, and soccer star Julie Foudy have served as Women's Sports Foundation presidents. Zina Garrison has talked openly about a troubling feminist issue: the body/self hatred that in her case led to bulimia.

According to a survey of working women, about 50 percent of women of color believe their sports participation helps them to access decision-making channels outside the office, be accepted by co-workers, advance their careers, and tap into business networks. About 36 percent of white women agree.[15]

Women who played college sports rate themselves higher in their abilities to set objectives, lead a group, motivate others, share credit, and feel comfortable in a competitive environment. Former high school athletes also rated themselves fairly highly in these abilities, followed by former youth-sport athletes. Women with no childhood competitive experience felt least adept.[16]

---

14. Simone de Beauvoir, *The Second Sex* (New York: Vintage Books, 1952), 331.
15. Don Sabo and Marjorie Snyder, "Miller Lite Report on Sports and Fitness in the Lives of Working Women," in cooperation with the Women's Sports Foundation and *Working Woman*, March 8, 1993, 13–15.
16. Ibid., 5–7.

Psychologists say that the best antidote to depression and helplessness is action. Athletes, with their proud muscles and trained minds, are poised to take those actions, and to provide leadership for women who are sick of living in fear. Sport, by definition, strengthens. The athlete dedicates herself to women's rights, beginning with her own. The team athlete become appreciative of women's bodies, beginning with her own. She cares for women, respects women, and becomes willing to take physical risks for and with women. Sport for women represents autonomy, strength, pleasure, community, control, justice, and power. It disrupts men's attempts to elevate themselves above women. It changes everything.

Collaborate Despite the awkward history with the word, Nelson argues that sports are feminist issues and that female athletes are feminists. In small groups, discuss how you understand Nelson defining feminism and why she understands female athletes as feminists. Note particular passages from the excerpt where Nelson explains her argument. Do you agree or disagree? Why or why not?

Compose Write an essay in which you reflect on your understanding of gender and sport. Was there a particular experience as a child that made you think of sport as something good or bad for girls to do? Why? What kinds of media have contributed to your understanding of women and sport? Do you feel like girls benefit from coed sports. Why or why not? If you were a parent, would you encourage your daughters to play a sport? Which one would it be and why?

Explore This exercise will prepare you for Major Assignment #5: The Persuasive Research Paper. How do women in your local community feel about sport and why? Similarly, how do men in your local community feel about women and sport? Create a questionnaire in which you ask open ended questions. Then, try and survey different groups of people including students on campus, your parents, people from the local community, and coaches of local and/or school teams. Analyze your findings. What insights do you discover from the results? Do the men and women in your local community support women and sport? Why or why not?

Ariel Levy was a contributing editor at New York Magazine *before joining* The New Yorker *as a staff writer in 2008. Among other awards, Levy's work has been anthologized in* The Best American Essays 2008. *In this compelling feature story, Levy reflects on the complexities of sport as a gender-segregated activity, and of its consequences for intersex athletes like Olympian track medalist Caster Semenya.*

EITHER/OR: SPORTS, SEX, AND THE CASE OF CASTER SEMENYA

By Ariel Levy

When people in South Africa say "Limpopo," they mean the middle of nowhere. They are referring to the northernmost province of the country, along the border with Botswana, Zimbabwe, and Mozambique, where few people have cars or running water or opportunities for greatness. The members of the Moletjie Athletics Club, who live throughout the area in villages of small brick houses and mud-and-dung huts, have high hopes nonetheless.

One day in late September, twenty teen-age athletes gathered for practice on a dirt road in front of Rametlwana Lower Primary School, after walking half an hour through yellow cornfields from their homes, to meet their coach, Jeremiah Mokaba. The school's track is not graded, and donkeys and goats kept walking across it to graze on the new grass that was sprouting as the South African winter gave way to spring. "During the rainy season, we can't train," said Mokaba, a short man wearing a brown corduroy jacket with a golden Zion Christian Church pin on the lapel. "We have nowhere to go inside."

For cross-country, Mokaba and his co-coach, Phineas Sako, train their runners in the miles of bush that spread out behind the track, toward the mountains in the distance. The land is webbed with brambles, and the thorns are a serious problem for the athletes, who train barefoot. "They run on loose stones, scraping them, making a wound, making a scar," Sako, a tall, bald man with rheumy eyes and a big gap between his two front teeth, said. "We can't stop and say we don't have running shoes, because we don't have money. The parents don't have money. So what must we do? We just go on."

From *The New Yorker* (2009).

The athletes and their coaches apologized for not having a clubhouse in which to serve tea. They didn't like talking out in the wind and the dust. There was music playing down the road at a brick-front bar, and chickens squawking in people's front yards, where they are kept in enclosures made out of tree branches. "The most disadvantaged rural area," Sako said, laughing a little and stretching his arms out wide. "That is where you are."

The fastest runner in the club now is a seventeen-year-old named Andrew who recently became the district champion in the fifteen-hundred-metre event. The average monthly income for black Africans in Limpopo—more than ninety-seven per cent of the local population—is less than a thousand rand per month, roughly a hundred and thirty-five dollars. (For white residents, who make up two per cent of the population, it is more than four times that amount.) "I think I will go to the Olympics," Andrew said, with conviction.

Joyce, a tiny girl in a pink sweater who is eighteen but looked much younger, was similarly optimistic. "I want to be the world champion," she said, her voice so soft it was almost a whisper. "I will be the world champion. I want to participate in athletics and have a scholarship. Caster is making me proud. She won. She put our club on the map."

Caster Semenya, the current world champion in the eight hundred metres, was a member of the Moletjie Athletics Club until a year ago. She was born in Ga-Masehlong, a village about fifteen miles from the track, and she was, Coach Sako said, "a natural." Even before Semenya left Limpopo for college, in Pretoria, she had won a gold medal in her event at the 2008 Commonwealth Youth Games, in Pune, India, with a time of 2:04, eleven seconds behind the senior world record set by the Czech runner Jarmila Kratochvílová in 1983. "I used to tell Caster that she must try her level best," Sako said. "By performing the best, maybe good guys with big stomachs full of money will see her and then help her with schooling and the likes. That is the motivation." He added, "And she *always* tried her level best." Semenya won another gold medal in July, in Mauritius, at the African Junior Athletics Championships, lowering her time by a remarkable seven and a half seconds, to come in at 1:56.72. This beat the South African record for that event, held by Zola Budd, and qualified Semenya for her first senior competition, the 2009 World Championships, in Berlin.

Semenya won the eight-hundred-metre title by nearly two and a half seconds, finishing in 1:55.45. After the first lap of the race, she cruised past her competitors like a machine. She has a powerful stride and remarkable efficiency of movement: in footage of the World Championships, you can see the other runners thrashing behind her, but her trunk stays still, even as she is pumping her muscle-bound arms up and down. Her win looks effortless, inevitable. "Even when we were training, I used to pair her with the males," Sako told me. "I feel like she was too powerful for ladies." It was a stunning victory for Semenya, for the Moletjie Athletics Club, and for South Africa.

After the race, Semenya told reporters, "Oh, man, I don't know what to say. It's pretty good to win a gold medal and bring it home." (Her voice is surprising. As Semenya's father, Jacob, has put it, "If you speak to her on the telephone, you might mistake her for a man.") She continued, "I didn't know I could win that race, but for the first time in my life the experience, the World Championships . . ." She broke into a grin. "I couldn't believe it, man."

Since the day Semenya broke Zola Budd's record, people in South Africa had been talking about her. Semenya does not look like most female athletes. People questioned whether she was really a woman. Some even e-mailed the International Association of Athletics Federations, the worldwide governing body for track and field, with their doubts. Before Semenya was awarded her gold medal in Berlin, on August 20th, a reporter asked about a story that had been circulating at the Championships, that Semenya's sex was unclear and that she had been required to undergo gender-verification testing before the race. The I.A.A.F. confirmed the rumor, arguably in violation of its confidentiality policies. ("The choice is that you lie, which we don't like to do," Nick Davies, the communications director, told *The New York Times*.) The story ripped around the world. Several of Semenya's competitors in the race were incensed that she had been allowed to participate. "These kind of people should not run with us," Elisa Cusma, of Italy, who came in sixth, said. "For me, she is not a woman. She is a man."

"Just look at her," Mariya Savinova, of Russia, who finished fifth, said.

Semenya is breathtakingly butch. Her torso is like the chest plate on a suit of armor. She has a strong jawline, and a build that slides straight from her ribs to her hips. "What I knew is that wherever we go, whenever she made her first appearance, people were somehow gossiping, saying, 'No, no, she is not a girl,'" Phineas Sako said, rubbing the gray stubble on his chin. "'It looks like a boy'—that's the right words—they used to say, 'It looks like a boy.' Some even asked me as a coach, and I would confirm: it's a girl. At times, she'd get upset. But, eventually, she was just used to such things." Semenya became accustomed to visiting the bathroom with a member of a competing team so that they could look at her private parts and then get on with the race. "They are doubting me," she would explain to her coaches, as she headed off the field toward the lavatory.

South Africa has eleven official languages. The majority of people in Limpopo speak the Pedi language, and many also speak English and Afrikaans, which schoolchildren were required to learn under apartheid. Sako's English was fluent but rough, and he frequently referred to Semenya as "he." "Caster was very free when he is in the male company," Sako said. "I remember one day I asked her, 'Why are you always in the company of men?' He said, 'No, man, I don't have something to say to girls, they talks nonsense. They are always out of order.'"

On September 11th, Australia's *Daily Telegraph*, a tabloid owned by Rupert Murdoch, reported that Semenya's test results had been leaked, and that they showed that Semenya, though she was brought up as a girl and had external female genitalia, did not have ovaries or a uterus. Semenya was born with undescended testes, the report said, which provided her with three times the amount of testosterone present in an average female—and so a potential advantage over competitors.

"I know what Caster has got," her aunt Johanna Lamola told the *Times*. "I've changed her nappies." Semenya's father said, "I don't even know how they do this gender testing. I don't know what a chromosome is. This is all very painful for us—we live by simple rules." Semenya did not cheat. She has not been evasive. It is very common for élite female athletes, who exert themselves to their physical limits as a matter of course, not to menstruate. There's no reason that Semenya or her coaches would have been alarmed if she were amenorrheic. "Maybe it's because we come from a disadvantaged area," Jeremiah Mokaba said. "They couldn't believe in us."

The I.A.A.F. has yet to inform Semenya whether she can continue running in international female competitions. I asked Sako what he thought would happen. "Caster," he said firmly, "will remain Caster."

Sports have played an important role in modern South African history. A crucial part of the African National Congress's strategy to end apartheid during "the struggle," as everyone calls it, was to secure international condemnation of South Africa's government through boycotts and the banning of South African athletes from all international competitions. Conversely, during the 1995 rugby World Cup Nelson Mandela managed to unite the entire country behind the Springboks, the South African team, which had been a hated symbol of Afrikaner white supremacism. It was pivotal to his success in avoiding civil war and in establishing a new sense of national solidarity. Sports are "more powerful than governments in breaking down racial barriers," Mandela said. "Sport has the power to change the world. It has the power to inspire, the power to unite people that little else has." Sometimes it can unite people against other people. The South African Minister of Sport and Recreation, Makhenkesi Stofile, has warned, "If the I.A.A.F. expels or excludes Semenya from competition or withdraws the medal, I think it would be the Third World War."

In August, when Semenya returned from Germany, thousands of cheering supporters waited to welcome her at O. R. Tambo Airport, outside Johannesburg. President Jacob Zuma met with her to offer his congratulations, as did Nelson Mandela.

Phat Joe, one of the most famous radio DJs in the country, was fired by Kaya FM for suggesting on his show that Semenya might have testicles. Lolly Jackson, the owner of a chain of strip clubs called Teazers, put up an enormous billboard in a suburb of

Johannesburg picturing a naked woman lying flat on her back above the words "No Need for Gender Testing!" Jackson subsequently claimed that the billboard had nothing to do with Semenya, but he sent her lawyers, at the firm of Dewey & LeBoeuf, a check for twenty thousand rand.

"I think it is the responsibility of South Africa to rally behind this child and tell the rest of the world she remains the hero she is and no one will take that away from her," Winnie Madikizela-Mandela, an ex-wife of Mandela's and a recently elected Member of Parliament, was quoted as saying in the London *Telegraph*. "There is nothing wrong with being a hermaphrodite. It is God's creation. She is God's child." By contrast, the African National Congress Youth League, a division of the African National Congress, issued a statement saying that it "will never accept the categorization of Caster Semenya as a hermaphrodite, because in South Africa and the entire world of sanity, such does not exist."

The African National Congress is part of the Tripartite Alliance, with the South African Communist Party and the Congress of South African Trade Unions. This year's meeting of the Congress happened to coincide with Heritage Day, and many of the hundreds of delegates who assembled at a conference center outside Johannesburg were in traditional tribal dress. Winnie Madikizela-Mandela wore a Xhosa turban and cape. A representative from the police and prison workers' union, wearing nothing but a loincloth made from springbok pelts and a Swazi necklace of red pompoms, mingled with fellow union members at the back of an enormous auditorium, where delegates were debating the items of the day: whether to support the legalization of prostitution in time for the soccer World Cup, which South Africa will host in 2010, and whether to pass a resolution in support of Caster Semenya.

The sessions are meant to evoke the African tradition of villagers gathering to share opinions on local matters. Everyone gets to speak, though men speak much more than women. The prostitution question was examined from every angle: some were concerned about "the downgrading of our women by capitalism"; others felt that every source of income was desperately needed and that sex workers, like everybody else, deserved the protection of a union. After several hours, the delegates decided that what was needed was more discussion.

The South African Minister of Women, Children, and Persons with Disabilities, Noluthando Mayende-Sibiya, went to the lectern dressed in red Xhosa regalia to speak about "the issue of our young star, Caster Semenya." Everyone applauded. "She is our own," Mayende-Sibiya said. "She comes from the working class." The crowd blew horns in support, and some people ululated. "You cannot be silent! The human rights of Caster have been violated," she concluded. The resolution passed with unusual alacrity.

South Africans have been appalled by the idea of a person who thinks she is one thing suddenly being told that she is something else. The classification and reclassification of human beings has a haunted history in this country. Starting with the Population Registration Act of 1950, teams of white people were engaged as census-takers. They usually had no training, but they had the power to decide a person's race, and race determined where and with whom you could live, whether you could get a decent education, whether you had political representation, whether you were even free to walk in certain areas at certain hours. The categories were fickle. In 1985, according to the census, more than a thousand people somehow changed race: nineteen whites turned Colored (as South Africans call people of mixed heritage); seven hundred and two Coloreds turned white, fifty Indians turned Colored, eleven Colored turned Chinese, and so on. (No blacks turned white, or vice versa.)

Taxonomy is an acutely sensitive subject, and its history is probably one of the reasons that South Africans—particularly black South Africans—have rallied behind their runner with such fervor. The government has decreed that Semenya can continue running with women in her own country, regardless of what the I.A.A.F. decides.

South Africans have compared the worldwide fascination with Semenya's gender to the dubious fame of another South African woman whose body captivated Europeans: Saartjie Baartman, the Hottentot Venus. Baartman, an orphan born on the rural Eastern Cape, was the servant of Dutch farmers near Cape Town. In 1810, they sent her to Europe to be exhibited in front of painters, naturalists, and oglers, who were fascinated by her unusually large buttocks and had heard rumors of her long labia. She supposedly became a prostitute and an alcoholic, and she died in France in her mid-twenties. Until 1974, her skeleton and preserved genitals were displayed at the Musée de l'Homme, in Paris. Many South Africans feel that white foreigners are yet again scrutinizing a black female body as though it did not contain a human being.

Mayende-Sibiya has asked that the United Nations get involved in Semenya's case, and I asked her what she thought it could do. "I would like to see it getting more information from the I.A.A.F.," she said over lunch at the Congress. "We wrote to the I.A.A.F. to ask a number of questions, including what precedents informed the action that it took on Caster. Why pick up on her? What were the reasons? The I.A.A.F. has not responded, and that to me raises questions on how it conducts business." Mayende-Sibiya is a big, warm woman, a grandmother and a former nurse, who hugs everyone she meets. She sighed. "There is a lot that has gone wrong in this process."

The I.A.A.F. has behaved erratically on the issue. On November 19th, the South African Ministry of Sport and Recreation announced that the I.A.A.F. had said that Semenya could keep her medal, but the I.A.A.F. refused to confirm this. Its president, Lamine Diack, was scheduled to visit South Africa several weeks ago to talk to Semenya and to representatives of the government, but he cancelled his trip at the last minute. In late October, I got in touch with the I.A.A.F., with questions about Semenya, and received a form-letter reply (dated September 11th) that it would not comment on the case until after its council meeting, at the end of November. Then, a few hours later, Nick Davies, the director of communications, wrote back by e-mail:

> Two things triggered the investigation. Firstly, the incredible improvement in this athlete's performance . . . and more bluntly, the fact that SOUTH AFRICAN sport web sites were alleging that she was a hermaphrodite athlete. One such blog (from sport24.co.za) stated, "Caster Semenya is an interesting revelation because the 18 year old was born a hermaphrodite and, through a series of tests, has been classified as female." With this blatant allegation, and bearing in mind the almost supernatural improvement, the I.A.A.F. believed that it was sensible to make sure, with help of A.S.A., that the athlete was negative in terms of doping test results, and also that there was no gender ambiguity which may have allowed her to have the benefits of male hormone levels, whilst competing against other women.

A.S.A. is the abbreviation for Athletics South Africa, the national governing body in charge of track and field. The group's president, Leonard Chuene, who was also on the board of the I.A.A.F., and had been in Berlin for the Championships, told reporters when he returned, "We are not going to allow Europeans to define and describe our children." South Africa would have no part in tests conducted by "some stupid university somewhere," Chuene, who also happens to be from Limpopo, said. "The only scientists I believe in are the parents of this child." He claimed to be shocked by the way that the I.A.A.F. had treated Semenya, and he resigned from the board in protest before he left Berlin. (A week later, Chuene wrote the I.A.A.F. a letter saying that his resignation had been hasty, and asked to be reinstated.)

In fact, Chuene was not only aware of the Berlin tests; he had authorized them, and, at the urging of the I.A.A.F., he had also had Semenya tested before she left Pretoria. On August 3rd, the I.A.A.F.'s anti-doping administrator, Dr. Gabriel Dollé, had sent an e-mail to Harold Adams, A.S.A.'s team doctor, citing the website posting that Nick Davies mentioned to me, which alleged that Semenya is a "hermaphrodite . . . classified as female." Dollé asked Adams if sex verification had been conducted—or ought to be. (Debora Patta, the host of a South African investigative program called "3rd Degree," obtained the e-mail exchange and forwarded it to me.) Adams then sent the following e-mail to Leonard Chuene and A.S.A.'s general manager, Molatelo Malehopo:

> After thinking about the current confidential matter I would suggest we make the following decisions.

1. We get a gynae opinion and take it to Berlin.

2. We do nothing and I will handle these issues if they come up in Berlin.
   Please think and get back to me A.S.A.P.

Malehopo replied the same day, agreeing to the exam. Semenya was taken to the Medforum Medi-Clinic, in Pretoria, for tests by a gynecologist.

"They did not even consult us as parents," Semenya's mother, Dorcus, told the *Star*, a South African daily. "They acted like thieves. They did whatever they wanted to do with our child without informing us."

On August 8th, Adams and Semenya flew to Germany to join the rest of the South African team and the A.S.A. staff at the training camp. Adams, who is also one of President Zuma's personal physicians, told Chuene that the Pretoria test results were "not good." He recommended that they withdraw Semenya from the competition, rather than subject her to further testing.

"The reason for my advice was that the tests might prove too traumatic for Ms. Semenya to handle, especially without the necessary support of family and friends around her," Harold Adams wrote in a subsequent report to Parliament. "The other reason was that being tested at the World Championships would not give her enough time to consult extensively and perhaps arrive at a decision to refuse the testing."

Leonard Chuene did not take Adams's advice. Instead, Semenya ran in a qualifying heat on August 16th and then in the semifinals, the next day. After her success in the semifinals, a television reporter outside the stadium blurted out, "With that comes rumors. I heard one that you were born a man?" The video is very hard to watch. As the reporter speaks, Semenya's breathing quickens, and she appears to be on the verge of panic. Then she looks at the ground and says, "I have no idea about that thing. . . . I don't give a damn about it," and walks away from the cameras. August 18th was supposed to be a rest day before the finals. Semenya spent it undergoing a second round of tests. The next day, after two weeks of confusion and scrutiny, Semenya won the gold medal.

In September, the Johannesburg weekly *Mail & Guardian* exposed Chuene's dishonesty about authorizing the tests in Pretoria and Berlin. Chuene contends that he was simply following I.A.A.F. procedure, and that his deceit was a well-intentioned attempt to maintain confidentiality. After the story broke, he held a press conference to apologize for lying to the nation, but the apology was not unconditional. "Tell me someone," he said, "who has not lied to protect a child."

Semenya is back at the University of Pretoria now, training with her coach, Michael Seme. I asked Seme how he thought she was doing. "Sometimes you can look at somebody thinking he is O.K.," Seme said. "But you find out in his heart, maybe it is complaining. I can't see what's happening in her heart."

At a meeting of the British Gynaecological Society on April 25, 1888, Dr. Fancourt Barnes declared that he had "in the next room a living specimen of a hermaphrodite." The person was nineteen years old, and had always believed that she was female. Barnes thought otherwise. He cited "1) the appearance of the head, 2) the *timbre* of the voice, 3) the non-development of the breasts," and "the utter absence of anything like a uterus or ovaries," as evidence of the subject's insufficient femininity.

Other members of the society who examined the patient disagreed. Dr. James Aveling asserted that "the face was feminine, the throat was decidedly that of a woman." Dr. Charles Henry Felix Routh argued that Barnes's diagnosis was "guess work," and claimed that "the mere fact" that this patient might not have a uterus was "no argument against its being a woman." (Routh was not entirely convinced that the patient lacked a uterus and suggested that unless Barnes tried to "pass his entire hand into her rectum" they could not be sure.) Dr. Heywood Smith finally "suggested that the Society should divide on the question of sex," and so it did. Before the doctors sent their patient home with her mother, they took a photograph. In the foreground, a "medical man" holds the "living specimen" 's genitals with his thumb and forefinger for the camera, between her spread legs. In the background is the blurred image of the subject's head, not quite obscured by the blanket that covers her torso. The subject's face is grainy, but it is set in an unmistakable expression of powerless panic.

The society's inability to reach consensus was due, in part, to its failure to locate either testicles or ovaries in the patient. Until 1915, that was the generally accepted determining factor for sex. In "Hermaphrodites and the Medical Invention of Sex," Alice Domurat Dreger calls the period from 1870 to 1915 "the Age of Gonads."

The way doctors, scientists, and sports officials have determined sex has changed radically over the years. Before 1968, the International Olympic Committee verified the sex of female athletes by looking between their legs. Athletes complained about these humiliating inspections—which weren't always conclusive—and, for the 1968 Olympics, in Mexico City, the I.O.C. decided to implement chromosomal testing. (There were rumors that some men from Eastern Bloc nations had plans to masquerade as women.) These assessments proved problematic, too.

In normal human development, when a zygote has XY, or male, chromosomes, the SRY—sex-determining region Y—gene on the Y chromosome "instructs" the zygote's protogonads to develop as testes, rather than as ovaries. The testes then produce testosterone, which issues a second set of developmental instructions: for a scrotal sac to develop and for the testes to descend into it, for a penis to grow, and so on. But the process can get derailed. A person can be born with one ovary and one testicle. The SRY gene can end up on an X chromosome. A person with a penis who thinks he is male can one day find out that he has a uterus and ovaries. "Then, there is chromosomal variability that is invisible," Anne Fausto-Sterling, the author of "Sexing the Body," told me. "You could go your whole life and never know."

All sorts of things can happen, and do. An embryo that is chromosomally male but suffers from an enzyme deficiency that partially prevents it from "reading" testosterone can develop into a baby who appears female. Then, at puberty, the person's testes will produce a rush of hormones and this time the body won't need the enzyme (called 5-alpha-reductase) to successfully read the testosterone. The little girl will start to become hairier and more muscular. Her voice may deepen, and her testes may descend into what she thought were her labia. Her clitoris will grow into something like a penis. Is she still a girl? Was she ever?

If a chromosomally male embryo has androgen-insensitivity syndrome, or A.I.S., the cells' receptors for testosterone, an androgen, are deaf to the testosterone's instructions, and will thus develop the default external sexual characteristics of a female. An individual with androgen-insensitivity syndrome has XY chromosomes, a vagina, and undescended testes, but her body develops without the ability to respond to the testosterone it produces. In fact, people with complete A.I.S. are less able to process testosterone than average women. Consequently, they tend to have exceptionally "smooth-skinned bodies with rounded hips and breasts and long limbs," Dreger writes in "Hermaphrodites."

People with incomplete A.I.S., on the other hand, could end up looking and sounding like Caster Semenya. Their bodies hear some of the instructions that the testosterone inside them is issuing. But that does not necessarily mean that they would have an athletic advantage.

For example, the Spanish hurdler Maria Patiño, who had A.I.S., went to the World University Games in Kobe, Japan, in 1985, and forgot to bring a letter from her doctor verifying that she was female. Until 1999, gender verification was compulsory for all female athletes. Officials scraped some cells from the inside of her cheek for chromatin testing. If visual inspection had still been the standard, Patiño's gender never would have been questioned. Her genitals, and the rest of her, looked female, but according to the test she was male. The story got out, and she was stripped of her past titles. Her boyfriend left her. Her scholarship was revoked, and she was evicted from the national athletic residence.

In 1991, the International Association of Athletics Federations abandoned this method as unreliable, and, nine years later, so did the International Olympic Committee. Patiño was requalified in 1988, when she was able to prove that her body could not make use of its testosterone, and that she had developed as a woman. "I knew I was a woman," Patiño said, "in the eyes of medicine, God, and most of all in my own eyes."

The approach that the I.A.A.F. appears to be taking in its review of Semenya's test results from Berlin is not unlike the British Gynaecological Society's muddled attempt to determine the sex of its living specimen. The I.A.A.F.'s gender policy states that an athlete "can be asked to attend a medical evaluation before a panel comprising gynecologist, endocrinologist, psychologist, internal medicine specialist, expert on gender/transgender issues." It has not come up with a single litmus test for sex; its goal, like that of the I.O.C. in such situations, is to reach consensus. The federation does not define the criteria that its group of experts must use to reach their determination, however. "It seems to be working with a kind of 'I know it when I see it' policy," Dreger, a professor of clinical medical humanities and bioethics at Northwestern University's Feinberg School of Medicine, told me. The policy does not indicate who should be tested and on what grounds. An athlete will be examined if "there is any 'suspicion' or if there is a 'challenge'" to her sex. Evidently, a blog post qualifies as a challenge.

In conjunction with other sports bodies, the I.A.A.F. will hold a special conference, in January, 2010, to review the policy. On November 18th, it sent out a press release stating that there would be "no discussion of Caster Semenya's case" at the November council meeting, despite its earlier promise to resolve the issue there.

Unfortunately for I.A.A.F. officials, they are faced with a question that no one has ever been able to answer: what is the ultimate difference between a man and a woman? "This is not a solvable problem," Alice Dreger said. "People always press me: 'Isn't there one marker we can use?' No. We couldn't then and we can't now, and science is making it more difficult and not less, because it ends up showing us how much blending there is and how many nuances, and it becomes impossible to point to one thing, or even a set of things, and say that's what it means to be male."

In 2000, Anne Fausto-Sterling, a professor of biology at Brown University, conducted what remains the study of record on the frequency of intersexuality, and concluded that 1.7 per cent of the population develops in a way that deviates from the standard definition of male or female. (Some scholars have argued that Fausto-Sterling's categories are too broad, because they include individuals who show no noticeable expression of their chromosomal irregularity.) Based on this figure, intersexuality is much more common than Down syndrome or albinism, though it can be harder to keep track of: every baby born in the United States is registered as "male" or "female."

The word "hermaphrodite" is as outdated and offensive to the people it once described as the word "mulatto." In one Greek myth, Hermes, the son of Zeus, and Aphrodite, the goddess of love, have a child endowed with all the attributes of both of them.

"Hermaphrodite" implies a double-sexed creature, fully male and fully female, which is a physical impossibility for human beings. (You can be half and half, but you can't be all and all.)

In the nineteen-nineties, a movement spearheaded by an activist who used to call herself Cheryl Chase, and now goes by the name Bo Laurent, insisted that what was needed was a new identity. Chase founded the Intersex Society of North America (now defunct) to draw attention to the frequently tragic consequences of doctors' performing irreversible surgery on newborns to enforce a sex—one that the baby might just as easily as not grow up to reject. The society advocated assigning intersex children a gender at birth but leaving their bodies intact, so that upon adulthood they could make their own choices about whether they wished to undergo surgical modification.

Then something unexpected happened. "The intersex identity started getting inhabited by people who weren't really intersex," Dreger said. "The people who accumulated around the intersex identity tended to be queer and out and comfortable with this identity outside the gender binary." They felt that refraining from interfering with infants' ambiguous genitalia was the first step on a desirable path to dissolving gender altogether. To them, this idea was "as politically inspiring as it is utterly disconnected from the actual experience of intersex people or the heart-wrenching decisions their parents have to make when an intersex child is born," as Vernon A. Rosario, a professor of psychiatry at U.C.L.A., put it in a recent issue of *The Gay and Lesbian Review*.

Semenya, whether she wants to be or not, has become a hero to many people who "don't fit the sex and gender boxes," as Jarvis, from Winnipeg, posted on the website casterrunsforme.com. A person named Megan Ewart wrote, "I'll bet you've got a lot more transgendered allies than just me that are feeling your pain."

Now there is an even newer term of art for people born with ambiguously sexed bodies who do not wish to be connected with the "L.G.B.T.Q.I."—lesbian, gay, bisexual, transgender, queer, intersex—camp: "disorders of sex development," or D.S.D. By naming the condition a medical "disorder," advocates of the D.S.D. label hope to make the people it describes seem less aberrant. "Oddly enough, it does normalize it in a certain way," Fausto-Sterling said. "It's putting it on the same plane as other anomalous development—like congenital anomalies of the heart." Advocates of the D.S.D. label are not seeking to create a third sex. Rather, they want disorders of sex development to be treated like any other physical abnormality: something for doctors to monitor but not to operate on, unless the patient is in physical discomfort or danger.

In science and medicine, categories are imperative, but they are also inflected by social concerns. "Mammals," for example, were so named by Linnaeus, in the eighteenth century, because their females produce milk to suckle their young. Was it irrelevant that scientists like Linnaeus sought to encourage mothers to breast-feed their own children, and to do away with the "unnatural" custom of wet-nursing? "There are philosophers of science who argue that when scientists make categories in the natural world—shapes, species—they are simply making a list of things that exist: natural kinds," Fausto-Sterling said. "It's scientist as discoverer. The phrase that people use is 'cutting nature at its joint.' There are other people, myself included, who think that, almost always, what we're doing in biology is creating categories that work pretty well for certain things that we want to do with them. But there is no joint."

If sex is not precisely definable, how else might sports be organized? Theoretically, athletes could be categorized by size, as they are in wrestling and boxing. But then women would usually lose to men. Or athletes could be categorized by skill level. Almost always, this would mean that the strongest élite female athletes would compete against the weakest élite male athletes, which would be pretty demoralizing all the way around.

Another option would be to divide athletes biochemically. Testosterone is, for an athlete, truly important stuff. Developmentally, testosterone spurs linear bone growth in adolescents. Fully grown people use testosterone in doping because it helps create muscle mass and increases red-blood-cell production, which, in turn, increases cellular oxygen-carrying capacity. The more oxygen an athlete has in her cells, the more efficiently her muscles operate and the longer it takes for her body to start producing lactic acid, the substance that causes cramps and pain. Testosterone makes a faster, better athlete, and enables a body to recover more quickly from exhaustion. Hypothetically, according to Eric Vilain, a professor of human genetics and pediatrics at U.C.L.A., those with a certain level of functional testosterone (testosterone that the body can actually make use of) could be in one group, and those below it could be in another. Although the first group would be almost all male and the second group would be almost all female, the division would be determined not by gender but by actual physical advantages that gender supposedly, yet unreliably, supplies.

But, setting aside the issue of gender, there is still no such thing as a level playing field in sports. Different bodies have physical attributes, even abnormalities, that may provide a distinct advantage in one sport or another. The N.B.A., for instance, has had several players with acromegaly—the overproduction of growth hormone. Michael Phelps, who has won fourteen Olympic gold medals, has unusually long arms and is said to have double-jointed elbows, knees, and ankles. Is Caster Semenya's alleged extra testosterone really so different?

There is much more at stake in organizing sports by gender than just making things fair. If we were to admit that at some level we don't know the difference between men and women, we might start to wonder about the way we've organized our entire world. Who gets to use what bathroom? Who is allowed to get married? (Currently, the United States government recognizes the marriage of a woman to a female-to-male transsexual who has had a double mastectomy and takes testosterone tablets but still has a vagina, but not to a woman who hasn't done those things.) We depend on gender to make sense of sexuality, society, and ourselves. We do not wish to see it dissolve.

What the I.A.A.F. concludes about Caster Semenya could have ramifications for sports in general and for South Africa in particular. This is true not only because it is Semenya's place of origin. South Africa has an unusually high level of intersex births. Nobody knows why.

During apartheid, for every white town there was a black township. Only the white towns appeared on maps, though the townships were nearly always more populous. John Carlin, in his account of the 1995 rugby World Cup, "Playing the Enemy: Nelson Mandela and the Game That Made a Nation," describes townships as "the black shadows of the towns." Khayelitsha is the black shadow of Cape Town. According to the most recent census, half a million people live there, but in reality the number is probably much higher. Many of their parents and grandparents settled in the Cape Flats, outside of Cape Town, after the Group Areas Acts of the nineteen-fifties made it illegal for them to live in the city. "Khayelitsha" is Xhosa for "New Home." Shacks made of corrugated tin, cardboard, and scrap wood, many without electricity or running water, sprawl for miles along mostly unmarked dirt roads, punctuated by beauty parlors and fruit stands in structures no bigger than British telephone booths.

By Khayelitsha standards, Funeka Soldaat's small home, with its solid brick walls and tiled floor, is very fine. Soldaat is an L.G.B.Q.T.I. activist. Both she and a cousin—whom Soldaat, following local custom, referred to as her sister—were born with anomalous genitalia, and both underwent "corrective" partial clitoridectomies when they were young, which they now regret. This is the standard "treatment" for babies born with a clitoris longer than one centimetre but smaller than 2.5 centimetres, at which point it becomes a medically acceptable penis. The scar tissue that forms after such a procedure can impede sensation for the rest of a person's life.

"My sister, she look just like Caster," Soldaat said, smiling. "She don't have the breasts. She never get a period. Everybody thinks she's a guy, just like Caster. We call them, in Xhosa, *italasi*. It is not a new thing—everybody has a word for it." That there is a name for intersex does not mean it is a condition that is ever spoken about. "One thing that is so difficult for African people: there's no way that you can discuss about something that's happened below the belt," Soldaat said. "All the time you don't know what's happening in your body, and there's nobody that try to explain to you. *Then* it becomes a problem. If my mom would know that I'm intersex and there's nothing wrong about it, then there was nothing going to make me panic."

Particularly in remote areas, where babies tend to be born in the presence of a mother, a grandmother, and maybe a midwife, it is easy to keep a baby's genitalia a secret. People want to insulate their children from the shame of being different, so they simply pretend that they are not. "Limpopo and Eastern Cape are the high incidence of intersex people," Soldaat said. "And when you grow up in the rural areas it's a mess, because people don't even go to doctors." The determination of gender is made very simply. "It depends what they do when they go to the loo," Soldaat said. "That's what makes their children to be women. If they go to the loo and they sit, that's it."

On her coffee table, Soldaat had a photocopy of the South African magazine *You*, which featured a photo spread showing Caster Semenya dressed in high heels and a short skirt, her hair fluffed out and her face made up. Her expression was painfully uncomfortable, and the pictures were garish.

"My sister was crying when she saw this whole thing on paper," Soldaat said, flipping through the pages. "It's a disaster. She look like a drag queen! I can just imagine her at night when she's alone, looking at these pictures."

Soldaat tossed the papers on the floor. "When we are really, really poor sometimes, and we really, really want to protect ourselves, people take an advantage," she said. "That's why it was easy for people to force her to do this, for A.S.A. to do this." Athletics South Africa received a payment from *You* in exchange for Semenya's appearance in its pages. "To say that she enjoyed doing this, that's a lie! There is no way. There is no way!"

Soldaat has a shaved head and was wearing big jeans and a baseball cap with the words "Mama Cash," the name of a Dutch women's-rights organization, on it. She is a lesbian, and she said that she suspected Semenya is, too.

"Everyone! Everyone who is like this likes women," Soldaat said, laughing. "Everyone!" ("Caster has never cared about men other than as friends," her father told a reporter. "Her sisters were always after boys in the way that I, too, was always after girls when I was younger. But Caster has never been interested in any of that.") If Soldaat is right, then Semenya's life may well get more difficult. Soldaat was going to court later that day to listen to the proceedings against several men accused of raping and murdering a lesbian in Khayelitsha. "They are raping lesbians to correct them," she said. "In order they can be a proper woman."

Soldaat said that Semenya should run with women. "It will never be like intersex women have their own Olympic Games—that's ridiculous!" she said. Soldaat has a big, raucous laugh, and the idea of that imaginary competition absolutely killed her. Soldaat was a runner herself when she was young. "If she can't run in the Olympics, Caster has to continue running with other girls in South Africa. Because, really, that's what she wants, that's what she is, that's what keeps her alive: that's running."

The only thing more slippery than the science in the Semenya case is the agendas of the men who have involved themselves in it. There is a bounty of political gain for whoever spins the story most successfully.

Julius Malema, the president of the A.N.C. Youth League, has said that he does not believe in the existence of intersex people, and has tried to frame the concept as a suspect and unwelcome import from abroad. "Hermaphrodite, what is that?" Malema asked at a press conference in October. "Somebody tell me, what is 'hermaphrodite' in Pedi? There's no such thing. So don't impose your hermaphrodite concepts on us." (The word is *tarasi*, according to a professor of South African languages at Yale.) The Youth League issued a press release decrying a "racist attack on Semenya" orchestrated by the media in "Australia, which is the most lucrative destination for South Africa's racists and fascists who refused to live under a black democratic government."

Julius Malema is not known for being levelheaded. He won the presidency of the Youth League in a highly contested election in 2008. Just a few months later, while Jacob Zuma was fending off charges of racketeering and fraud (the charges have since been dropped), Malema became notorious for vowing, "We are prepared to die for Zuma. Not only that, we are prepared to take up arms and kill for Zuma." (Zuma also beat a rape charge, in 2006.) Zuma has called Malema "a leader in the making," worthy of "inheriting the A.N.C." one day. Malema has demonstrated an ability to mobilize people and an almost reckless willingness to use charges of racism to do so. He has been Leonard Chuene's most steadfast defender.

Chuene has, since the revelation of his deceit, become almost as controversial a figure in South Africa as Caster Semenya. Countless editorials have accused Chuene of sacrificing her in his quest for a gold medal and have demanded his ouster. In Dr. Harold Adams's report to Parliament, he calls Chuene's decision "short-sighted and grossly irresponsible." Though Chuene received a vote of confidence from Athletics South Africa's board after his admission, the A.N.C. asked him to apologize; its rival party, the Democratic Alliance, demanded his resignation, and the Deputy Minister of Sport called him a liar. Minister Mayende-Sibiya told me that Chuene's behavior was "totally unacceptable."

Julius Malema has continued to paint any criticism of Chuene as racist. In early October, one of A.S.A.'s biggest sponsors, Nedbank, announced that it would withdraw its support pending a change in A.S.A.'s leadership. Malema retaliated by calling for a boycott of the bank. "We will teach them a lesson about the power of the masses," Malema said. "They may have money, but we can defeat them because we have the masses."

On three occasions, Leonard Chuene's personal assistant made an appointment for me to interview "the president," as she calls her boss. She always called or e-mailed at the last minute to cancel. We had several calls scheduled, but Chuene never picked up his phone at the appointed time. Then, one day, I got on an airplane going to Polokwane, a small northern city. Sitting in an empty row, in a navy blazer and pressed jeans, was Leonard Chuene.

Chuene wanted to know how I recognized him. Only minutes before, I had been looking at his photograph in a newspaper, alongside a story about Nedbank's withdrawal of funds from A.S.A. and A.S.A.'s failing finances. "I have become more famous than Caster," he said, and chuckled. Chuene has a shiny bald head and a little gut. He was once a serious runner and has completed more than a hundred marathons, he told me. He said he had no choice but to get Semenya tested. "You cannot just argue like a fool and say no. This is not the law of the jungle!" He speaks very quickly. He explained why he had not heeded Adams's advice to withdraw Semenya from the race.

"I don't have the results in my hand!" he said. "How did you expect me to take an informed decision?"

Indeed, Adams had had word from the Pretoria clinic but no actual documentation of the test results. "Where is the evidence?" Chuene said. "Now I come back home and they will say, 'When this black child from the rural be No. 1, why do you deprive her?'"

Chuene shrugged. "They say I lied. That's what they are saying. I said no. There is confidentiality! I.A.A.F. is in trouble for breaching that. Who was going to be Leonard to say that?" The engines started roaring as the small plane took off. "It was 22-Catch situation!" Chuene shouted over the noise. "If I will do this, it's 'Why did you withdraw her?' If I did not, 'Why did you allow her to run?' Whatever way you look at it, I'm judged. I'm judged!"

There were around twenty people on the plane. We were airborne, and the engines quieted. Chuene did not. "The stupid leader is the one who says, 'I'm not sure; I don't know.' I had to take a decision! She must run. If Chuene didn't allow her, it meant she was going to stay in South Africa. This thing has given her more opportunity! Everybody knows her. The world is out there to say, 'Your problems are our problems.' Imagine if I had not let her win!" As we touched down in Polokwane, he said, "If there is to be help, it is because of the opportunity created by Leonard Chuene."

Recently, Semenya told the *Guardian*, "It's not so easy. The university is O.K. but there is not many other places I can go. People want to stare at me now. They want to touch me. I'm supposed to be famous." She added, "I don't think I like it so much."

The law firm Dewey & LeBoeuf announced in September that it was taking on Caster Semenya as a client. It is still sorting through what happened and deciding whom to sue. One afternoon, I drove with Benedict Phiri, an associate in the firm's Johannesburg office, across the Blood River from Polokwane to Ga-Masehlong to meet Semenya's mother.

Ga-Masehlong is a small village dotted with jacaranda trees; goats graze on the garbage and the grass on the roadsides. The houses have tin roofs, and people put rocks on top of them to keep them from blowing away. There are satellite dishes in several yards, but most people have dug their own wells and collect firewood from the bush for cooking. Everyone knows everyone else in Ga-Masehlong, and it was easy to get directions to the house of the champion.

At the Semenya home, there was a flyer tacked to the front door promoting a lecture that Julius Malema was giving at the local elementary school. Phiri knocked. We heard shuffling and then the sound of locks turning and bolts sliding. Phiri called out that he was Caster's lawyer, but nobody came to the door.

A few minutes later, a pretty girl wearing an orange fleece jacket walked into the yard and introduced herself as Maphela. She said she was fourteen. "Do you want my story?" she asked in English. "I am Caster's sister! But I am not like her. I am different from Caster." I asked her what she meant, and Maphela replied emphatically, "I am not that way."

Maphela looked toward the window where her mother, Dorcus, was hiding her face behind the curtain and motioning vigorously for her daughter to stop speaking with us. We asked Maphela if she would tell her mother that Phiri was Caster's lawyer. Maphela ran off toward the back door.

We sat on the stoop of a cooking hut in the Semenyas' front yard, and waited with the chickens and the goats. An elderly neighbor named Ike came into the yard. "Caster has done a wonderful thing," he said. "This has brought to mind when the Philistines were persecuting the Israelites." Ike told us that he just wanted to check on the family and see how their visit from Julius Malema the previous evening had gone. This made Phiri nervous.

After a few minutes, Maphela returned. She told us that her mother would not meet with Phiri, because she did not agree that Caster should have a lawyer.

As we drove away through the bush, Phiri called his boss in Johannesburg, a white former rugby player named Greg Nott. I could hear Nott yelling through the phone. "We knew this would happen all along," Phiri said, trying to calm him. "Julius Malema is Chuene's ally, and Julius is giving Caster money."

On the occasion of the A.N.C. Youth League's sixty-fifth anniversary, in October, Julius Malema presented Caster Semenya with a hundred and twenty thousand rand (about sixteen thousand dollars) at a gala dinner in Johannesburg. "I can even see it," Phiri said on the phone. "They probably told the mom, 'People will come and say they're her lawyer. Don't believe it.'" Phiri was afraid that Malema would step in and persuade the family to side with Chuene, who comes from the same region, and whose interests might not be served by lawyers poking around. One of the first things that Dewey & LeBoeuf did when the firm took the case was to ask both A.S.A. and the I.A.A.F. to provide documentation of the tests and any other pertinent paperwork; neither organization has fully complied.

The firm is representing Semenya pro bono, so good publicity will be its only reward. "And that," Phiri said, "could blow up in our faces."

Nobody wants Chuene out of office more than an old friend and colleague named Wilfred Daniels, who started at A.S.A. with him, sixteen years ago. "From day one we connected, in the struggle days, you know?" Daniels said. "We were like, we *belong* together." Both Daniels, fifty-eight, and Chuene, fifty-seven, grew up as promising athletes who could never compete internationally because of apartheid. They understood each other then, but not anymore.

Daniels—whom everyone calls Wilfie—is the unofficial mayor of Stellenbosch, a leafy college town in the wine country. He likes to hold court at the Jan Cats restaurant, in front of the elegant Stellenbosch Hotel. As he sat at his street-front table on a sunny afternoon in a green Izod jacket and track pants, drinking a bottle of Chenin blanc, every other person who passed by stopped to pay his respects, or at least waved at him driving by. Daniels was a famous athlete in his youth, and he is even more famous now. In early September, he resigned from A.S.A. in protest over its handling of Caster Semenya, and had since been in the papers constantly. "We allowed it," he said. "If we as management were on our game, we would've objected. We accompanied her to the slaughter. And that is my dilemma."

Daniels was not directly involved in the testing or the coverup. During the first training session in Berlin, "while she was warming up and stretching, putting on her spikes, she told me they had done tests on her. I said, 'What tests?'" Semenya told him that she didn't know what they were for, but she described what had happened. "They put her feet in straps and 'they work down there,' she said. They told her it was dope tests." Semenya had undergone routine doping tests many times before. She knew that this was something very different.

"If you and me who come from the big cities, if we find it repulsive, I mean, what about a rural girl," Daniels said. "She doesn't know what's happening around her. She's seven, eight months in the city now, in Pretoria, a new life altogether, and nobody takes the time to explain to her?" He shook his head in disgust. "It was unprovoked talk, and she's not somebody who talks, normally. And she spoke to me as a Colored guy, as a man, about intimate, female things. That to me was like a cry for help."

The sins of A.S.A., as Daniels sees it, are, first, not giving Semenya adequate information about the Pretoria tests—including her right to refuse them—and, second, not pulling her out of the competition in Berlin.

"It's the day before the championships," Daniels said. "Eighteen years old, your first World Championships, the greatest race of your life. You can't focus, because you have to go for gender testing. And you come back and you have to watch on TV: they are explaining the possibilities. I found her in her room, sitting in front of the TV like this," Daniels put his hand up to his face to show how close she was to the screen. "And they're talking about her and she's trying to understand what they're saying. Because nobody has spoken to her, to tell her, Look, this is what these tests might mean. I felt so ashamed."

Daniels has worked in various capacities at A.S.A. over the years, first in management, then as a coach, and, most recently, as A.S.A.'s coördinator with the High Performance Centre, the program at the University of Pretoria where Semenya is now. Daniels does not agree with the I.A.A.F.'s assessment that Semenya's seven-and-a-half-second improvement was "supernatural." She went from training on the dirt roads of Limpopo to a world-class facility. She is also an extraordinarily hard worker. "Understand: Maria Mutola is her hero," Daniels said. "So she had wonderful goals and ideals for herself; she was really trying to emulate her hero one day." Maria Mutola is a runner from Mozambique whose event, like Semenya's, was the eight hundred metres. Mutola also happened to have a strikingly masculine appearance.

Daniels believes that the best that can happen for Semenya at this point is to have a career like his. He has travelled the world and met many of his heroes. He has a cellar with more than two thousand bottles of red wine. He eats his grilled springbok at Jan Cats and clearly enjoys being a local eminence. But it is probably not the life he would have led if apartheid hadn't prevented him from competing internationally; and it is not the life that was in front of Caster Semenya before she went to Germany. "I understand that her running days are over," Daniels said.

There's another scenario, in which Semenya's story could become one of against-all-odds victory. The I.A.A.F. could apologize and decree Semenya female. Kobus van der Walt, the director of sport at the High Performance Centre, pointed out that though Semenya has beaten the South African record for her event, she hasn't come anywhere near Kratochvílová's world record, which means that there are plenty of women with a chance of besting Semenya. Conceivably, one day we will see Caster Semenya at the Olympics with a medal hanging from her neck. She could be the poster child for triumphant transgression.

But that is not what Daniels thinks will happen. "Now her life is over," he said. "Not only as an athlete but as a human being. Even if the I.A.A.F. says there's nothing wrong with her, people will always look at her twice. There should be hell to pay for those responsible."

He pounded his fist on the table. "I've got a daughter. If that was my daughter, what would I have done as a father? Somebody might have been dead by now."

On November 5th, Chuene and the entire board of A.S.A. were suspended by the South African Sports Confederation and Olympic Committee, pending an investigation into how they handled Caster Semenya.

One afternoon at the High Performance Centre, I sat up in the bleachers, killing time before a meeting with Kobus Van der Walt. I was surrounded by a spread of neatly partitioned fields, like a Brueghel painting: there are twenty-four cricket nets, six rugby fields, twenty-two outdoor tennis courts, nine soccer fields, seven squash courts, and a track surrounded by a three-thousand-seat stadium, all kept in impeccable condition. Runners in little packs zoomed around the fields and into the distance. Spring sunlight flicked along the blue of the swimming pool.

A figure in a black sweatshirt with the hood up walked along the path about thirty yards in front of me. There was something about this person's build and movements that drew my attention. I got up and followed along the path, until I caught up to the person where he or she was stopped behind the cafeteria, talking to a waiter and a cook, both of whom were much shorter than she was. It was Caster Semenya.

She wore sandals and track pants and kept her hood up. When she shook my hand, I noticed that she had long nails. She didn't look like an eighteen-year-old girl, or an eighteen-year-old boy. She looked like something else, something magnificent.

I told her I had come from New York City to write about her, and she asked me why.

"Because you're the champion," I said.

She snorted and said, "You make me laugh."

I asked her if she would talk to me, not about the tests or Chuene but about her evolution as an athlete, her progression from Limpopo to the world stage. She shook her head vigorously. "No," she said. "I can't talk to you. I can't talk to anyone. I can't say to anyone how I feel or what's in my mind."

I said I thought that must suck.

"No," she said, very firmly. Her voice was strong and low. "That doesn't suck. It sucks when I was running and they were writing those things. That sucked. That is when it sucks. Now I just have to walk away. That's all I can do." She smiled a small, bemused smile. "Walk away from all of this, maybe forever. Now I just walk away." Then she took a few steps backward, turned around, and did.

Outline Levy's article and its concerns. What are its main claims and how does she organize these throughout the piece? What kinds of evidence does she provide in support of certain claims? How does Levy's *New Yorker* audience determine how she covers the topic, both in terms of tone and reasoning?

In small groups discuss how you feel about Caster Semenya's case. Take a few minutes and research some articles on Caster and her Olympic legacy. Do you agree or disagree with the IOC's decision regarding Semenya's medals? Why? Come up with clear arguments for your case and present to the class. Can you think of other intersex and/or transgender athletes facing similar challenges?

The issue of transgender and intersex athletes is highly controversial in sports, particularly at elite levels, because sports are gender segregated. How do you feel about transgender and intersex screening in athletes? What advantages or disadvantages do you think this poses for athletes competing as males or as females? Are there different consequences? Why? Historically, only females have been subject to official gender verification testing. What biases and presuppositions inform this choice and what should be done in the future? Note: You might watch the *ESPN* documentary *Renee*, which looks at the issue of transgender athletes and the historical legacy of tennis player Renee, formerly Richard, Raskin as a precursor to this exercise. Write a short (250-word) response to the film and your evolving understanding of transgender and intersex athletes in sport.

After reading Levy's article, do you find you look at sports and/or intersex athletes differently? Are you more or less inclined to support sport as a gender-segregated event? Why or why not? Write a reflective journal in which you explore these issues more fully.

Education associate professor Keith Storey has written and published on school and community inclusion. In the following piece, he takes a somewhat unexpected approach to the Special Olympics, asking policy makers and the public to rethink how the current structure of the event may in fact do more harm than good for people with disabilities.

THE CASE AGAINST THE SPECIAL OLYMPICS

By Keith Storey

The Special Olympics has been a controversial program for persons with disabilities. Research has often found negative results concerning the Special Olympics, and there have been numerous discussions in the literature concerning pros and cons of the Special Olympics. The purpose of this article is to articulate and elaborate on concerns regarding the Special Olympics, to promote discussion about these issues, and to suggest future directions for service delivery.

What appropriate and state-of-the-art recreational services are for people with developmental disabilities has changed dramatically over the past 30 years (Schilling & Coles, 1997; Schleien, 1993; Schleien, Heyne, Rynders, & McAvoy, 1990; Schleien, Meyer, Heyne, & Brandt, 1995). The change has been from specialized, segregated services to services in inclusive settings with appropriate supports (Mactavish & Schleien, 2000; Modell & Valdez, 2002; Polloway, Smith, Patton, & Smith, 1996; Schleien, Green, & Heyne, 1993; Schleien & Ray, 1997). However, segregated recreational services still predominate (Dattilo, 2002). Segregated activities are often seen as the norm, and special associations have the responsibility for providing recreational services for people with disabilities. Thus, there is a scarcity of requests for integrated services and few resources to provide them, while people with developmental disabilities often have an abundance of unstructured free time (Schleien & Ray, 1997).

One of the most popular recreational programs for people with developmental disabilities has been the Special Olympics. The Special Olympics is a popular program with more than 1 million participants and 500,000 volunteers. The Special Olympics started when there

From *The Journal of Disability Policy Studies* (2004).

were few recreational services for people with disabilities. The mission of the Special Olympics is to provide year-round sports training and athletic competition in a variety of Olympic-type sports for children and adults with mental retardation, giving them continuing opportunities to develop physical fitness, demonstrate courage, experience joy and participate in a sharing of gifts, skills and friendship with their families, other Special Olympics athletes and the community. (Special Olympics, 2004)

However, over the years, several articles have raised a variety of problems and concerns about the Special Olympics and have suggested possible solutions or policy changes that need to be made (Brickley, 1984; Hourcade, 1989; Orelove, Wehman, & Wood, 1982; "Troubling Questions," 1987). At the same time, there have been articles that have promoted the Special Olympics as a valuable program for people with developmental disabilities (Block & Moon, 1992; Hingsburger, 1997; Privett, 1999).

OVERVIEW OF CONCERNS

The purpose of this article is to articulate and elaborate on concerns regarding the Special Olympics, to promote discussion about these issues, and to suggest future directions for service delivery. Many of the examples provided are from popular press sources, as these highlight the issues being discussed and also reflect on how the general population is provided with information regarding these issues.

Segregation

In the disability field, four different components of integration have generally been considered (Mank & Buckley, 1989; Storey, 1993). These are physical integration, social integration, relationships, and social networks. Wehman (1988) defined integrated settings as "situations where nonhandicapped workers or members of the public at large predominate" (p. 5). Without physical integration there cannot be social integration, relationships, or social networks. However, mere physical presence may not necessarily lead to other forms of integration (Rosenthal-Malek, 1998; Storey & Horner, 1991).

Social interactions that do occur between people with and without disabilities at the Special Olympics are likely to be short term and unlikely to develop into friendships or social networks. Here is an example:

> My name is Jacob Dickinson. I'm 13 years old, and I live in North Haven, Connecticut. I got to work at the 1995 Special Olympics World Games. ...When the games finally started, I helped out at different events. I worked at track and field. I carried athletes' warm-up clothes in baskets from the starting line to the finish line. I kicked a ball around with a soccer team from Barbados to help them warm up before a game. I made new friends. I became good pals with a volunteer from Australia. I met

athletes. We talked about their sports. On the last day of the games, I wasn't too happy. All of my fun was over. I went to the closing ceremony and saw all of my new friends one last time. We said good-bye. We promised to write to one another. ("Let me tell you," 1995, p. 62)

Smart (2001) reviewed research indicating that superficial and casual interactions, such as those that occur in the Special Olympics between people with and without developmental disabilities, do not lead to a reduction in prejudice and may actually reinforce negative stereotypes regarding people with disabilities. As Johnson (2003) noted, events such as the Special Olympics foster the "us against them" attitude (with "them" being people with disabilities), and there has been a backlash against disability rights in part due to people with disabilities being in segregated settings and events and not being part of mainstream society.

At best, the Special Olympics provide mere physical presence of nondisabled persons. There is no way around it; the Special Olympics are a segregated event (Hourcade, 1989; Storey, 1993; Wolfensberger, 1995). You can participate only if you have a disability. The Special Olympics stand in contrast with efforts to integrate people with disabilities into normalized recreational settings (Schleien et al., 1993; Schleien, Green, & Stone, 1999; Williams & Dattilo, 1997).

Lack of Functional Skills

Functional curricula consist of teaching skills that have direct and immediate utility in people's lives within their communities and contribute directly to the attainment of greater independence, self-sufficiency, and quality of life (F. Brown, Evans, Weed, & Owens, 1987; L. Brown et al., 1979; L. Brown, Nietupski, & Hamre-Nietupski, 1976; Wehman, Renzaglia, & Bates, 1985). A basic analysis of functionality is whether an individual who does not learn to perform a particular activity needs to have someone else do it for him or her. If the answer is yes, the activity is likely to be functional. Many of the Special Olympics events are of doubtful functional value and do not prepare people for the criterion of ultimate functioning (Orelove et al., 1982). How functional are some events, such as the softball throw, where the participant throws to a spot on the ground rather than to a person? It is important to note that form refers to a specific motor act, whereas function focuses on the outcomes that the activity achieves (F. Brown et al., 1987). Thus, it is possible to teach a skill that achieves a certain form (passing a basketball) but does not achieve the function (the person is unable to pass a ball quickly and accurately to teammates during a basketball game). L. Brown et al. (1976) have suggested a series of questions to ask of any activity or skill being taught to students. These include,

> Could students function as adults if they did not acquire the skill? Is there a different activity that will allow students to approximate realization of

the criterion of ultimate functioning more quickly and more efficiently? Will this activity impede, restrict, or reduce the probability that students will ultimately function in community settings? (p. 9)

In the Special Olympics, there is a lack of skill acquisition, and much precious teaching time of functional activities is lost. For example, one newspaper article reported that "many of the athletes spent two days a week for the past eight months training for the event" in which many persons participate once a year (Gardiner, 1998, p. B1).

Age Inappropriateness

Age-appropriate curricula involve materials and activities that are consistent with a person's chronological age (McDonnell, Mathot-Buckner, & Ferguson, 1996; Wehman et al., 1985). As Wilcox and Bellamy (1982) noted, because the goals of best practices are in part to minimize the discrepancies between individuals with and without disabilities, educational arrangements that exaggerate or highlight deviance labels should be avoided, and age-inappropriate activities and materials stigmatize the individual with a disability. Calhoun and Calhoun (1993) found that chronological-age-appropriate activities had an effect on how a person with a disability was perceived by others, and that the use of age-inappropriate activities decreased the positive perceptions of people without disabilities.

The adult participants in the Special Olympics are often perceived as children because both children and adults compete at the same event, which often leads to the infantilization of adults with disabilities. This infantilization leads to participants' being denied adult status and dignity (Fleischer & Zames, 2001; Smart, 2001). This has especially been reflected in newspaper reports of the Special Olympics. Each of the following quotes labels adults with disabilities as children, thus reinforcing this stereotype for the general public:

> "It just proves that something can be done for these children," said Doreen Selekane, one of the volunteers. (DePalma, 1997, p. A6)

> The event gives kids the chance to compete. (Cowles, 1998, p. 3)

> Special day for special kids…About 200 people between the ages of 3 and 50 competed in the event. ("Special Day," 1999)

> Rogers [intern director of Ventura County's special Olympics] said she and her co-workers cry every year at the ceremonies. "It's the spirit and excitement," she said. "The kids have just given their all." (Surman, 1999, p. B-1)

The impact of these articles may be long term in how the general public views adults with developmental disabilities.

Lack of Normalization

In the Special Olympics, everyone wins (McGhee, 2002). In real life, such is not always the case. It has been advocated that individuals with disabilities should be allowed the dignity of risk. As Perske (1972) noted, overprotection endangers the person's human dignity and tends to keep people with developmental disabilities from experiencing the normal taking of risks in life, which is necessary for normal human growth and development, and in which winning an event is a common occurrence. Learning how to accept and behave in these circumstances can be helpful for an individual. In other words, the Special Olympics set up an artificial environment where the rules are not the same as in integrated settings, which can limit the generalization of skills.

There is also the problem of "huggers." For example, in a newspaper article titled " 'Huggers' ready for Winter Special Olympics," it was noted that "the huggers are an important part of the Special Olympics program, according to Susan Wessinger of the Oregon Special Olympics office in Portland" (Shotwell, 1989, p. B2). A *New York Times* article had a picture of a person being hugged, with the caption, "The second-place winner in a 3,000 meter run, Ludmila Kanushevskaj of the Ukrainian team, got a hug from Rose Marie Spatafore, who with Rose Carotenuto had come from Ansonia, Conn., to watch the games" (Martin, 1995, p. 30). The Fresno Bee quoted two Special Olympic directors: " 'We get paid,' says Carolyn. 'All the smiles and hugs we can get.' 'We're big huggers,' says her husband. 'The kids love it. So do we' " (Barberich, 2001, p. E1).

People with developmental disabilities often have difficulties engaging in appropriate social behavior (Chadsey & Shelden, 1998; Hanley-Maxwell, Rusch, Chadsey-Rusch, & Renzaglia, 1986). So here you have athletes being hugged by complete strangers. The huggers set up a dilemma of teaching inappropriate social behavior, where participants are encouraged to hug strangers. This can be especially problematic if participants generalize this behavior to other settings and situations.

Coach in Dominant Role

In sports, the coach is expected to direct players as to what they are to do. In the Special Olympics, the coach is a person without a disability, and this means that the athletes are in a role of being less able, more dependent, and unequal. This arrangement makes it more difficult to establish friendships and social networks between participants with disabilities and coaches without disabilities, because it is difficult to get around the coach–athlete relationship. Research has found that equality is a key ingredient to forming relationships (Amado, 1993; Anthony, 1972; Newton, Olson, Horner, & Ard, 1996; Smart, 2001).

Promotion of Negative Images

Popular press accounts of the Special Olympics often reinforce a negative, self-fulfilling prophecy that evokes sympathy, pity, or stigma and promote negative stereotypes of people with developmental disabilities (Polloway & Smith, 1978; Shapiro, 1993; Wolfensberger, 1995). Here are a few examples:

> Chad McFarlane, 13, of Medford triumphs over retardation and his own hesitance in cross-country skiing at the Special Olympics.... Part of a worldwide network, the Oregon games this year drew about 400 athletes who suffer from mental retardation to Mount Bachelor during the weekend to ski, skate and even dance just for fun at a party in Sunriver. (Ellis, 1989, p. B2)

> Suppose behind the vacant, empty eyes, the gold medal on the red, white and blue ribbon dazzled them and meant something. Is it possible that the mouth that could not control saliva was willed by the brain to smile, but the muscles just couldn't do it? (Bombeck, 1987)

The *Pittsburgh Press* had a picture of a person being hugged, with the caption "Special Hug" (Mellon, 1990, p. A1). The *Syracuse Herald-American* said that it was difficult "deciding where the 'special' ends and the 'Olympics' begins" (Brieaddy, 1993, p. C1). An editorial in the same paper noted that Special Olympics volunteers learn that "the mentally retarded are 'great kids'" ("A gift," 1993, p. A8). A headline in the *Eugene Register-Guard* stated, "Athletes win more than medals." A photo showed an athlete being hugged after participating (Hurt, 1997, p. 1C). A headline in the *Oakland Tribune* remarked "Special Olympics athletes win smiles: Races belong to not-so-swift, not-so-strong" (Gardiner, 1998, p. B1).

Each of these examples reinforces negative stereotypes of people with disabilities through their descriptions and use of language, especially with phrases like "suffers from" (Blaska, 1993; Longmore, 1985; Vocational Rehabilitation Research Institutes, 1997). These examples are consistent with the analysis by Smart (2001) that language used by the broader society to speak about devalued people has the following characteristics:

1. the words used to describe these people are both offensive and demeaning;

2. the identifying words that are used to set these people apart from the broader society make very clear that these people do not "belong" with everybody else (this is called "distancing" or "polarization");

3. usually the language is not a self-identification—people don't use these terms to describe themselves;

4. the language usually "lumps" all the people perceived to be in the group together regardless of individual differences;

5. the labels used to describe people with disabilities describe, often inaccurately, only one aspect of an individual's identity (this is called "reductionism"); and

6. society is very reluctant to change individual language use, using the defense of ease of use or of freedom of speech. (p. 56)

Promotion of Handicappism

Handicappism is a theory and set of practices that promote unequal and unjust treatment of people because of apparent or assumed physical or mental disability (Bogdan & Biklen, 1977; Bogdan & Knoll, 1995; Smart, 2001). Because the Special Olympics were designed to serve only people with disabilities, they focus the attention of the public on the disability rather than on the person. Therefore, the Special Olympics perpetuate the belief that there are two classes of people—"normal" and "disabled"—and that people with disabilities need a recreation program different from that provided to people without disabilities (Orelove & Moon, 1984).

Lack of Empirically Verifiable Lifestyle Outcomes

It is surprising that there has been very little research concerning the Special Olympics. There are no data indicating that the Special Olympics provide quality-of-life outcomes for participants, such as friendships, social networks, community participation, and positive attitudes. The few published studies show limited or mixed results (Brundige, Hautala, & Squires, 1990; Dykens & Cohen, 1996; Klein, Gilman, & Zigler, 1993; Lord & Lord, 2000; Ninot, Bilard, & Sokolowski, 2000; Wilhite & Kleiber, 1992). It is interesting to note that there has been little assessment of the perception of the individuals with disabilities who participate in the Special Olympics or of the individuals who choose not to participate.

Negative Outcomes

Several studies have reported negative findings regarding the Special Olympics. These studies have included volunteers and perceptions of the general public. For instance, Roper (1990a, 1990b) found that perceptions toward people with mental retardation were not changed in a positive direction as a result of contact as a volunteer at the Special Olympics and found that certain features of the event reinforced negative perceptions.

Porretta, Gillespie, and Jansma (1996) used survey methodology to assess the perceptions of various agencies and organizations regarding the Special Olympics. Among their results was the finding that the Special Olympics needed to change its mission to place more emphasis on inclusion.

Storey, Stern, and Parker (1990) found that a person portrayed in Special Olympic activities was judged to be less competent than the same person portrayed in matched, integrated community activities. The respondents regarded the woman in the Special Olympics events as younger and felt that she should be in more segregated school and recreational settings.

Burns, Storey, and Certo (1999) found that high school service-learning students who volunteered at the Special Olympics did not have a change in their attitudes toward persons with severe disabilities as a result of their participation and had lower attitudes than nondisabled high school students involved in integrated service-learning activities.

Promotion of Corporations

Corporations will often provide fund-raising for nonprofit organizations along with promotion of the corporations (Stauber & Rampton, 1995). However, with the Special Olympics, these corporations are not promoting their hiring practices of people with developmental disabilities, and the promotions appear to be more for public relations value for the corporations (Fitzgerald, 1995;" The Coca-Cola Company," 2002). For example, the Special Olympics website lists corporations that have donated certain amounts to the Special Olympics and provides links to the website of these corporations (Special Olympics, 2004). Other examples include,

> The 28th annual summer games (1997) in Eugene was sponsored primarily by AT&T Wireless Services.... State Farm employees snapped instant photos of the athletes competing and receiving ribbons. (Hurt, 1997, p. 1C)

> Clark Refining & Marketing, Inc., announced today the kickoff of its 1999 Special Olympics Sponsorship Program. Clark's goal in 1999 is to raise $100,000 for the charity through company-wide involvement, store promotions and sponsorship with employees and communities." ("Clark announces," 1999, p. 1946)

A ShopKo event raised a record $2 million for the Special Olympics ("ShopKo event," 1999). Red Lobster and police volunteers raised $1 million for the Special Olympics through various promotions ("Red Lobster," 1999). Cingular Wireless has donated more than $2 million in an effort to raise $40 million ("The Coca-Cola Company," 2002).

Paternalism

Of the 48 members of the 2002 Board of Directors for the Special Olympics, only 2 are identified as having developmental disabilities. With other athletic competitions involving people with disabilities (Deaf Olympics, ParaOlympics), people with disabilities are in control of the organizations and activities (e.g., the board members of the U.S.A. Deaf Sports Federation are deaf). With the Special Olympics, people with disabilities are "receiving" services, whereas those with decision-making power are people without disabilities. This situation is in contrast to developments in the disability rights movement, where people with disabilities control the service delivery system (Charlton, 1997; Fleischer & Zames, 2001; Longmore, 1995; Shaw, 1994; Smart, 2001).

Athletic Ability

Many people with developmental disabilities are often quite capable of competing successfully in competitive sports with nondisabled participants (Bernabe & Block, 1994; Block & Malloy, 1998; Devine, McGovern, & Hermann, 1998; Lamplia, 1998; Roper & Silver, 1989). Other people with developmental disabilities have been successfully integrated into noncompetitive recreational activities (Cooper & Browder, 1997; Hamre-Nietupski et al., 1992; Schleien & Larson, 1986).

Financial Issues

Storey (1998) has raised concerns about the financial aspects of the Special Olympics based on the 1995 Internal Revenue Service (IRS) 990 reports (such as salary amounts and perks). Among these findings are that the Special Olympics paid Sargent Shriver, its CEO and chairman of the board, $5,640 for the use of a company car. Chief operating officer Edgar May received $135,633 in pay, plus $19,588 for the use of a company car and apartment. A look at their 2000 IRS 990 reports (the most recent available when this was written) shows continued concerns in regard to salaries and other perks. For instance, the salaries of the five highest paid employees other than officers ranged from $104,550 to $200,000, with expense accounts ranging from $1,820 to $2,708. Timothy Shriver, director, received $200,000 in salary, and Kimberly Elliott, the chief operating officer, received $175,000 in salary. The national Special Olympics office has 40 employees making more than $50,000 per year. Their compensation of their five highest paid independent contractors also raises concerns, with more than $4 million going to direct marketing agencies and $334,000 to investment managers.

DISCUSSION

There are three overall choices regarding the Special Olympics in terms of what, if anything, should be done to change the current system. The first option would be not to change what is happening and to keep the current structure in place. Given the preceding arguments, this does not appear to be a viable option.

The second option would be to reform the current structure but to keep the basic premise and conditions of the Special Olympics. However, the basic premise of the Special Olympics is wrong in regard to the inclusion of people with developmental disabilities and is not in keeping with best practices in the field. As Orelove et al. (1982) noted, "Many traditions in our culture are valuable and inspirational; however, when tradition infringes long-range social habilitation of a group of citizens, . . . its benefits wane considerably" (p. 329). From a systems change perspective, it does not appear to be logical to keep a dual system in place for recreational services for people with disabilities where one system promotes segregated services and the other promotes inclusive recreational services with appropriate supports (Lipsky & Gartner, 1997; Schleien & Meyer, 1988).

The third option would be to discontinue or replace the Special Olympics with programs in inclusive recreational leisure situations (Moon, 1994). Over the past 20 years, the field has moved from facilities to programs and then from programs to supports (Hagner, 2000). As Smith, Edelen-Smith, and Stodden (1998) noted, changing from the "old ways" to the "new ways" means taking away the familiar, and these changes can be difficult, but it is important to question the basic assumptions on which program and service systems are organized. Some authors have suggested concepts such as the "Kennedy games" (Hourcade, 1989) or the "National Youth Olympics" (Rice & Fleck, 1988), where there is a formalized structure for integrated recreational services. Others have advocated for supports and services in typical recreational settings, and there is an extensive empirical research base indicating that individuals with developmental disabilities can be successfully included with appropriate supports (Dattilo, 2002; Kozub & Porretta, 1996; Moon, 1994; Zhang, Gast, Horvat, & Dattilo, 1995). The continued support of segregated services can limit the availability of more inclusive services (Anderson & Heyne, 2000).

A growing research base indicates that services and supports in typical recreational settings may be the best way of achieving meaningful quality-of-life outcomes for people with disabilities (Dattilo, 2002; Schleien et al., 1993). As person-centered planning and self-determination become more prevalent, individually planned and supported recreational placements may replace more group- and center-oriented services such as the Special Olympics (Browder, Cooper, & Lim, 1998; DiLeo, 1994; Garcia & Menchetti, 2003; Wehmeyer, Agran, & Hughes, 1998).

REFERENCES

Amado, A. N. (1993). *Friendships and community connections between people with and without developmental disabilities.* Baltimore: Brookes.

Anderson, L., & Heyne, L. (2000). A statewide assessment using focus groups: Perceived challenges and goals in providing inclusive recreation services in rural communities. *Journal of Park and Recreation Administration, 18,* 17–37.

Anthony, W. (1972). Societal rehabilitation: Changing society's attitudes toward the physically and mentally disabled. *Rehabilitation Psychology, 19,* 117–126.

Barberich, K. (2001, July 1). Caring makes couple special. *The Fresno Bee,* p. E1.

Bernabe, E. A., & Block, M. E. (1994). Modifying rules of a regular girls softball league to facilitate the inclusion of a child with severe disabilities. *Journal of the Association for Persons with Severe Handicaps, 19,* 24–31.

Blaska, J. (1993). The power of language: Speak and write using "person first." In M. Nagler (Ed.), *Perspectives on disability* (2nd ed., pp. 25–32). Palo Alto, CA: Health Markets Research.

Block, M. E., & Malloy, M. (1998). Attitudes on inclusion of a player with disabilities in a regular softball league. *Mental Retardation, 36,* 137–144.

Block, M. E., & Moon, M. S. (1992). Orelove, Wehman, and Wood revisited: An evaluative review of Special Olympics ten years later. *Education and Training in Mental Retardation, 27,* 379–386.

Bogdan, R., & Biklen, D. (1977). Handicapism. *Social Policy, 7,* 59–63.

Bogdan, R., & Knoll, J. (1995). The sociology of disability. In E. L. Meyen & T. M. Skrtic (Eds.), *Special education and student disability* (pp. 675–711). Denver: Love.

Bombeck, E. (1987, September 17). Special Olympians make valiant efforts. *Los Angeles Times.*

Brickley, M. (1984). Normalizing the Special Olympics. *The Journal of Physical Education, Recreation, and Dance, 55*(8), 28–29, 75–76.

Brieaddy, F. (1993, June 20). Olympians run and jump for joy. *Syracuse Herald-American,* pp. C1, C2.

Browder, D. M., Cooper, K., & Lim, L. (1998). Teaching adults with severe disabilities to express their choice of settings for leisure activities. *Education and Training in Mental Retardation and Developmental Disabilities, 33,* 226–236.

Brown, F., Evans, I. M., Weed, K. A., & Owens, V. (1987). Delineating functional competencies: A component model. *Journal of the Association for Persons with Severe Handicaps, 12,* 117–124.

Brown, L., Branston, M. B., Hamre-Nietupski, S., Pumpian, I., Certo, N., & Gruenewald, L. (1979). A strategy for developing chronological age–appropriate and functional curricular content for severely handicapped adolescents and young adults. *The Journal of Special Education, 13,* 81–90.

Brown, L., Nietupski, J., & Hamre-Nietupski, S. (1976). Criterion of ultimate functioning. In M. A. Thomas (Ed.), *Hey, don't forget about me!* (pp. 2–15). Reston, VA: Council for Exceptional Children.

Brundige, T. L., Hautala, R. M., & Squires, S. (1990). The Special Olympics developmental sports program for persons with severe and profound disabilities: An assessment of its effectiveness. *Education and Training in Mental Retardation, 25,* 376–380.

Burns, M., Storey, K., & Certo, N. J. (1999). The effect of service learning on attitudes towards students with severe disabilities. *Education and Training in Mental Retardation and Developmental Disabilities, 34,* 58–65.

Calhoun, M. L., & Calhoun, L. G. (1993). Age-appropriate activities: Effects on the social perception of adults with mental retardation. *Education and Training in Mental Retardation, 28,* 143–148.

Chadsey, J. G., & Shelden, D. (1998). Moving toward social inclusion in employment and postsecondary school settings. In F. R. Rusch & J. G. Chadsey (Eds.), *Beyond high school: Transition from school to work* (pp. 406–437). Belmont, CA: Wadsworth.

Charlton, J. I. (1997). *Nothing about us without us: Disability oppression and empowerment.* Berkeley: University of California Press.

Clark announces 1999 Special Olympics sponsorship. (1999, January 4). *PR Newswire*, p. 1946.

The Coca-Cola Company extends long-standing partnership with Special Olympics Inc. (2002, November 19). *PR Newswire*, p. ATTU00519112002.

Cooper, K. J., & Browder, D. M. (1997). The use of a personal trainer to enhance participation of older adults with severe disabilities in community water exercise classes. *Journal of Behavioral Education, 7*, 421–434.

Cowles, A. (1998, April 9). Benefit earns Special Olympics funds. *The Atlanta Constitution, XJI*, p. 3.

Dattilo, J. (2002). *Leisure education program planning: A systematic approach* (2nd ed.). State College, PA: Venture.

DePalma, A. (1997, February 10). Special winter games warm hearts in Toronto. *The New York Times*, p. A6.

Devine, M. A., McGovern, J. N., & Hermann, P. (1998). Inclusion in youth sports. *Journal of Park and Recreation Administration, 17*, 56–72.

DiLeo, D. (1994). *Reaching for the dream: Developing individual service plans for persons with disabilities.* St. Augustine, FL: Training Resources Network.

Dykens, E. M., & Cohen, D. J. (1996). Effect of Special Olympics International on social competence in persons with mental retardation. *Journal of the American Academy of Child and Adolescent Psychiatry, 35*, 223–229.

Ellis, B. C. (1989, March 5). Great! No. 199 finds his spot. *The Oregonian*, p. B2. Fitzgerald, K. (1995, April 10). Special Olympics wins over sponsors. *Advertising Age*, p. 2.

Fleischer, D. Z., & Zames, F. (2001). *The disability rights movement: From charity to confrontation.* Philadelphia: Temple University Press.

Garcia, L. A., & Menchetti, B. M. (2003). The adult lifestyles planning cycle: A continual process for planning personally satisfying adult lifestyles. In D. L. Ryndak & S. Alper (Eds.), *Curriculum and instruction for students with significant disabilities in inclusive settings* (pp. 277–306). Boston: Allyn & Bacon.

Gardiner, L. (1998, May 3). Special Olympics' athletes win smiles: Races belong to not-so-swift, not-so-strong. *The Oakland Tribune*, p. B1. A gift for spectators, volunteers. (1993, May 10). *Syracuse Herald-American*, p. A8.

Hagner, D. (2000). Supporting people as part of the community: Possibilities and prospects for change. In J. Nisbet & D. Hagner (Eds.), *Part of the community: Strategies for including everyone* (pp. 15–42). Baltimore: Brookes.

Hamre-Nietupski, S., Krajewski, L., Riehle, R., Sensor, K., Nietupski, J., Moravec, J., et al. (1992). Enhancing integration during the summer: Combined educational and community recreation options for students with severe disabilities. *Education and Training in Mental Retardation, 27*, 68–74.

Hanley-Maxwell, C., Rusch, F. R., Chadsey-Rusch, J., & Renzaglia, A. (1986). Reported factors contributing to job termination of individuals with severe disabilities. *Journal of the Association for Persons with Severe Handicaps, 11*, 45–52.

Hingsburger, D. (1997). Dave Hingsburger's 'hot fudge Sunday.' *TASH Newsletter, 23*, 10–11.

Hourcade, J. J. (1989). Special Olympics: A review and critical analysis. *Therapeutic Recreation Journal, 23*, 58–65.

Hurt, S. (1997, June 8). Athletes win more than medals: Special Olympics: Participants succeed each time they compete. *Eugene Register-Guard*, p. 1C.

Johnson, M. (2003). *Make them go away: Clint Eastwood, Christopher Reeve & the case against disability rights.* Louisville, KY: Advocado Press.

Klein, T., Gilman, E., & Zigler, E. (1993). Special Olympics: An evaluation by professionals andparents. *Mental Retardation, 31,* 15–23.

Kozub, F. M., & Porretta, D. (1996). Including athletes with disabilities: Interscholastic benefits for all. *The Journal of Physical Education, Recreation, and Dance, 67,* 19–24.

Lamplia, L. (1998). Special athletes in "normal" athletics. *AAMR News and Notes, 11*(3), 3–9.

Let me tell you about the Special Olympics. (1995, September). *Sports Illustrated for Kids, 7*(9), 62–64.

Lipsky, D., & Gartner, A. (1997). *Inclusion and school reform: Transforming America's classrooms.* Baltimore: Brookes.

Longmore, P. (1985). A note on language and the social identity of disabled people. *American Behavioral Scientist, 28,* 419–423.

Longmore, P. K. (1995). The second phase: From disability rights to disability culture. *The Disability Rag & ReSource, 16*(5), 4–11.

Lord, M. A., & Lord, W. J. (2000). Effects of the Special Olympics of Texas athletes for outreach program on communication competence among individuals with mental retardation. *Communication Education, 49,* 267–283.

Mactavish, J. B., & Schleien, S. J. (2000). Exploring family recreation activities in families that include children with developmental disabilities. *Therapeutic Recreation Journal, 34,* 132–153.

Mank, D. M., & Buckley, J. (1989). Strategies for integrating employment environments. In W. Kiernan & R. Schalock (Eds.), *Economics, industry, and disability: A look ahead* (pp. 319–335). Baltimore: Brookes.

Martin, D. (1995, July 2). I may not be a victor, but let me try bravely: Special Olympians give games their all. *The New York Times,* p. 30.

McDonnell, J., Mathot-Buckner, C., & Ferguson, B. (1996). *Transition programs for students with moderate/ severe disabilities.* Pacific Grove, CA: Brooks/Cole.

McGhee, L. (2002, May 20). Qualifying for Special Olympics. *The Oakland Tribune,* pp. A1, A4.

Mellon, S. (2000, May 13). Special hug. *The Pittsburgh Press,* p. A1.

Modell, S. J., & Valdez, L. A. (2002). Beyond bowling: Transition planning for students with disabilities. *Teaching Exceptional Children, 34,* 46–52.

Moon, S. (1994). *Making school and community recreation fun for everyone: Places and ways to integrate.* Baltimore: Brookes.

Newton, J. S., Olson, D., Horner, R. H., & Ard, W. R. (1996). Social skills and the stability of social relationships between individuals with intellectual disabilities and other community members. *Research in Developmental Disabilities, 17,* 15–26.

Ninot, G., Bilard, J., & Sokolowski, M. (2000). Athletic competition: A means of improving the self-image of the mentally retarded adolescent? *International Journal of Rehabilitation Research, 23,* 111–117.

Orelove, F. P., & Moon, M. S. (1984). The Special Olympics program: Effects on retarded persons and society. *Arena Review, 8*(1), 41–45.

Orelove, F. P., Wehman, P., & Wood, J. (1982). An evaluative review of Special Olympics: Implications for community integration. *Education and Training of the Mentally Retarded, 17,* 325–329.

Perske, R. (1972). The dignity of risk and the mentally retarded. *Mental Retardation, 10,* 24–26.

Polloway, E. A., & Smith, J. D. (1978). Special Olympics: A second look. *Education and Training of the Mentally Retarded, 13,* 432–433.

Polloway, E. A., Smith, J. D., Patton, J. R., & Smith, T. E. C. (1996). Historic changes in mental retardation and developmental disabilities. *Education and Training in Mental Retardation and Developmental Disabilities, 31,* 3–12.

Porretta, D. L., Gillespie, M., & Jansma, P. (1996). Perceptions about Special Olympics from service delivery groups in the United States: A preliminary investigation. *Education and Training in Mental Retardation and Developmental Disabilities, 31,* 44–54.

Privett, C. (1999). The Special Olympics: A tradition of excellence. *The Exceptional Parent, 29,* 28–31.

Red Lobster, police volunteers, raise $1m for Special Olympics. (1999, May 24). *Nation's Restaurant News, 33,* p. 28.

Rice, T., & Fleck, L. (1988). Moving into the 90s with TASH and the Special Olympics. *TASH Newsletter, 14,* 1–2.

Roper, P. (1990a). Changing perceptions through contact. *Disability, Handicap, and Society, 5,* 243–255.

Roper, P. (1990b). Special Olympics volunteers' perceptions of people with mental retardation. *Education and Training in Mental Retardation, 25,* 164–175.

Roper, P. A., & Silver, C. (1989). Regular track competition for athletes with mental retardation. *Palaestra, 5,* 14–16, 42–43, 58–59.

Rosenthal-Malek, A. (1998). Development of friendships and social competence. In A. Hilton & R. Ringlaben (Eds.), *Best and promising practices in developmental disabilities* (pp. 107–115). Austin, TX: PRO-ED.

Schilling, M. L., & Coles, R. (1997). From exclusion to inclusion: A historical glimpse at the past and reflection of the future. *The Journal of Physical Education, Recreation, & Dance, 68,* 42–45.

Schleien, S. J. (1993). Access and inclusion in community leisure services. *Park and Recreation, 28,* 66–72.

Schleien, S. J., Green, F. P., & Heyne, L. A. (1993). Integrated community recreation. In M. E. Snell (Ed.), *Instruction of students with severe disabilities* (pp. 526–555). Columbus, OH: Merrill.

Schleien, S., Green, F., & Stone, C. (1999). Making friends within inclusive community recreation programs. *Journal of Leisurability, 26,* 33–43.

Schleien, S. J., Heyne, L. A., Rynders, J. E., & McAvoy, L.H. (1990). Equity and excellence: Serving all children in community recreation and leisure services in a community setting. *The Journal of Physical Education, Recreation, and Dance, 61,* 45–48.

Schleien, S. J., & Larson, A. (1986). Adult leisure education for the independent use of a community recreation center. Journal of the Association for Persons with Severe Handicaps, 11, 39–44.

Schleien, S. J., & Meyer, L. H. (1988). Community-based recreation programs for persons with severe developmental disabilities. In M.D. Powers (Ed.), *Expanding systems of service delivery for persons with developmental disabilities* (pp. 93–112). Baltimore: Brookes.

Schleien, S., Meyer, L., Heyne, L., & Brandt, B. (1995). *Lifelong leisure skills and lifestyles for persons with developmental disabilities.* Baltimore: Brookes.

Schleien, S. J., & Ray, M. T. (1997). Leisure education for a quality transition to adulthood. *Journal of Vocational Rehabilitation, 8,* 155–169.

Shapiro, J. P. (1993). *No pity: People with disabilities forging a new civil rights movement.* New York: Times Books.

Shaw, B. (1994). *The ragged edge: The disability experience from the pages of the first fifteen years of the Disability Rag.* Louisville, KY: Advocado Press.

ShopKo event raises record $2 mil. for Special Olympics. (1999). *Home Textiles Today, 20,* p. 9.

Shotwell, R. E. (1989, March 1). Huggers ready for winter Special Olympics. *The Oregonian,* p. B2.

Smart, J. (2001). *Disability, society, and the individual.* Gaithersburg, MD: Aspen.

Smith, G. J., Edelen-Smith, P. J., & Stodden, R. A. (1998). Effective practice for generating outcomes of significance: The complexities of transformational change. In A. Hilton & R. Ringlaben (Eds.), *Best and promising practices in developmental disabilities* (pp. 331–342). Austin, TX: PRO-ED.

Special day for special kids. (1999, 18 November). *The New Orleans Times-Picayune*, p. 1G.

Special Olympics. *About the Special Olympics.* Retrieved from http://www.specialolympics.org/about_special_olympics/index.html

Special Olympics. *Corporate Sponsors.* Retrieved from http://www.specialolympics.org/corporate_sponsors/index.html

Stauber, J., & Rampton, S. (1995). *Toxic sludge is good for you! Lies, damn lies and the public relations industry.* Monroe, ME: Common Courage Press.

Storey, K. (1993). A proposal for assessing integration. *Education and Training in Mental Retardation, 28,* 279–287.

Storey, K. (1998). Telethons and the Special Olympics: Where does that money go? Some revelations and how to get more information. *Ragged Edge, 19*(2), 30–33.

Storey, K., & Horner, R. H. (1991). Social interactions in three supported employment options: A comparative analysis. *Journal of Applied Behavior Analysis, 24,* 349–360.

Storey, K., Stern, R., & Parker, R. (1990). A comparison of attitudes towards typical recreational activities versus the Special Olympics. *Education and Training in Mental Retardation, 25,* 94-99.

Surman, M. (1999, June 11). Shedding some light on winning: Special Olympics athletes and their supporters carry symbolic torch 79 miles through county en route to the summer games in Long Beach. *The Los Angeles Times (Ventura County Edition)*, p. B1.

Troubling questions about Special Olympics. (1987, September/October). *The Disability Rag*, p. 32.

Vocational and Rehabilitation Research Institute. (1997). A rose by any other name . . . ? *Rehabilitation Review, 8,* 1–2.

Wehman, P. (1988). Supported employment: Toward zero exclusion of persons with severe disabilities. In P. Wehman & M. S. Moon (Eds.), *Vocational rehabilitation and supported employment* (pp. 3–16). Baltimore: Brookes.

Wehman, P., Renzaglia, A., & Bates, P. (1985). *Functional living skills for moderately and severely handicapped individuals.* Austin, TX: PRO-ED.

Wehmeyer, M. L., Agran, M., & Hughes, C. (1998). *Teaching self-determination to youth with disabilities: Basic skills for successful transition.* Baltimore: Brookes.

Wilcox, B., & Bellamy, G. T. (1982). *Design of high school programs for severely handicapped students.* Baltimore: Brookes.

Wilhite, B., & Kleiber, D. A. (1992). The effect of Special Olympics participation on community integration. *Therapeutic Recreation Journal, 26,* 9–20.

Williams, R., & Dattilo, J. (1997). Effects of leisure education on choice making, social interaction, and positive affect of young adults with mental retardation. *Therapeutic Recreation Journal, 31,* 244–258.

Wolfensberger, W. (1995). Of "normalization," lifestyles, the Special Olympics, deinstitutionalization, mainstreaming, integration, and cabbages and kings. *Mental Retardation, 33,* 128–131.

Zhang, J., Gast, D., Horvat, M., & Dattilo, J. (1995). The effectiveness of a constant time delay procedure on teaching lifetime sport skills to adolescents with severe to profound intellectual disabilities. *Education and Training in Mental Retardation and Developmental Disabilities, 30,* 51–64.

Storey's approach to the Special Olympics seems, at first, to buck the common sense notion that the platform is a good way to promote awareness and inclusion for people with disabilities. How does Storey develop his argument that the Special Olympics, in fact, may exaggerate social stigmas against people with disabilities. Make a list of all the claims and evidence Storey uses to forward his argument. Do you agree or disagree? Why?

In small groups discuss your own experiences with and impressions of the Special Olympics. Then, reflect as a group on how these impressions articulate to some of Storey's concerns. For example, do any of you share examples of the Special Olympics that reify segregation, age inappropriate training curricula, unbalanced power relations between coaches and participants, corporatization, paternalism, or the promotion of negative images? In what ways do the stories that we tell and the images that we circulate about Special Olympics contribute to these concerns voiced by Storey? Share your findings with the class.

Storey lists several possible alternatives for the Special Olympics. Pick one and spend some time researching a little more about this approach. You might look to scholarly journal articles, news media coverage, organizational materials, and media. Jot down your findings and reflect on how your ideas about the Special Olympics are changing as a result of your initial research.

This exercise will prepare you for Major Assignment #5: The Persuasive Research Paper. Write a short essay in which you argue for one of Storey's three recommended approaches to the Special Olympics. Be sure to make claims in support of your argument and integrate supporting evidence to support your reasoning.

Michael Behar is a freelance writer and editor who writes about science, the environment, and extreme sports. His publications have appeared in, among other publications, Wired, National Geographic Adventure, The Economist, *and* Discover, *in which this article originally appeared.*

WILL GENETICS DESTROY SPORTS?

By Michael Behar

A new age of biotechnology promises bigger, faster, better bodies—and blood, urine, and saliva tests can't stop the cheating.

The chime on H. Lee Sweeney's laptop dings again—another e-mail. He doesn't rush to open it. He knows what it's about. He knows what they are *all* about. The molecular geneticist gets dozens every week, all begging for the same thing—a miracle. *Ding.* A woman with carpal tunnel syndrome wants a cure. *Ding.* A man offers $100,000, his house, and all his possessions to save his wife from dying of a degenerative muscle disease. *Ding, ding, ding.* Jocks, lots of jocks, plead for quick cures for strained muscles or torn tendons. Weight lifters press for larger deltoids. Sprinters seek a split second against the clock. People volunteer to be guinea pigs.

Sweeney has the same reply for each ding: "I tell them it's illegal and maybe not safe, but they write back and say they don't care. A high school coach contacted me and wanted to know if we could make enough serum to inject his whole football team. He wanted them to be bigger and stronger and come back from injuries faster, and he thought those were good things."

The coach was wrong. Gene therapy is risky. In one recent experiment, a patient died. In another the therapy worked, but 2 of the 10 human subjects—infants—got leukemia. To some, such setbacks are minor hiccups, nothing to worry about if you want to cure the incurable or win big. In the last few years, Sweeney, a professor of physiology and medicine at the University of Pennsylvania, and a small cadre of other researchers have learned how to create genes that repair weak, deteriorating, or damaged muscles, bones, tendons, and cartilage in a relatively short period of time. They can also significantly increase the strength

From *Discover Magazine* (2004).

and size of undamaged muscles with little more than an injection. So far, they have worked with only small laboratory rodents—mice and rats. Clinical trials on larger animals, like dogs and cats, are currently not being funded. Human testing is years away, but gene therapy has already become a controversy in professional and amateur sports, where steroids, human growth hormones, and other performance-enhancing drugs have been a problem for years. With the Olympics opening in Athens on August 13, the subject is only going to get hotter. "It's the natural evolution of medicine, and it's inevitable that people will use it for athletics," Sweeney says. "It's not clear that we will be able to stop it."

Sweeney became interested in gene therapy in 1988, shortly after scientists pinpointed the gene responsible for Duchenne muscular dystrophy. He decided to find out if there was a way to counteract the disease genetically. Children with muscular dystrophy lack the gene required to regulate dystrophin, a protein for muscle growth and stability. Without dystrophin, muscle cells atrophy, wither, and die. Sweeney's plan was to introduce the dystrophin gene by hitching it to the DNA of a virus that can transport genes into cells. As it turned out, viruses were too small to carry that gene. So Sweeney began searching for a smaller gene that would fit inside a virus and at least mimic dystrophin. He settled on a gene that produces insulin-like growth factor (IGF-I), a powerful hormone that drives muscle growth and repair. The IGF-I gene fit nicely inside a virus and was more appealing because it could potentially treat several kinds of dystrophies. In a series of experiments beginning in 1998, Sweeney and his team at Penn injected IGF-I genes into mice and rats and watched in wonder as damaged muscle tissue repaired itself.

Today Sweeney spends much of his time scrutinizing the rats and mice he has injected with IGF-I genes. He puts them through a rigorous exercise program, strapping weights to their hind legs and repeatedly prodding them up a three-foot-high ladder. After two months, the rodents can lift 30 percent more weight, and their muscle mass has swollen by a third—double what his control group of mice (those without IGF-I) can achieve with weight training alone. In another experiment Sweeney gives IGF-I to mice but curbs their exercise. They too bulk up, jumping 15 percent in muscle volume and strength.

On a recent visit to Penn, I asked Sweeney to show me the mice. He led me to a cramped lab where a bubbling tank of liquid nitrogen spewed a cold fog across the floor. Rows of transparent plastic shoebox-size containers were stacked on a chrome pushcart, a pungent, musky odor emanating from each box. Inside were several chocolate-colored mice. Sweeney pointed out two groups in neighboring pens and asked, "Which set do you think we've given IGF-I?" I lean in for a closer look. The mice in the left box no doubt have been watching *Buns of Steel* videos. Each mouse boasts a rock-hard rump and shockingly large and perfectly chiseled gastrocnemius and soleus muscles (which, in humans, make up the calf). In the adjacent cage, two control mice look scrawny by comparison. The results are impressive and make me wonder just how easy it would be for someone to reproduce Sweeney's results in a human. "I wouldn't be surprised if someone was actively setting up to do it right now," he says. "It's not that expensive, especially if you are just going to do it to a small population of athletes."

That is exactly what worries officials at the World Anti-Doping Agency and the U.S. Anti-Doping Agency. The world agency has put gene doping on the International Olympic Committee's 2004 list of prohibited substances, which includes everything from cough syrup to cocaine. The prohibition defines gene doping as "the non-therapeutic use of genes, genetic elements and/or cells that have the capacity to enhance athletic performance." But no one thinks for a minute that gene doping isn't happening. "Sport is supposed to be fun," says former Olympic swimmer Richard Pound, now president of the world agency and chancellor of McGill University in Montreal. "But it is surrounded by people who are conspiring to destroy the athlete and the game."

Gene doping is different from other performance-enhancing techniques. Human growth hormone, for example, occurs naturally in the body and will accelerate cell division in many types of tissue. Taken in high doses, it can provide a head-to-toe muscle boost and can even add a few extra inches of height. Anabolic steroids, which President Bush attacked in his State of the Union address in January, are chemical relatives of testosterone. They are believed to be in wide use in professional sports such as baseball, football, basketball, and hockey—although most players deny it. They are also popular with weight lifters because they foster new muscle growth in the upper body. Synthetic erythropoietin, or EPO, a chemical naturally produced by the kidneys, is a favorite of cyclists, triathletes, marathon runners, and people who engage in long periods of aerobic activity. EPO flushes fatigued muscles with oxygen to stave off exhaustion.

These and other substances can be detected in blood and urine tests because they drift through the circulatory system for hours, days, or months. But gene doping is not as easy to spot. Genetic modifications become an indistinguishable element of DNA in targeted muscles. The only way to prove that someone has experimented with gene doping is to biopsy a suspicious muscle and look for signs of DNA tampering. It's not hard to imagine that most athletes will object to having bits of flesh sliced from the very muscles they've spent years honing. "Athletes aren't going to say, 'Hey, take a muscle biopsy before my 100-meter run,'" quips Johnny Huard, who developed his own set of muscle-building genes as professor of molecular genetics, biochemistry, and bioengineering at the University of Pittsburgh School of Medicine.

Gene doping involves incorporating healthy growth-factor genes with the DNA in a viral carrier. The virus is then injected into the muscle, where it readily infects the target cell and delivers growth-factor genes to the nucleus. After integrating with chromosomes, the genes exit the nucleus via messenger RNA (mRNA). These strands serve as templates for the production of growth-factor proteins, and ribosomes assist in the conversion. The proteins affect surrounding muscle tissues, helping them to strengthen and to heal.

Lack of detection makes gene doping extremely attractive to athletes. But its muscle-building powers are the big draw. Sweeney predicts gene-doped athletes would readily surpass their personal best and could even smash world records. Sprinters and weight lifters would see the most benefits, their peak speeds and maximum strength amplified. "Athletes could push their muscles harder than ever before because their muscles will repair themselves so much faster," he says. "And they won't have to retire when they're 32."

The anti-doping agency officials are convinced that athletes will try gene doping, despite its dangers. "In the current climate there is even more pressure than when I was competing," says Norway's 1994 Olympic speed skating gold medalist Johann Koss, a physician and former member of the world agency's executive board. "People will take shortcuts. The reward at being the best in the world offers huge financial gains." Pound cites a poll of American athletes who said they would take any drug that would help them win, even if they knew the drug would eventually kill them.

"Nobody ever said athletes are the smartest people in the world," Pound says. "This is why there has to be parentalism. This is why I don't let my kids drive the car at age 13, even though they tell me they can do it safely."

Pound has good reason to worry. The newest therapies work on mice and rats with no apparent adversity. Until clinical trials, however, it's impossible to know exactly what the effects will be on humans. Sweeney acknowledges that IGF-I could make precancerous cells grow faster and stronger.

Huard says "we have absolutely no clue" about side effects, but he and others are worried about an immunologic reaction to the virus that serves as a carrier. That is what killed 18-year-old Jesse Gelsinger, who had a rare liver disease and was participating in gene therapy research at the University of Pennsylvania. The Food and Drug Administration immediately terminated all gene therapy trials at Penn, and the incident prompted federal regulators to establish new rules for human gene therapy research. Another concern is that the vector virus might run amok. Scientists believe that's what happened during a 1999 French gene therapy trial on a group of 10 infants with X-SCID, an immune deficiency disorder known as boy-in-the-bubble syndrome. Researchers engineered a virus to carry a replacement gene to repair the immune systems of the sick children. The technique cured nine of the children, and scientists deemed the trial an overwhelming success. Nearly three years later, however, doctors diagnosed two boys in the study with T-cell leukemia. Somehow the virus carrier—not the replacement gene—had managed to touch off the blood disease. In future tests doctors will either modify or change the carrier.

Those two incidents sparked widespread condemnation that stifled nascent research initiatives. Today some clinical gene therapy trials on humans are under way with tighter safeguards, but most experiments are confined to rodents. Despite the medical and regulatory setbacks, the largest roadblock to commercializing the technology is money. "We've been struggling with getting dog studies [under way] because of the cost," says Sweeney. But once he gets funding, he's ready to go. His team has already made a version of the IGF-I vector to test on dogs with muscular dystrophy. If successful, he'll begin trials on children with muscular dystrophy sometime before the end of the decade. Sweeney keeps a list of telephone numbers from desperate parents who've contacted him.

Meanwhile, amateur athletics is trying to come to grips with gene doping. In March 2002, Theodore Friedmann, who directs the program in human gene therapy at the University of California at San Diego and has advised the National Institutes of Health and congressional leaders on gene-related issues, organized a three-day workshop for the world agency. Scientists, regulatory officials, and athletes gathered in Cold Spring Harbor on Long Island to discuss gene doping. "People intent on subverting the gene therapy will do so," says Friedmann. "The technology is too easy. It's just graduate student science."

That bothers Arne Ljungqvist, the world agency's health, medical, and research committee chairman, who doles out several million dollars in grant money every year to research groups looking at gene doping and its detection. Additionally, Friedmann, who serves on the agency's anti-doping commission, is working to establish testing protocols. "So far the results are sitting in the form of research advances," he says, "but not in the form of real detection methods." One concept is to hunt for what Friedmann calls physiological fingerprints. Introducing foreign genes into muscles, he says, "is going to produce changes in the way muscles secrete things into the blood and, therefore, into the urine." In the same way breast and colon cancer alter the pattern of proteins in the bloodstream, genes linked to IGF-I or EPO will, in theory, leave traces. Surveillance organizations like the U.S. and world agencies "will look for those signatures and patterns that can be tied, with confidence, to the existence of a foreign gene," Friedmann says. Although it may be years yet in development, Friedmann envisions a noninvasive imaging device akin to an X-ray that detects bits and pieces of leftover viruses used to introduce performance-enhancing genes.

Ironically, the misuse of gene doping in sports is more clearly defined than its proper use. When physicians begin curing athletic injuries with gene therapy, the boundaries of healing and enhancement will blur. "There will be a fuzzy line between what is a medically justifiable treatment of injuries and what is performance enhancement," says Friedmann. "There is nothing terribly noble about an athlete destroying a career with an injury if one can medically prevent or correct it. I would be hard-pressed to say that athletes are not eligible for this or that manipulation. It has always been obvious that there are therapeutic-use exceptions. There is no reason to think that therapeutic-use exceptions would be disallowed for genetic tools."

That, of course, opens the door for abuse. In some instances, athletes would require only minuscule improvements to nudge them into the winner's circle. "For Olympic athletes, they don't need to see a drastic change," says Johnny Huard. "Sometimes the gold medalist is only a fraction of a second over the silver." It would be very easy for a team physician to let therapeutic genes continue working for a few hours, days, or weeks after an officially sanctioned treatment ends.

With no viable testing mechanism on the horizon, the possibility remains that at least one of the 10,000-plus Olympic competitors in Athens this summer will have experimented with gene doping. By the 2006 Winter Games in Turin, Italy, it's even more likely. And by the time Beijing 2008 rolls around, it could easily be a sure thing.

This exercise will prepare you for Major Assignment #5: The Persuasive Research Paper. How does the audience for which Behar writes (*Discover* is a scientific audience) inform his approach to discussing the "gene doping" controversy in sport? How does he present gene therapy in a logical, credible, and/or emotional way to the reader? Do you feel the author sufficiently and equally covers the technical, ethical, and safety issues involved in gene therapy? How does Behar translate the complicated science behind gene therapy in a way that is easy to understand for *Discover's* scientifically-minded lay audience?

Behar interviews leading expert Dr. H. Lee Sweeney on his views of gene therapy for this article. Sweeney has since been consulted by a variety of media regarding his opinions on the issue. Listen to his and other's comments on gene therapy a decade later in the *BBC* 5 Live Investigates podcast on gene therapy (00:00-26:00): http://downloads.bbc.co.uk/podcasts/5live/5linvestigates/5linvestigates_20140112-1300b.mp3. As you listen to the podcast, make note of the different interviewees weighing in and their respective arguments. What are their backgrounds and what are their respective interests in gene therapy and sport? After listening to the podcast, how do *you* feel about gene therapy in sport? Why? How did the evidence and arguments provided in the podcast by the experts on the topic inform your opinion? What was the most compelling evidence for you and why? Or, read Tim Frank's *BBC* article, "*Gene doping: Sport's biggest battle*" (11 Jan 2014) at http://www.bbc.com/news/magazine-25687002 and compare and contrast the types of arguments Behar and Frank make about sports genetics and doping.

Collaborate

The primary focus of Behar's article is to explain the potential uses of gene therapy in athletes as a form of injury rehabilitation, for example using IGF-I to repair damaged muscle tissue. However, some skeptics worry that gene therapy can quickly lead to "gene doping" to gain competitive advantage and that it may have unknown health consequences on humans. Work in small groups to explore the different sides to the gene therapy in sport controversy. For example, have one group search "gene therapy and sport" and another group search "gene doping and sport" in Google. Have the groups share the results and, as a class, discuss what similarities and differences can be found in the results by switching the word from "therapy" to "doping." Meanwhile, have other groups quickly search "gene therapy and sports" across a couple of credible news sources, like the digital archives for the *New York Times, Washington Post*, and *BBC*, and share their findings. Together as a class, make a list of five to six promising texts on the issue and quickly summarize their main opinions and arguments.

Compose

Drawing on Behar's article and the other sources discovered in the Explore exercise, write a two to three page essay in which you explore the different arguments and evidence for and against gene therapy.

Juliet Macur is a New York Times sports columnist who has regularly covered the Olympics and doping in sports. Her work has been anthologized in the Best American Sportswriting *series and she has received numerous honors for her work, including distinctions from the Associated Press Sports Editors and the Society of Professional Journalists.*

BORN TO RUN? LITTLE ONES GET TEST FOR SPORTS GENE

By Juliet Macur

BOULDER, Colo. – When Donna Campiglia learned recently that a genetic test might be able to determine which sports suit the talents of her 2 ½-year-old son, Noah, she instantly said, Where can I get it and how much does it cost?

"I could see how some people might think the test would pigeonhole your child into doing fewer sports or being exposed to fewer things, but I still think it's good to match them with the right activity," Ms. Campiglia, 36, said she watched a toddler class at Boulder Indoor Soccer in which Noah struggled to take direction from the coach between juice and potty breaks.

"I think it would prevent a lot of parental frustration," she said.

In health-conscious, sports-oriented Boulder, Atlas Sports Genetics is playing into the obsessions of parents by offering a $149 test that aims to predict a child's natural athletic strengths. The process is simple. Swab inside the child's cheek and along the gums to collect DNA and return it to a lab for analysis of ACTN3, one gene among more than 20,000 in the human genome.

The test's goal is to determine whether a person would be best at speed and power sports like sprinting or football, or endurance sports like distance running, or a combination of the two. A 2003 study discovered the link between ACTN3 and those athletic abilities.

From *The New York Times* (2008).

In this era of genetic testing, DNA is being analyzed to determine predispositions to disease, but experts raise serious questions about marketing it as a first step in finding a child's sports niche, which some parents consider the road to a college scholarship or a career as a professional athlete.

Atlas executives acknowledge that their test has limitations but say that it could provide guidelines for placing youngsters in sports. The company is focused on testing children from infancy to about 8 years old because physical tests to gauge future sports performance at that age are, at best, unreliable.

Some experts say ACTN3 testing is in its infancy and virtually useless. Dr. Theodore Friedmann, the director of the University of California-San Diego Medical Center's interdepartmental gene therapy program, called it "an opportunity to sell new versions of snake oil."

"This may or may not be quite that venal, but I would like to see a lot more research done before it is offered to the general public," he said. "I don't deny that these genes have a role in athletic success, but it's not that black and white."

Dr. Stephen M. Roth, director of the functional genomics laboratory at the University of Maryland's School of Public Health who has studied ACTN3, said he thought the test would become popular. But he had reservations.

"The idea that it will be one or two genes that are contributing to the Michael Phelpses or the Usain Bolts of the world I think is shortsighted because it's much more complex than that," he said, adding that athletic performance has been found to be affected by at least 200 genes.

Dr. Roth called ACTN3 "one of the most exciting and eyebrow-raising genes out there in the sports-performance arena," but he said that any test for the gene would be best used only on top athletes looking to tailor workouts to their body types.

"It seems to be important at very elite levels of competition," Dr. Roth said. "But is it going to affect little Johnny when he participates in soccer, or Suzy's ability to perform sixth grade track and field? There's very little evidence to suggest that."

The study that identified the connection between ACTN3 and elite athletic performance was published in 2003 by researchers primarily based in Australia.

Those scientists looked at the gene's combinations, one copy provided by each parent. The R variant of ACTN3 instructs the body to produce a protein, alpha-actinin-3, found specifically in fast-twitch muscles. Those muscles are capable of the forceful, quick contractions necessary in speed and power sports. The X variant prevents production of the protein.

The ACTN3 study looked at 429 elite white athletes, including 50 Olympians, and found that 50 percent of the 107 sprint athletes had two copies of the R variant. Even more telling, no female elite sprinter had two copies of the X variant. All male Olympians in power sports had at least one copy of the R variant.

Conversely, nearly 25 percent of the elite endurance athletes had two copies of the X variant—only slightly higher than the control group at 18 percent. That means people with two X copies are more likely to be suited for endurance sports.

Still, some athletes prove science, and seemingly their genetics, wrong. Research on an Olympic long jumper from Spain showed that he had no copies of the R variant, indicating that athletic success is probably affected by a combination of genes as well as factors like environment, training, nutrition and luck.

"Just think if that Spanish kid's parents had done the test and said, 'No, your genes show that you are going to be a bad long jumper, so we are going to make you a golfer,'" said Carl Foster, a co-author of the study, who is the director of the human performance laboratory at the University of Wisconsin-La Crosse. "Now look at him. He's the springiest guy in Spain. He's Tigger. We don't yet understand what combination of genes creates that kind of explosiveness."

Dr. Foster suggested another way to determine if a child will be good at sprint and power sports. "Just line them up with their classmates for a race and see which ones are the fastest," he said.

Kevin Reilly, the president of Atlas Sports Genetics and a former weight-lifting coach, expected the test to be controversial. He said some people were concerned that it would cause "a rebirth of eugenics, similar to what Hitler did in trying to create this race of perfect athletes."

Mr. Reilly said he feared what he called misuse by parents who go overboard with the results and specialize their children too quickly and fervently.

"I'm nervous about people who get back results that don't match their expectations," he said. "What will they do if their son would not be good at football? How will they mentally and emotionally deal with that?"

Mr. Reilly insisted that the test is one tool of many that can help children realize their athletic potential. It may even keep an overzealous father from pushing his son to be a quarterback if his genes indicate otherwise, Mr. Reilly said.

If ACTN3 suggests a child may be a great athlete, he said, parents should take a step back and nurture that potential Olympian or N.F.L. star with careful nutrition, coaching and planning. He also said they should hold off on placing a child in a competitive environment until about the age of 8 to avoid burnout.

"Based on the test of a 5-year-old or a newborn, you are not going to see if you have the next Michael Johnson; that's just not going to happen," Mr. Reilly said. "But if you wait until high school or college to find out if you have a good athlete on your hands, by then it will be too late. We need to identify these kids from 1 and up, so we can give the parents some guidelines on where to go from there."

Boyd Epley, a former strength and conditioning coach at the University of Nebraska, said the next step would be a physical test he devised. Atlas plans to direct children to Epic Athletic Performance, a talent identification company that uses Mr. Epley's index. He founded the company; Mr. Reilly is its president.

China and Russia, Mr. Epley said, identify talent in the very young and whittle the pool of athletes until only the best remain for the national teams.

"This is how we could stay competitive with the rest of the world," Mr. Epley said of genetic and physical testing. "It could, at the very least, provide you with realistic goals for you and your children."

The ACTN3 test has been available through the Australian company Genetic Technologies since 2004. The company has marketed the test in Australia, Europe and Japan, but is now entering the United States through Atlas. The testing kit was scheduled to be available starting Monday through the website atlasgene.com.

The analysis takes two to three weeks, and the results arrive in the form of a certificate announcing Your Genetic Advantage, whether it is in sprint, power and strength sports; endurance sports; or activity sports (for those with one copy of each variant, and perhaps a combination of strengths). A packet of educational information suggests sports that are most appropriate and what paths to follow so the child reaches his or her potential.

"I find it worrisome because I don't think parents will be very clear-minded about this," said William Morgan, an expert on the philosophy of ethics and sport and author of "Why Sports Morally Matter." "This just contributes to the madness about sports because there are some parents who will just go nuts over the results.

"The problem here is that the kids are not old enough to make rational autonomous decisions about their own life," he said.

Some parents will steer clear of the test for that reason.

Dr. Ray Howe, a general practitioner in Denver, said he would rather see his 2-year-old, Joseph, find his own way in life and discover what sports he likes the best. Dr. Howe, a former professional cyclist, likened ACTN3 testing to gene testing for breast cancer or other diseases.

"You might be able to find those things out, but do you really want to know?" he said.

Others, like Lori Lacy, 36, said genetic testing would be inevitable. Ms. Lacy, who lives in Broomfield, Colo., has three children ranging in age from 2 months to 5 years.

"Parents will start to say, 'I know one mom who's doing the test on her son, so maybe we should do the test too,'" she said.

"Peer pressure and curiosity would send people over the edge. What if my son could be a pro football player and I don't know it?"

What is Macur's tone and stylistic approach in this piece? How does she use interviews and direct quotes to underscore and frame her opinion on the issue? What other types of evidence and strategies does Macur use and what effect do they have on you as a reader?

Visuals are important sources of information and argument. Look at the photograph by Kevin Maloney selected to frame Macur's opinion editorial in the online version of the article here: http://www.nytimes.com/2008/11/30/sports/30genetics.html?pagewanted=all&_r=0. In what ways does the image forecast Macur's argument? What specific mood, tone, or feeling do you get from looking at the image? Why? How does the image affect the way you respond to Macur's argument?

Macur's editorial is interested in the ethics of specialization in youth sport and the uses of advances in sports genetics to predetermine athletic opportunities for youth. With your peers, watch the documentary *The Marinovich Project*. What are your responses to the protagonist? How does your understanding of Macur's argument evolve after watching the film? What do you understand to be some of the main risks of overspecialization of youth in sports, and how might new advances in genetic testing exacerbate these risks? What rights do parents and children have to this information? Or, work in groups that are assigned different identities: the scientists, the children, the parents, the testing agencies, and devise arguments that hypothetically represent these various stakeholders' stances on the issue. As a class, deliberate and engage in a flash debate over the ethics of using genetic science to test youth for sports in the manner presented by Macur. How many different arguments can you come up with as a class? Who has the most interesting position and why? What evidence can you offer in support of your side of the debate?

Communication Currents is the National Communication Association's online web magazine that translates scholarly research on communication for a general audience. In the following essay, communications scholar Michael Butterworth discusses the complex relationships between sport, identity, and cultural memory, specifically focusing on the role of the NFL in memorializing 9/11 through its traveling museum exhibit, "Pro Football and the American Spirit."

MILITARISM, PUBLIC MEMORY, AND THE PRO FOOTBALL HALL OF FAME

By Michael L. Butterworth

In the wake of the September 11, 2001 terrorist attacks and the subsequent declaration of a "war on terror," references and tributes to the military were ubiquitous in American popular culture. Political scientist Jamesder Derian has referred to the conflation of media, entertainment, and militarism as the "military-industrial-media-entertainment network," or "MIME-NET." This phenomenon is not new, but has been amplified in recent years. Even as the United States has ended its war in Iraq and announced plans to do the same in Afghanistan, popular culture celebrations of the military have intensified. This has especially been the case in sports.

Sports leagues and media have produced an almost endless list of military-themed events and programming, including flyovers, ceremonial first-pitches and coin tosses by military personnel, songs performed by members of the Armed Forces, collaborations with military charities, games sponsored by military organizations or contractors, on-field enlistment ceremonies, and near-constant platitudes from broadcasters designed to "support the troops." Among the more recent iterations of this is a traveling museum exhibit for the Pro Football Hall of Fame called, "Pro Football and the American Spirit." This exhibit, housed in the Hall of Fame throughout 2008 and 2009, and currently traveling throughout the country, features multiple points of identification between the game—especially in the National Football League (NFL)—and the military. As such, it shapes an audience that is positioned to view war as necessary and noble, with the mythological warrior ethos of professional football serving as rhetorical support.

From *Communication Currents* (2012).

As a part of a museum, "Pro Football and the American Spirit," invites consideration from the perspective of memory studies. Numerous scholars across various disciplines have noted a growing interest in memory or, in the terminology of rhetorical studies, *public memory*. Put simply, how a culture remembers or memorializes the past reveals much about that culture's anxieties and political concerns in the *present*. This explains why trauma generally, and war specifically, occupy a central place in public memory, especially in the United States.

The sport of football is already linked rhetorically to war and militarism. Much of this discourse is based on the mythology of the "warrior," a term that conveniently conflates soldiers and football players. Key to this myth is *sacrifice*, for in both endeavors the warrior must give up his body for a greater cause. Although many sports depend on individual deference to team, the physical toll of football and the metaphorical "war" over territory makes it an ideal vehicle for affirming the virtues of war.

Sacrifice is related to memory, for those who have sacrificed—their lives in war and their bodies in football—are those who earn the greatest honor. "Pro Football and the American Spirit" thus makes use of the warrior myth and the theme of sacrifice in an exhibit that, in the words of the Hall of Fame's website, "recalls the stories of triumphs, tragedy, and personal sacrifice made by the more than 1,200 players, coaches, and administrators who interrupted or delayed their pro football careers to serve their country during times of military conflict." I visited the exhibit in Canton, OH on March 12, 2009, before it embarked on its tour. Based on this visit, I argue that "Pro Football and the American Spirit" exploits the football/war metaphor in ways that affirm the necessity of war and marginalize any competing images of heroism and citizenship.

The traveling exhibit details the military service of professional football players from World War II to the present day. Each conflict was presented in a circular chronology, which meant that World War II and the War on Terror were next to one another. Although an argument can be made this was simply a matter of chance, it is also important to note these wars have been compared regularly in the past decade, both because 9/11 was frequently compared to the bombing of Pearl Harbor and because these two wars are largely understood as "just" or "virtuous" causes for the United States. The flip side of this equation is the ambiguity symbolized by the wars in Korea and especially Vietnam, and it is striking that these two conflicts were less visibly displayed than other moments of war or patriotism.

Given that 9/11 is a relatively recent tragedy and that the War on Terror continues to affect American life, perhaps the most striking display was the tribute to Pat Tillman, called "Duty and Courage." After the 2001 terrorist attacks, Tillman gave up his lucrative National Football League contract to join the U.S. Army Rangers. He was subsequently killed in Afghanistan in 2004 and his death was initially used to valorize the "ultimate sacrifice" made by many in the name of "freedom" and "democracy." However, this story was later revealed to be incomplete and the discovery that Tillman was ambivalent about the war and that he had been killed by "friendly fire" diminished the myth's potency. More damaging were allegations that the military and members of the Bush administration knowingly manipulated his memory in service of their rhetorical justifications for the War on Terror.

The complexity of this story, however, was simplified and sanitized in "Pro Football and the American Spirit." Although biographical text noted Tillman's death by fratricide, the visuals contained in the display were far more powerful. Indeed, the glass case prominently displayed his Arizona Cardinals jersey and Army Ranger uniform, as well as a large copy of what has now become an iconic photograph of Tillman running onto the field, helmet in hand and hair flying from his head. This image, which first appeared on the cover of *Sports Illustrated* after his death, provided the blueprint for the 8-foot tall statue of Pat Tillman located in the "Freedom Plaza" outside of the University of Phoenix Stadium where the Arizona Cardinals play. Thus, the inclusion of the image in the exhibit echoes uses of the photo elsewhere, all of which articulate with one another to cement the mythologizing of his death.

The display of Pat Tillman is representative of the overall effect of the exhibit. Throughout "Pro Football and the American Spirit" visitors are invited to valorize war and militarism. Accordingly, citizenship is understood in narrow terms of patriotism, with football serving as the most vocal supporter of America's cause. At no point in the exhibit are those with dissenting views acknowledged, resulting in an implicit argument that dissent from war must be antithetical to the "American spirit." In this way, the public memory of football's contributions to war serves not only to memorialize the past but also to discipline acceptable modes of behavior in the present.

Throughout the exhibit, video kiosks play short features that show various instances of football's wartime nobility. In Canton, one such kiosk was located immediately behind the Pat Tillman exhibit. In the narration provided by legendary broadcaster Pat Summerall, visitors are told, "Whenever America called, the mighty of the NFL responded with courage and sacrifice, showing they treasure freedom above all else…In war and in football, the will to win and the will to excel are the things that endure." These words provide an appropriate summary of the exhibit as a whole, for "Pro Football and the American Spirit" offers a full-throated endorsement of the conflation of football with war while celebrating the sport's symbolic importance to American identity.

Outline Butterworth's article. How is he arranging his argument for a general audience and what conventions of language and style does Butterworth attend to in writing for a lay reader? Make a list of all the important textual strategies you see that suggest Butterworth's attempt at "translating" a scholarly concept.

This exercise will prepare you for Major Assignment #5: The Persuasive Research Paper. *Communication Currents* asks researchers to translate and abbreviate recently published work on communication. Butterworth's essay is thus a translation of his longer scholarly article: Butterworth, M.L. (2012). "Militarism and memorializing at the Pro Football Hall of Fame." *Communication and Critical/Cultural Studies*, 9, 241-258. Using your library's database, search for and read Butterworth's original scholarly article. First, note your search process: Did you look for the article in a general article database? Or, did you try to search for the article through the journal's archives? Next, compare and contrast the two articles. Is it the same argument? What is "translated" from the original journal article to the web essay? What gets lost in translation? What value is added by writing a shorter piece for a public audience? What strategies does Butterworth use to write for a general audience and how are these different than his approach to writing for a scholarly audience in his longer piece?

Communication Currents is directed at a general audience. In small groups discuss the following: What does this "general readership" look like? Who would be interested in reading about communication issues? What kind of demographic comprises this readership? What is their education level, income, sex, class, an race? How does Butterworth's piece demonstrate a "translation" of scholarly ideas into everyday intelligible prose for a public readership? What is the value of translating academic scholarship for the public? What is gained/lost in this process? Why should the public care about an issue like public memory and its relationship to the NFL? Take notes and share your findings as a class.

This exercise is designed to help you better understand the concept of "translation" and the differences in writing for public and scholarly audiences. Write two short essays (1,000-1,500 words) on an important topic related to sport. In one version, imagine you are writing for *Communication Currents* and a lay audience. In the other version, imagine you are writing for a scholarly audience. In a cover memo, address the differences in your two approaches and how you understood the concepts of translation and audience dictating your approach to each essay. How do your tone, arrangement, syntax, thesis, and examples vary from the two pieces and why?

Rick Telander is the lead sports columnists for the Chicago Sun-Times *who previously worked as a senior writer for both* Sports Illustrated *and* ESPN, The Magazine. *One of his eight books, his acclaimed* Heaven is a Playground *was made into a motion picture. In "Senseless," Telander discusses the darker side of sports, however, when corporate sport clashes with structural inequality and urban culture.*

SENSELESS

BY RICK TELANDER

In America's cities, kids are killing kids over sneakers and other sports apparel favored by drug dealers. Who's to blame?

For 15-year-old Michael Eugene Thomas, it definitely was the shoes. A ninth-grader at Meade Senior High School in Anne Arundel County, MD, Thomas was found strangled on May 2, 1989. Charged with first-degree murder was James David Martin, 17, a basketball buddy who allegedly took Thomas's two-week-old Air Jordan basketball shoes and left Thomas's barefoot body in the woods near school.

Thomas loved Michael Jordan, as well as the shoes Jordan endorses, and he cleaned his own pair each evening. He kept the cardboard shoe box with Jordan's silhouette on it in a place of honor in his room. Inside the box was the sales ticket for the shoes. It showed he paid $115.50, the price of a product touched by deity.

"We told him not to wear the shoes to school," said Michael's grandmother, Birdie Thomas. "We said somebody might like them, and he said, 'Granny, before I let anyone take those shoes, they'll have to kill me.'"

Michael Jordan sits in the locked press room before a workout at the Chicago Bulls' practice facility in suburban Deerfield, Ill. He is wearing his practice uniform and a pair of black Air Jordans similar to the ones young Thomas wore, except that these have Jordan's number, 23, stitched on the sides. On the shoelaces Jordan wears plastic toggles to prevent the shoes from loosening if the laces should come untied. Two toggles come in each box of Air

From *Sports Illustrated Vault* (1999).

Jordans, and if kids knew that Jordan actually wears them, they would never step out the door without their own toggles securely in place. The door is locked to keep out the horde of fans, journalists and favor seekers who dog Jordan wherever he goes. Jordan needs a quiet moment. He is reading an account of Thomas's death that a reporter has shown him.

For just an instant it looks as though Jordan might cry. He has so carefully nurtured his image as the all-American role model that he refuses to go anywhere, get into any situation, that might detract from that image. He moves swiftly and smoothly from the court to home to charity events to the golf course, all in an aura of untarnished integrity. "I can't believe it," Jordan says in a low voice.

"Choked to death. By his friend." He sighs deeply. Sweat trickles down one temple.

He asks if there have been other such crimes. Yes, he is told. Plenty, unfortunately. Not only for Air Jordans, but also for other brands of athletic shoes, as well as for jackets and caps bearing sports insignia—apparel that Jordan and other athlete endorsers have encouraged American youth to buy.

The killings aren't new. In 1983, 14-year-old Dewitt Duckett was shot to death in the hallway of Harlem Park Junior High in Baltimore by someone who apparently wanted Duckett's silky blue Georgetown jacket. In 1985, 13-year-old Shawn Jones was shot in Detroit after five youths took his Fila sneakers. But lately the pace of the carnage has quickened. In January 1988, an unidentified 14-year-old Houston boy, a star athlete in various sports, allegedly stabbed and killed 22-year-old Eric Allen with a butcher knife after the two argued over a pair of tennis shoes in the home the youths shared with their mothers. Seven months later a gunman in Atlanta allegedly robbed an unnamed 17-year-old of his Mercedes-Benz hat and Avia hightops after shooting to death the boy's 25-year-old friend, Carl Middlebrooks, as Middlebrooks pedaled away on his bike.

Last November, Raheem Wells, the quarterback for Detroit Kettering High, was murdered, allegedly by six teenagers who swiped his Nike sneakers. A month later, 17-year-old Tyrone Brown of Hapeville, Ga., was fatally shot in the head, allegedly by two acquaintances who robbed him of money, cocaine and his sneakers. In Baltimore last summer 18-year-old Ronnell Ridgeway was robbed of his $40 sweatpants and then shot and killed. In March, Chris Demby, a 10th-grader at Franklin Learning Center in West Philadelphia, was shot and killed for his new Nikes.

In April 1989, 16-year-old Johnny Bates was shot to death in Houston by 17-year-old Demetrick Walker after Johnny refused to turn over his Air Jordan hightops. In March, Demetrick was sentenced to life in prison. Said prosecutor Mark Vinson, "It's bad when we create an image of luxury about athletic gear that it forces people to kill over it."

Jordan shakes his head.

"I thought I'd be helping out others and everything would be positive," he says. "I thought people would try to emulate the good things I do, they'd try to achieve, to be better. Nothing bad. I never thought because of my endorsement of a shoe, or any product, that people would harm each other. Everyone likes to be admired, but when it comes to kids actually killing each other"—he pauses—"then you have to reevaluate things."

We certainly do. In a country that has long been hung up on style over substance, flash over depth, the athletic shoe and sportswear industries (a projected $5.5 billion in domestic sales of name-brand shoes in 1990; more than $2 billion in sweatpants, sweatshirts and warm-up suits) suddenly have come to represent the pinnacle of consumer exploitation. In recent months the industries, which include heavyweights Nike and Reebok as well as smaller players Adidas, Asics, British Knights, Brooks, Converse, Ellesse, Etonic, Fila, L.A. Gear, New Balance, Pony, Puma, Starter and numerous other makers of sports shoes, caps and jackets, have been accused of creating a fantasy-fueled market for luxury items in the economically blasted inner cities and willingly tapping into the flow of drug and gang money. This has led to a frightening outbreak of crimes among poor black kids trying to make their mark by "busting fresh," or dressing at the height of fashion.

In some cities muggings for sportswear are commonplace—Atlanta police, for instance, estimate they have handled more than 50 such robberies in the last four months. Yet it is not only the number of violent acts but also the seeming triviality of the booty that has stunned the public. In February, 19-year-old Calvin Wash was about to cross Central Park Avenue on Chicago's West Side when, according to police, two youths drove up in a van and demanded that he give them the Cincinnati Bengal jacket he was wearing. When Wash resisted, one of the youths is alleged to have fatally shot him in the back—through the A in BENGALS.

Chicago police sergeant Michael Chasen, who works in the violent crimes division in Area Four, which covers four of Chicago's 25 police districts, says his districts have about 50 reported incidents involving jackets and about a dozen involving gym shoes each month. "When you really think about the crime itself—taking someone's clothes off their body—you can't get much more basic," he says. But, of course, these assailants aren't simply taking clothes from their victims. They're taking status. Something is very wrong with a society that has created an underclass that is slipping into economic and moral oblivion, an underclass in which pieces of rubber and plastic held together by shoelaces are sometimes worth more than a human life. The shoe companies have played a direct role in this. With their million-dollar advertising campaigns, superstar spokesmen and over-designed, high-priced products aimed at impressionable young people, they are creating status from thin air to feed those who are starving for self-esteem. "No one person is responsible for this type of violence," says Patricia Graham, principal of Chicago's Simeon High, one of the city's perennial basketball powers. "It's a combination of circumstances. It's about values and training. Society's values are out of sync, which is why these things have become important."

"The classic explanation in sociology is that these people are driven by peer pressure," says Mervin Daniel, a sociology professor at Morgan State. "What is advertised on TV and whatever your peers are doing, you do it too." Most assuredly, the shoe industry relies heavily on advertising; it spends more than $200 million annually to promote and advertise its products, churning out a blizzard of images and words that make its shoes seem preternaturally hip, cool and necessary. Nike alone will spend $60 million in 1990 on TV and print ads that have built such slogans as "Bo knows," and "Just do it," and "Do you know? Do you know? Do you know?" into mantras of consumerism.

What is baffling, however, is the strength of certain sporting products as icons for drug dealers and gangs. In Boston the Greenwood Street gang wears Green Bay Packer garb, the Vamp Hill Kings wear Los Angeles Kings and Raider gear, and the Castlegate gang wears Cincinnati Reds clothes. "The Intervale gang uses all Adidas stuff, exclusively—hats, jackets, sweatpants, shoes," says Bill Stewart III, the probation officer at the Dorchester District Court in Boston, one of the busiest criminal courts in the nation. "They even have an Adidas handshake, copying the three stripes on the product. They extend three fingers when they shake hands."

Stewart knows how certain young drug dealers feverishly load up on the latest models of sneakers, tossing out any old ones that are scuffed or even slightly worn and replacing them with new pairs. "I was in a kid's apartment recently and there were about 50 pairs of brand-new sneakers, all top-of-the-line stuff—Adidas, Reebok and so forth," he says. "I asked the kid's mother how he came into all this stuff. She said she didn't know."

The use of Major League Baseball hats by gangs has prompted some high schools around the nation to ban them from school grounds, and expensive gold chains, major league or major college team jackets and other ostentatious, potentially troublesome items have also been prohibited. "When I look around sometimes, I think I'm in spring training in Florida," says Stewart.

When informed that baseball caps are being used by gangs as part of their uniforms, Major League Baseball public relations director Richard Levin seemed shocked. "I'm not aware of it at all, nor would I understand why," he said. "Obviously, we don't support it in any way."

Could any respectable U.S. corporation support the use of its products in this way? Absolutely not, said most shoe company executives contacted for this article. You better believe it, said a number of sports apparel retailers, as well as some of the more candid shoe execs.

Among the retailers is Wally Grigo, the owner of three sportswear shops in and near New Haven, Conn. Last August, Grigo put a sign in the front window of his inner-city store that reads, IF YOU DEAL DRUGS, WE DON'T WANT YOUR BUSINESS. SPEND YOUR MONEY SOMEWHERE ELSE.

"Unfortunately, it'll probably have to stay up forever," says Grigo. "I was doing, I'd say, $2,000 a week in drug money sales that disappeared after the sign went up. Our industry is sick, addicted to drug money. We're going through the first phase of addiction, which is total denial."

Before he put up the sign, Grigo had been told by sales reps from two sportswear companies that he should "hook up" the local drug dealers to expose the companies' new products to the neighborhood clientele. After the sign went up, Grigo says, the rep from the smaller company returned and said, "Wally, we're thinking about giving you the line. But, you know, I can't do anything until you cut out the crap and take that sign out of your window. The bulk of our business is done with drug dealers. Wake up!"

Grigo was so stunned that he thought of wearing a wire to record the rep making similar statements. He didn't do so, though, figuring the company's officials would dismiss any evidence by saying the rep was a loose cannon. But Grigo says the companies know what's going on, because the reps are "in the trenches, and they go back and report."

Grigo doesn't want to publicly state the names of the suppliers, for economic reasons. "I'm not afraid of the drug dealers," he says. "But the shoe companies could put me out of business anytime, just by canceling my credit."

One obvious question: How does Grigo, or anyone, know when a drug dealer and not a law-abiding citizen is making a buy? "Hey, spend 10 minutes in any city store," says Grigo. "When an 18-year-old kid pulls up in a BMW, walks down the aisle saying, 'I want this, this, this and this,' then peels off 50's from a stack of bills three inches thick, maybe doesn't even wait for change, then comes back a couple weeks later and does the same thing, hey…you know what I'm saying?"

And what about all those good guys advertising the shoes? What about Nike's Jordan and Spike Lee, the gifted filmmaker and actor who portrays Mars Blackmon, the hero-worshipping nerd in the company's Air Jordan ads? Are they and other pitchmen at fault, too? "Maybe the problem is those guys don't know what's going on," says Grigo. "There are stores doing $5,000 to $10,000 a week in drug money, all over. Drug money is part of the economic landscape these days. Even if the companies don't consciously go after the money, they're still getting it. Hey, all inner-city kids aren't drug dealers. Most of them are good, honest kids. Drug dealers are a very small percent. But the drug dealers, man, they set the fashion trends."

Liz Dolan, director of public relations for Nike, hits the ceiling when she hears such talk. "Our commercials are about sport, they're not about fashion," she says.

But the industry's own figures make that assertion extremely questionable. At least 80% of the athletic shoes sold in the U.S. are not used for their avowed purpose—that is, playing sports. Dolan sighs. She says that all of Nike's athlete-endorsers are quality citizens as well as superjocks. "We're not putting Leon Spinks in the commercials," she says. Then she says that the people who raise the alarm that Nike, as well as other sports apparel companies, is exploiting the poor and creating crime just to make money are bizarre and openly racist. "What's baffling to us is how easily people accept the assumption that black youth is an unruly mob that will do anything to get its hands on what it wants," she says, excitedly. "They'll say, 'Show a black kid something he wants, and he'll kill for it.' I think it's racist hysteria, just like the Charles Stuart case in Boston or the way the Bush campaign used Willie Horton."

Lee also says he has heard such panic before. "Everybody said last summer that my movie Do the Right Thing was going to cause 30 million black people to riot," he says angrily. "But I haven't heard of one garbage can being thrown through a pizzeria window, have you? I want to work with Nike to address the special problems of inner-city black youths, but the problem is not shoes."

Lee is particularly irate because he has been singled out by New York Post sports columnist Phil Mushnick as being untrue to the very people Lee champions in his films. In Mushnick's April 6 column headlined, SHADDUP, I'M SELLIN' OUT… SHADDUP, he sharply criticized Lee for leading the hype. The caption under four photos—one of Lee; the others of soaring pairs of Air Jordans—said, "While Spike Lee watches Michael Jordan (or at least his shoes) dunk all over the world, parents around the country are watching their kids get mugged, or even killed, over the same sneakers Lee and Jordan are promoting." In his column Mushnick said, "It's murder, gentlemen. No rhyme, no reason, just murder. For sneakers. For jackets. Get it, Spike? Murder."

Lee wrote a response in *The National,* the daily sports newspaper, in which he angrily accused Mushnick of "thinly veiled racism" for going after him and other high-profile black endorsers and not white endorsers like Larry Bird or Joe Montana. Lee also questioned Mushnick's sudden "great outpouring of concern for Afro-American youths." Lee wrote, "The Nike commercials Michael Jordan and I do have never gotten anyone killed…The deal is this: Let's try to effectively deal with the conditions that make a kid put so much importance on a pair of sneakers, a jacket and gold. These kids feel they have no options, no opportunities."

Certainly Lee is right about that. Elijah Anderson, a University of Pennsylvania sociologist who specializes in ethnography, the study of individual cultures, links the scourge of apparel-related crimes among young black males to "inequality in race and class. The uneducated, inner-city kids don't have a sense of opportunity. They feel the system is closed off to them. And yet they're bombarded with the same cultural apparatus that the white middle class is. They don't have the means to attain the things offered, and yet they have the same desire. So they value these 'emblems,' these symbols of supposed success. The gold, the shoes, the drug dealer's outfit—those things all belie the real situation, but it's a symbolic display that seems to say that things are all right.

"Advertising fans this whole process by presenting the images that appeal to the kids, and the shoe companies capitalize on the situation, because it exists. Are the companies abdicating responsibility by doing this? That's a hard one to speak to. This is, after all, a free market."

But what about social responsibility? One particularly important issue is the high price of the shoes—many companies have models retailing for considerably more than $100, with the Reebok Pump leading the parade at $170. There is also the specific targeting of young black males as buyers, through the use of seductive, macho-loaded sales pitches presented by black stars.

"You can quibble about our tactics, but we don't stand for the drug trade," says Dolan. She points out that Nike's fall promotion campaign will include $5 million worth of "strictly pro-education, stay-in-school" public service commercials that will "not run late at night, but on the same major sporting events as the prime-time ads."

Nike is not alone in playing the good corporate citizen.

Reebok recently gave $750,000 to fund Project Teamwork, a program designed to combat racism that is administered by the Center for the Study of Sport in Society at Northeastern University.

Nevertheless, certain products wind up having dubious associations—some products more than others. John Hazard, the head buyer for the chain of City Sports stores in Boston, says, "We used to have brawls in here, robberies, a tremendous amount of stealing. But we cut back on 90 percent of it by getting rid of certain products. We don't carry Adidas, Fila, British Knights. Those things bring in the gangs.

"There's a store not far away that carries all that stuff. They have after-hours sales to show the new lines to big drug dealers. They even have guys on beepers, to let them know when the latest shoes have come in. It would be nothing for those guys to buy 20, 30 pair of shoes to give to all their 12-year-old runners."

He thinks for a moment. "I don't know if you can really blame the shoe companies for what happens. Not long ago there was a murder, a gang deal, here in Boston. The cops had the murderer, and they were walking him somewhere. It was on TV. The murderer was bent over at first, and then the cops stood him up, and—I couldn't believe it—all of a sudden you could see he was wearing a City Sports T-shirt. There's no way you can control what people wear."

John Donahoe, manager of a Foot Locker store in Chicago's Loop, agrees. "Right now, this is the hottest thing we've got," he says, holding up a simple, ugly, blue nylon running shoe. Behind him are shelves filled with more than 100 different model or color variations. "Nike Cortez: $39," he says. "Been around for 20 years. Why is it hot now?" He shrugs. "I don't know."

Assistant manager James Crowder chimes in helpfully, "It's not the price, or who's endorsing it. It's just…what's happening."

Keeping up with what's happening has shoe manufacturers scrambling these days. "It used to be you could have a product out and fiddle with it for years, to get it just right," says Roger Morningstar, the assistant vice-president of promotions at Converse. "Now, if you don't come out with two or three new models every month, you're dead."

At home I go to my closet and pull out my own meager assortment of sports shoes—nine pairs, all told. A pair of ancient turf football shoes; some nubbed softball shoes; a pair of old running shoes; a pair of original, hideous red-and-black Air Jordans, kept for historical reasons; a pair of Avia volleyball shoes, worn-out, though they were never used for their intended purpose; two pairs of low-cut tennis shoes (or are they walking shoes?); a pair of Nike cross-training shoes (though I don't cross-train or even know what it means) in bad shape; a pair of sweat-stained, yet still awe-inspiring hightop basketball Reebok Pumps, a Christmas gift from my sister and brother-in-law. I pick these up. They are happening.

There are three colors on them, and the words REEBOK BASKETBALL are stitched in the tongue, right below the wondrous pump itself, colored orange and pebbled to resemble a basketball. On the bottom of the shoes are three colors of textured rubber. And there is an indented section in the heel with clear plastic laid over four orange tubes, and embossed with the words REEBOK ENERGY RETURN SYSTEM. On the back of the hightops there is the orange release valve that, when touched, decompresses the whole shebang.

The shoes haven't changed my hoops game at all, though they are comfortable, unless I pump them up too much and my toes slowly go numb. While I could never bring myself to pay for a pair out of my own pocket, I will admit that when I opened the shoe box on Christmas Day, I was thrilled by the sheer techno-glitz of the things. It was identical to the way I felt when, at the age of eight, I received a Robert-the-Robot.

But can promoting athletic shoes possibly be wrong in a capitalist society? Reebok chairman Paul Fireman was recently quoted as describing the Pump as "a product that's aspirational to a young person"—that is, something to be desired. He added, if prospective buyers couldn't afford the shoes, "that's the place for a kid to get a job after school." What, indeed, is the point of ads if not to inform the public of products that it may or may not need, but that it may wish to buy? Should we demand that the sports shoe industry be held to a higher standard than, say, the junk food industry? The advertising community itself thought so highly of Nike's "Bo knows" spot with Bo Jackson and Bo Diddley that Advertising Age named Jackson its Star Presenter of 1989.

What are we looking for here, anyway?

"Responsibility," says Grigo, the New Haven store owner. "Have Spike Lee and Michael Jordan look at the camera and say, 'Drug dealers, don't you dare wear my shoes!' Put antidrug labels on the box. I already do at my stores."

"Everybody wants us to do everything," says Nike's Dolan. "It's naive to think an antidrug message on the shoe box is going to change anyone's behavior. Our theme is 'Just do it!' because we want people playing sports, because they'll need more shoes. The healthier people are, the more shoes we'll sell."

Trouble is, young black males—a significant portion of the market—are not healthy right now. In fact, 23% of black males between the ages of 20 and 29 are under the supervision of the criminal justice system—incarcerated, paroled or on probation. According to a 1989 study in the Journal of the American Medical Association, a black male is six times more likely to be a homicide victim than a white male. Writes Washington Post columnist William Raspberry: "The inability of so many young black men to see themselves as providers, or even as necessary to their families, may be one explanation for their irresponsible behavior." Marc Mauer, of the Sentencing Project, a nonprofit group concerned with disparities in the administration of criminal justice, says, "We now risk the possibility of writing off an entire generation of black men."

Obviously we are talking about something bigger than shoes here. Jordan sits up straight in his chair. It's time for practice to start. "I'd rather eliminate the product ((the shoes)) than know drug dealers are providing the funds that pay me," he says. Of course drug money is, to a troubling extent, supporting the product, as well as other brands of sneakers and sports apparel. And kids are being killed for them. So what should the shoe companies, the schools, the advertising industry, the endorsers, the media, parents—all of us—do about it?

Do you know? Do you know? Do you know?

Take some inventory on the cover article. How does Telander structure his argument, and who is his intended audience? What is his style and tone, and is it effective or not? What kind of evidence (facts, statistics, interviews, anecdotes…) does he use and what are their effects? How does Telander's attention to the surface features of language and writing affect you as a reader?

The cultural legacy of the Air Jordan has been controversial and legend for decades. But not everyone agrees with Telander's point of view. Spend a few minutes searching Google for "Air Jordans" followed by a couple of key words of interest. What other sources and texts do you find on the topic? How do these compare and contrast with Telander's point of view? For starters, look at the following opinion editorial, "25 years later, the Air Jordan's footprint remains" (2010), written by Kevin McNutt for the *Daily News* as a response to Telander's cover story, found at: http://www.nydailynews.com/opinion/25-years-air-jordan-footprint-remains-article-1.164887.

Drawing on evidence from Telander's article, write an essay in which you explore your own thoughts about the Air Jordan's "controversy," being sure to acknowledge multiple viewpoints. What evidence do you find the most compelling? What evidence do you find the most disturbing? What potential media bias do you see in the reporting and how might we look at the issue another way? What was your own relationship to the Air Jordan as a child, and how does this affect how you understand Telander's perspective?

Pat Garofalo is the economic policy editor for ThinkProgress.org. Travis Waldron is the economics and sports reporter for ThinkProgress.org, and the winner of a journalism excellence award from the Sydney Hillman Foundation (2008).

IF YOU BUILD IT, THEY MIGHT NOT COME: THE RISKY ECONOMICS OF SPORT STADIUMS

BY PAT GAROFALO AND TRAVIS WALDRON

The trials of the Phoenix Coyotes, the least popular hockey team in the NHL, offer a lesson in public debt and defeat.

In June, the city council of Glendale, Arizona, decided to spend $324 million on the Phoenix Coyotes, an ice hockey team that plays in Glendale's Jobing.com Arena.

The team has been owned by the league itself since its former owner, Jerry Moyes, declared bankruptcy in 2009. For each of the past two seasons, Glendale has paid $25 million to the league to manage the Coyotes, even as the city faced millions of dollars in budget deficits. Now, Greg Jamison, who is also part of the organization that owns the NHL's San Jose Sharks, is making a bid for the team, and would therefore be the beneficiary of the subsidies.

To put the deal in perspective, Glendale's budget gap for 2012 is about $35 million. As the city voted to give a future Coyotes owner hundreds of millions of taxpayer dollars, it laid off 49 public workers, and even considered putting its city hall and police station up as collateral to obtain a loan, according to the Arizona Republic. (The latter plan was ultimately scrapped.)

Overall, Glendale is not only on the hook for $15 million per year over two decades to a potential Coyotes owner, but also a $12 million annual debt payment for construction of its arena. In return, according to the Republic, the city receives a measly "$2.2 million in annual rent payments, ticket surcharges, sales taxes and other fees." Even if the Coyotes

From *The Atlantic* (2012).

were to dominate the league like no other in recent memory and return to the Stanley Cup Finals year after year, the city would still lose $9 million annually.

This is an altogether too common problem in professional sports. Across the country, franchises are able to extract taxpayer funding to build and maintain private facilities, promising huge returns for the public in the form of economic development.

For instance, just three of the NFL's 31 stadiums were originally built without public funds. In two of those cases, public funding was later used to upgrade the stadium or surrounding facilities, even as all 32 of the NFL's teams ranked among Forbes' 50 most valuable sporting franchises in the world in 2012. (Only MetLife Stadium, shared by the New York Jets and New York Giants, received no public funding.)

Time after time, politicians wary of letting a local franchise relocate—as the NBA's Seattle Supersonics did, to Oklahoma City before the 2008-2009 season—approve public funds, selling the stadiums as public works projects that will boost the local economy and provide a windfall of growth.

However, according to leading sports economists, stadiums and arenas rarely bring about the promised prosperity, and instead leave cities and states mired in debt that they can't pay back before the franchise comes calling for more.

"The basic idea is that sports stadiums typically aren't a good tool for economic development," said Victor Matheson, an economist at Holy Cross who has studied the economic impact of stadium construction for decades. When cities cite studies (often produced by parties with an interest in building the stadium) touting the impact of such projects, there is a simple rule for determining the actual return on investment, Matheson said: "Take whatever number the sports promoter says, take it and move the decimal one place to the left. Divide it by ten, and that's a pretty good estimate of the actual economic impact."

Others agree. While "it is inarguable that within a few blocks you'll have an effect," the results are questionable for metro areas as a whole, Stefan Szymanski, a sports economist at the University of Michigan, said.

PUBLIC MONEY BALL

There are numerous reasons for the muted economic effects. The biggest is that arenas often sit empty for a significant portion of the year. Jobing.com Arena is guaranteed 41 hockey games annually. The other 324 nights, it must find concerts, conventions or other events to fill the schedule, and in Glendale, where the arena competes with facilities in nearby Phoenix, that can be tough to do.

"We've looked at tons of these things, and the one that we found that seemed to make sense is the Staples Center in Los Angeles," Matheson said. "But they use it 250 dates a year. They don't make sense when you're using it 41 times a year and competing with another venue down the street."

Another reason the projects rarely make sense is because of the way they are structured. Stadiums and arenas are financed with long-term bonds, meaning cities and states will be stuck with the debt for long periods of time (often 30 years). And while cities make 30-year commitments to finance stadiums, their commitments to government workers and other local investments are often made on a year-to-year basis, meaning that, just as in Glendale, it becomes easier to eliminate public sector jobs and programs than to default on debt incurred from arenas.

The counterargument—made by council member Joyce Clark, who voted for the subsidies, and Glendale First, an organization in favor of the package—is that the Coyotes and their arena provide support to the local economy that otherwise wouldn't be there.

"It's a huge economic engine for Glendale," Bea Wyatt, a spokesperson for Glendale First said. According to Wyatt, who doesn't live in Glendale but frequents the city for Coyotes games, sales tax revenue made up 41 percent of Glendale's budget last year, and a significant portion was derived from sales around the arena. Supporters also claim the deal with Jamison is a good one for the city, since he will eventually pay for the arena's management and employ local workers.

But again, economists don't seem to buy the argument. While Glendale First claims that more than 600,000 visitors—three times Glendale's population—came to the city for hockey last year, the Coyotes finished last in the NHL in attendance. And it is unclear how many of those visitors were, like Wyatt, residents of nearby communities who may patronize restaurants but don't spend money shopping or staying in hotels.

Matheson estimates that 20 percent of fans for a Major League Baseball game come from outside the local area, and that the figure for hockey games is likely much smaller. That's hardly enough to fill the local hotels or to add outside spending to the local economy in other ways, he said.

"It's not generating new revenue. This is local spending on a local event," Matheson said, adding that most of the money spent in and around arenas and stadiums would likely be spent elsewhere in the local economy if there were no sporting events to attend.

Though it is clear that new facilities are not a wise investment for taxpayers, the argument from Glendale First stems from the fact that Jobing.com Arena is already there. Refusing to use more public financing—and potentially allowing the Coyotes to leave for a new town—Wyatt said, would amount to the city turning its back on its initial investment and risking the failure of hotels, restaurants, and other businesses.

Glendale "jumped in with both feet, and to now change course would be detrimental to the city," Wyatt said. "Finding a management company that's going to [run the arena] for nothing, relying on acts of god, I don't think that's the way the world works anymore," added Clark, who objected to the characterization of the $324 million as a subsidy, instead called it a "lease management agreement."

Even faced with that question, though, Szymanski was skeptical of the decision to continue financing the team. Yes, Glendale made a sizeable investment—one that went bad surprisingly fast—but that doesn't mean it should throw more good money into a project that likely isn't sustainable.

"The argument here seems to be that if you only put a little more in, even though the initial investment wasn't viable, we now have a plan," Szymanski said. "It's kind of a perverse argument that taxpayers should subsidize this because businesses depend on this deal that isn't viable."

"It's like doubling up in gambling to get your money back," he added. "At some point, you have to say stop."

HOCKEY IN ARIZONA?

If Glendale lets the Coyotes walk to another city, it won't be alone. The NHL's experiment to bring hockey to southern America has had mixed results, succeeding in cities like Nashville and Raleigh, but failing miserably in Atlanta, which lost the Thrashers to Winnipeg last year.

By all indications, the Coyotes are more Atlanta than they are Nashville, particularly in the sense that they have yet to be embraced by the local population even during periods of success. "This is hockey in a non-hockey city where the average resident hasn't seen ice outside of a margarita," Matheson said.

With the city shedding jobs and cutting services, the logical decision would seem to be to take back the funding it has promised to Coyotes in order to preserve those jobs and programs, a stance taken by city council member Phil Lieberman, who voted against the funding package. "I can use that $15 million [annual payment] for good things for Glendale," Lieberman said. "Open our libraries up again…Replace the 55 cops that we're short right now."

But if the city and its residents are desperate to keep the Coyotes in town, they have to understand that doing so comes at a cost that likely won't be replaced—not by sales tax revenue, not by economic growth, and not by outside spending. When the city subsidizes hockey, it reduces its ability to pay for public safety officials, public transportation, and services upon which its citizens rely.

That's a choice the city is free to make, of course, but it shouldn't pretend that the mere presence of the Coyotes is an economic investment. Doing so simply enables a further transfer of public dollars to a private enterprise, without much hope for a return.

Invent

Make a list of all the reasons/evidence offered in support of cities' support for building major sports stadia and the respective stakeholders whose interests are represented by these reasons as offered in Garofalo's and Waldron's article. Next, make a list of all the reasons/evidence offered against the building of sports stadia and their various stakeholders per Garofalo and Waldron. Which sets of evidence seem stronger or more convincing and why? Which, if any, seem weak or logically suspicious and why?

Collaborate

The financing of sports stadia has been a growing and expensive controversy in the past several decades. With your peers, watch the award-winning documentary *Battle for Brooklyn* (2001) and compare and contrast the arguments presented in the documentary to those made in Garofalo's and Waldron's article.

Explore

Watch the documentary *Battle for Brooklyn* (2011) and find three reviews by critics (one published in a newspaper or magazine, one by a professional film critic, and one provided by a viewer on a consumer site like Netflix.com). How do these reviews differ from one another in tone, style, length, organization, and content? How do the critics' reviews correspond to your own feelings about the issue? What criteria does each review seem to favor in its analysis of the issue and are these the same criteria you would use if you were to review the film?

Editor of The New Republic, *Franklin Foer's writing has also been published in the* New York Times, Spin, Slate, *and* The Atlantic Monthly. *In the final chapter of his book* How Soccer Explains the World, *Foer reflects on America's ongoing unease with the world's most popular sport.*

HOW SOCCER EXPLAINS THE AMERICAN CULTURE WARS

BY FRANKLIN FOER

I.

My soccer career began in 1982, at the age of eight. This was an entirely different moment in the history of American soccer, well before the youth game acquired its current, highly evolved infrastructure. Our teams didn't have names. We had jersey colors that we used to refer to ourselves: "Go Maroon!" Our couch, a bearded German named Gunter, would bark at us in continual nomenclature that didn't quite translate into English. Urging me to stop a ball with my upper body, he would cry out, "Use your breasts, Frankie!"

That I should end up a soccer player defied the tie-tested laws of sporting heredity. For generations, fathers bequeathed their sporting loves unto their sons. My father, like most men of his baby boom age, had grown up madly devoted to baseball. Why didn't my dad adhere to the practice of handing his game to his son? The answer has to do with the times and the class to which my parents belonged, by which I mean, they were children of the sixties and lived in the yuppie confines of Upper Northwest Washington, D.C., a dense aggregation of Ivy League lawyers with aggressively liberal politics and exceptionally protective parenting styles. Nearly everyone in our family's social set signed up their children to play soccer. It was the fashionable thing to do. On Monday mornings, at school, we'd each walk around in the same cheaply made pair of white shorts with the logo of our league, Montgomery Soccer Inc.

Steering your child into soccer may have been fashionable, but it wasn't a decision to be made lightly. When my father played sandlot baseball, he could walk three blocks to his

From *How Soccer Explains the American Culture Wars* (2004).

neighborhood diamond. With soccer, this simply wasn't possible. At this early moment in the youth soccer boom, the city of Washington didn't have any of its own leagues. My parents would load up our silver Honda Accord and drive me to fields deep in suburban Maryland, 40-minute drives made weekly across a landscape of oversized hardware stores and newly minted real estate developments. In part, these drives would take so long because my parents would circle, hopelessly lost, through neighborhoods they had never before visited and would likely never see again.

As I late discovered, my parents made this sacrifice of their leisure time because they believed that soccer could be transformational. I suffered from a painful, rather extreme case of shyness. I'm told that it extended beyond mere clinging to my mother's leg. On the sidelines of halftime, I would sit quietly on the edge of the other kid's conversations, never really interjecting myself. My parents had hoped that the game might necessitate my becoming more aggressive, a breaking through of inhibitions.

The idea that soccer could alleviate shyness was not an idiosyncratic parenting theory. It tapped into the conventional wisdom among yuppie parents. Soccer's appeal lay in its opposition to the other popular sports. For children of the sixties, there was something abhorrent about enrolling kids in American football, a game where violence wasn't just incidental but inherent. They didn't want to teach the acceptability of violence, let alone subject their precious children to the risk of physical maiming. Baseball, where each batter must stand center stage four or five times a game, entailed too many stressful, potentially ego-deflating encounters. Basketball, before Larry Bird's prime, still had the taint of the ghetto.

But soccer represented something very different. It was a tabula rasa, a sport onto which a generation of parents could project their values. Quickly, soccer came to represent the fundamental tenets of yuppie parenting, the spirit of *Sesame Street* and Dr. Benjamin Spock. Unlike the other sports, it would foster self-esteem, minimize the pain of competition while still teaching life lessons Dick Wilson, the executive director of the American Youth Soccer Organization since the early seventies, described the attitude this way: "We would like to provide the child a chance to participate in a less competitive, win-oriented atmosphere…We require that teams be balanced; and that teams not remain intact from year to year, that they be dissolved and totally reconstituted in the next season. This is done to preclude the adults from building their own dynasty 'win at all cost' situations."

This was typical of the thinking of a generation of post-'60s parenting theories, which were an extension of the counterculture spirit—Theodor Adorno's idea that strict, emotionally stultifying homes created authoritarian, bigoted kids. But for all the talk of freedom, the sixties parenting style had a far less laissez-faire side, too. Like the 1960s consumer movement which brought American car seat belts and air bags, the soccer movement felt like it could create a set of rules and regulations that would protect both the child's body and mind from damage. Leagues like the one I played in handed out "participation" trophies to every player, no matter how few games his (or her) team won. Other leagues had stopped posting the scores of games or keeping score altogether. Where most of the world accepts the practice of heading the ball as an essential element of the game, American soccer parents have fretted over the potential for injury to the brain. An entire industry sprouted to manufacture protective headgear, not that different-looking from a boxer's sparring helmet, to soften the blows. Even though very little medical evidence supports this fear, some youth leagues have prohibited headers altogether.

This reveals a more fundamental difference between American youth soccer and the game as practiced in the rest of the world. In every other part of the world, soccer's sociology varies little: it is the province of the working class. Sure, there might be aristocrats like Gianni Agnelli, who take an interest, and instances like Barca, where the game transcendently grips the community. But there cases are rare. The United States is even rarer. It inverts the class structure of the game. Here, aside from Latino immigrants, the professional classes follow the game most avidly and the working class couldn't give a toss about it. Surveys, done by the sporting goods manufacturers, consistently show that children of middle class and affluent families play the game disproportionately. Half the nation's soccer participants come from households earning over $50,000. That is, they come from the solid middle class and above.

Elites have never been especially well liked in post-war American politics—or at least they have been easy to take swipes at. But the generation of elites that adopted soccer has been an especially ripe target. That's because they came through college in the sixties and seventies, at a time when the counterculture self-consciously turned against the stultifying conformity of what it perceived as traditional America. Even as this group shed its youthful radical politics, it kept some of its old ideals, including its resolute cosmopolitanism and suspicions of middle America, "flyover country." When they adopted soccer, it gave the impression that they had turned their backs on the American pastime. This, naturally, produced even more disdain for them—and for their sport.

Pundits have employed many devices to sum up America's cultural division. During the 1980s, they talked about the "culture war"—the battle over textbooks, abortion, prayer in school, affirmative action, and funding of the arts. This war pitted conservative defenders of tradition and morality against liberal defenders of modernity and pluralism. More recently this debate has been described as the split between "red and blue America"—the two colors used to distinguish partisan preference in maps charting presidential election voting. But another explanatory device has yet to penetrate political science departments and the national desks of newspapers. There exists an important cleavage between the parts of the country that have adopted soccer as its pastime and the places that haven't. And this distinction lays bare an underrated source of American cultural cleavage: globalization.

II.

Other countries have greeted soccer with relative indifference. The Indian subcontinent and Australia come to mind. But the United States is perhaps the only place where a loud portion of the population actively disdains the game, even campaigns against it. This anti-soccer lobby believes, in the world of *USA Today*'s Tom Weir, "that hating soccer is more American than apple pie, driving a pickup, or spending Saturday afternoons channel surfing with the remote control." Weir exaggerates the pervasiveness of this sentiment. But the cadre of soccer haters has considerable sway. Their influence rests primarily with a legion of prestigious sportswriters and commentators, who use their column inches to fulminate against the game, especially on the occasions of World Cups.

Not just pundits buried in the C Section of the paper, but people with actual power believe that soccer represents a genuine threat to the American way of life. The former Buffalo Bills quarterback Jack Kemp, one of the most influential conservatives of the 1980s, a man once mentioned in the same breath as the presidency, holds this view. In 1986, he took to the floors of the United States Congress to orate against a resolution in support of an American bid to host the World Cup. Kemp intoned, "I think it is important for all those young out there, who someday hope to play real football, where you throw it and kick it and run with it and put it in your hands, a distinction should be made that football is democratic, capitalism, whereas soccer is a European socialist [sport]."

Lovers of the game usually can't resist dismissing these critics as xenophobes and reactionaries intoxicated with a sense of cultural superiority, the sporting wing of Pat Buchanan's American First conservatism. For a time, I believed this myself. But over the years I've met too many conservatives who violently disagree with Kemp's grafting of politics onto the game. And I've heard too many liberals take their shots at soccer, people who write for such publications as the *Village* and couldn't be plausibly grouped in the troglodyte camp of American politics. So if hatred of soccer has nothing to do with politics, conventionally defined, why do so many Americans feel threatened by the beautiful game?

For years, I have been collecting a file on this anti-soccer lobby. The person whose material mounts highest in my collection is the wildly popular radio shock jock Jim Rome. Rome arrived on the national scene in the mid-nineties and built an audience based on his self-congratulatory flouting of social norms. Rome has created his own subculture that has enraptured a broad swath of American males. They are united by their own vernacular, a Walter Winchell-like form of slang that Rome calls "smack," derived in part from the African American street and in part from the fraternity house. An important part of this subculture entails making fun of the people who aren't members of it. Rome can be cruelly cutting to callers who don't pass his muster, who talk the wrong king of smack or freeze up on air. These put-downs form a large chunk of his programs. The topics of his rants include such far-ranging subject matter as the quackery of chiropractors, cheap seafood restaurants, and, above all, soccer.

Where specific events trigger most soccer hating—a World Cup, news of hooligan catastrophes that arrive over the wires—Rome doesn't need a proximate cause to break into a tirade. He lets randomly rip with invective. "My son is not playing soccer. I will hand him ice skates and a shimmering sequined blouse before I hand him a soccer ball. Soccer is not a sport, does not need to be on TV, and my son will not be playing it." In moments of honesty, he more or less admits his illogic. "If it's incredibly stupid and soccer is in any way related, then soccer must be the root cause [of the stupidity]," he said in one segment, where he attacked the sporting goods manufacturer Umbro for putting out a line of clothing called Zyklon, the same name as the Auschwitz gas. (Zyklon translates as cyclone. By his logic, the words "concentration" or "camp" should be purged from conversational English for their Holocaust associations.) He often inadvertently endorses some repulsive arguments. One segment ripped into African soccer teams for deploying witch doctors. "So you can add this to the laundry list of reasons why I hate soccer," he frothed.

Such obvious flaws make it seem he is proud of his crassness, and that would be entirely in keeping with character. These arguments would be more easily dismissed were they the product of a single demented individual. But far smarter minds have devolved down to Rome's level. Allen Barra, a sportswriter for the *Wall Street Journal*, is one of these smarter minds. Usually, Barra distinguishes himself from his colleagues by making especially rarified, sharp arguments that follow clearly from the facts and have evidence backing his provocative claims. But on soccer, he slips from his moorings. He writes, "Yes, OK, soccer is the most 'popular' game in the world. And rice is the most 'popular' food in the world. So what? Maybe other countries can't afford football, basketball and baseball leagues: maybe if they could afford these other sports, they'd enjoy them even more."

Unlike Rome, Barra has some sense of why he flies off the handle on this subject. It has to do with his resentment of the game's yuppie promoters. He argues, "Americans are such suckers when it comes to something with a European label that many who have resisted thus far would give in to trendiness and push their kids into youth soccer programs." And more than that, he worried that the soccer enthusiasts want the U.S. to "get with the rest of the world's program."

As Barra makes clear, the anti-soccer lobby really articulates the same fears as Eurico Miranda and Alan Garrison, a phobia of globalization. To understand their fears, it is important to note that both Barra and Rome are proud aficionados of baseball. The United States, with its unashamedly dynamic culture, doesn't have too many deeply rooted, transgenerational traditions that it can claim as its own. Baseball is one of the few.

That's one reason why the game gets so much nostalgia-drenched celebration in Kevin Costner movies and Stephen Jay Gould books.

But Major League Baseball, let's face it, has been a loser in globalization. Unlike the NBA or NFL, it hasn't made the least attempt to market itself to a global audience. And the global audience has shown no hunger for the game. Because baseball failed to master the global economy, it has been beat back by it. According to the Sporting Goods Manufacturers Association of America, the number of teens playing baseball fell 47 percent between 1987 and 2000. During that same period, youth soccer grew exponentially. By 2002, 1.3 million more kids played soccer than Little League. And the demographic profile of baseball has grown ever more lily white. It has failed to draw African Americans and attracts few Latinos who didn't grow up playing the game in the Caribbean. The change can also be registered in the ballot box that matters most. Nielsen ratings show that, in most years, a World Series can no longer draw the same number of viewers as an inconsequential Monday night game in the NFL.

It's not surprising that Americans should split like this over soccer. Globalization increasingly provides the subtext for the American cultured split. This isn't to say America violently or even knowingly divides over globalization. But after September 11 opened new debates over foreign policy, two camps in American politics have clearly emerged. One camp believes in the essential tenets of the globalization religion as preached by European politicians that national governments should defer to institutions like the UN and WTO. These tend to be people who opposed the war in Iraq. And this opinion reflects a worldview. These Americans share cultural values with Europeans—an aggressive secularism, a more relaxed set of cultural mores that tolerates gays and pot smoking—which isn't surprising, considering that these Americans have jobs and tourist interests that put them in regular contact with the other side of the Atlantic. They consider themselves to be part of a cosmopolitan culture that transcends national boundaries.

On the other side, there is a group that believes in "American exceptionalism," an idea that America's history and singular form of government has given the nation a unique role to play in the world; that the U.S. should be above submitting to international laws and bodies. They view Europeans as degraded by their lax attitudes, and worry about the threat to American culture posed by secular tolerance. With so much relativism seeping into the American way of life, they fret that the country has lost the self-confidence to make basic moral judgments, to condemn evil. Soccer isn't exactly pernicious, but it's a symbol of the U.S. junking its tradition to "get with the rest of the world's program."

There are many conservatives who hate relativism, consider the French wussy, and still adore soccer. But it's not a coincidence that the game has become a small touchstone in this culture war.

III.

I wish that my side, the yuppie soccer fans, were blameless victims in these culture wars. But I've been around enough of America's soccer cognoscenti to know that they invite abuse. They are inveterate snobs, so snobbish, in fact, that they think nothing of turning against their comrades. According to their sneering critique, their fellow fans are dilettantes without any real understanding of the game; they are yuppies who admire soccer like a fine slab of imported goat cheese; they come from neighborhoods with spectacularly high Starbucks-per-capita, so they lack any semblance of burning working-class passion.

This self-loathing critique can be easily debunked. I've seen counterevidence with my own eyes. In the spring of 2001, the U.S. national team played Honduras in Washington's Robert Francis Kennedy stadium. This vital World Cup qualifying match had generated the packed, exuberant stadium that the occasion deserved. Fans wore their nation's jersey. Their singing and stomping caused the steel and concrete to undulate like the Mexican wave. In a country with lesser engineering standards, it would have been time to worry about a stadium collapse. On the field, stewards scampered to pick up scattered sneakers. Fans had removed them and thrown them at the opposing goalkeeper, a small gesture of homage to the madness of Glasgow and the passion of Barcelona. They mercilessly booed the linesman, softening him up by insulting his slut of a mother. It might not have quite ascended to the atmospheric wonders of a game played by the English nation team, but it wasn't far from that mark.

There is, however, an important difference between a home game in London and Washington. The majority of English fans will root for England. In Washington, more or less half the stadium wore the blue-and-white Honduran jersey, and they were the ones who shouted themselves hoarse and heaved their shoes. The American aspiration of appearing in the World Cup rested on this game. But on that day, the Washington stadium might as well have been in Tegucigalpa.

Traveling through Europe, you hear the same complaint repeated over and over: Americans are so "hyper-nationalistic." But is there any country in the world that would tolerate such animosity to their national team in their own national capital? In England or France or Italy, this would have been cause for unleashing hooligan hell.

Nor were the American fans what you'd expect of a hegemonic power. The *Washington Post* had published a message from the national soccer federation urging us to wear red shirts as a sign of support—and to clearly distinguish ourselves from the Hondurans. But most American soccer fans don't possess a red USA jersey and aren't about to go down to the sporting goods store to buy one. They do, however, own red Arsenal, Man U., and Ajax jerseys, or, in my case, an old Barcelona one, that they collected on continental travels. While we were giving a patriotic boost, we couldn't help revealing our Europhilic cosmopolitanism.

I mention this scene because many critics of globalization make America the wicked villain in the tale. They portray the U.S. forcing Nike, McDonald's and *Baywatch* down the throats of the unwilling world, shredding ancient cultures for the sake of empire and cash. But that version of events skirts the obvious truth: Multinational corporations are just that, multinational; they don't represent American interests or American culture. Just as much as they have changed the tastes and economies of other countries, they have tried to change the tastes and economy of the United States. Witness the Nike and Budweiser campaigns to sell soccer here. No other country has been as subjected to the free flows of capital and labor, so constantly remade by migration, and found its national identity so constantly changed. In short, America may be an exception, but it is not exceptionally immune to globalization. And we fight about it, whether we know it or not, just like everyone else.

What are the culture wars, as defined by Foer in this chapter, and how does soccer "explain" them? What arguments and evidence does Foer provide in support of his claims? How do you as a reader respond to his theory? Are you convinced? Why or why not?

In an unlikely twist, Foer actually defends America in the "globalization debate" by arguing that America's unease with soccer reflects a distrust of how globalization, and its multinational corporations, is changing American culture. He says that soccer is essentially "Anti-American." Do you agree or disagree? What tensions do you have with globalization? How do you understand globalization changing American culture and tastes? To further explore this issue, you might watch the film *Bend It Like Beckham* from the filmography and reflect on this argument from a different cultural perspective.

In small groups, explore the ways in which globalization impacts a particular "American" sporting culture: baseball, football, basketball. Browse the web, sports magazines, and sports columns in newspapers for articles, advertisements, and other signs of globalization's impact on the sport and assemble a collage of sorts—digital or hardcopy—and share your findings in class. Which other sports seem affected by globalization? Is this relationship viewed as positive or negative, and by whom? Are there some sports that seem more American than others, and what role does globalization seem to play in this process?

David Halberstam is a Pulitzer Prize-winning author of 12 bestsellers, including Summer of '49 *and* Playing for Keeps: Michael Jordan and the World He Made. *One of the most anthologized sports writers of our time, Halberstam also served as editor of the* The Best American Sports Writing of the Century *series. Occasionally, he wrote for ESPN's Page 2, the syndicate's early sports blog where literary titans like Hunter S. Thompson and Ralph Wiley weighed in on sport and culture. The following "post" is a sobering retrospective written by Halberstam a year out from Sept. 11 on the potential and limits of sport in the aftermath of tragedy.*

SPORTS CAN DISTRACT, BUT THEY DON'T HEAL

By David Halberstam

The question before us today is sports and tragedy, most particularly Sept. 11. Is there a connection, and how important is it? Does the world of sports heal, and does it make us stronger, and give us precious, badly needed relief from the darker concerns and burdens of our lives, as so many people (most of them connected to the world of sports, and therefore with no small amount of vested interest) keep saying?

We should be so lucky as to have something as simple as sports to offer relief from the grimmest of life's realities.

I have my doubts…strong ones, as a matter of fact. Serious readers of this space will note that I disappeared from it for some 10 months after Sept. 11, largely because I could not find it in me for a long time to want to write about sports. That world seemed to shrink on me overnight. Instead, I wrote about the men of our local firehouse, 12 of whom had perished on that apocalyptic day. So, along with my doubts, I have my prejudices.

I like sports, enjoy the artistry of them enormously. I love to watch great athletes compete against each other in big games or matches, like Sampras beating Agassi in the U.S. Open final. But I think there is an important faultline out there somewhere: The world of sports is the world of sports, and reality is reality.

Sometimes sports mirrors society, sometimes it allows us to understand the larger society a little better. But mostly, it is a world of entertainment, of talented and driven young men and women who do certain things with both skill and passion. I am always amused at playoff time by those obsessive superfans, who cast the players from their home team as the good guys, and the visitors as evil—they hate the opposing players and do not understand that, in most circumstances, the players they root for are closer to the players they hate than they are to their adoring fans, and would almost surely rather go out for dinner with the alleged enemy than they would with the home-team fans.

I am wary, as well, of those people who say after a given World Series or Super Bowl victory that it saved the city, made it whole and healed deep-seated racial grievances. When I hear things like that—and I often do—I usually think, "I'll give it about two weeks before it all unheals." In truth, if making your city whole demands a World Series victory on behalf of athletes who more often than not flee the city the moment the season is over, then your problems are probably harder to solve than you realize.

Nor did I think, during the Vietnam years, that the link between the NFL and the Pentagon (all those jet fighters flying overhead at the Super Bowl) greatly helped the war effort, nor factored into the WVA or the Viet Cong's schedules. I was not much moved by the Army's television recruitment commercials showing teamwork between NFL players, who most demonstrably had no intention of serving in the military.

So back to the question at hand—did sports help bind us in the days, weeks and months after Sept. 11? Did we need to be so bound? The answer to the first question is, I suspect, a little bit, and my answer to the second is, I fear, surprisingly negative. If, in the long run, you need sports to help you through a time of tragedy and to take your mind off a grimmer reality, then you are emotionally in so much trouble in not understanding what is real and what is fantasy that the prospects for your long-term emotional health are probably not very good.

Let me suggest that there are notable exceptions to this, and that many of us, at one time or another, have gotten some kind of lift—albeit usually a brief one—from the performance of a favorite sports team on an unusual roll. I am a New Yorker, and there is no doubt that in all the pain and grief that followed the assault on the World Trade Center, the last-minute run of the Yankees—particularly some of the late-inning rallies in the World Series—were unusually sweet, that for a short period of time, they lifted many people in the city, including a great number (such as my wife, who usually does not care very much). It was an aging Yankee team, trying for one last hurrah, the starting pitching was wearing a bit thin—as were some of the left-handed hitters—but it made one last wonderful run. I suspect the city boosted the team and the team, in turn, boosted the city. It surely made The Stadium a more difficult place to play for some of the visiting teams.

But for all the sportscasters who tried to push the point too hard, that the grief and passion of New York lifted the local athletes, we have these other reminders: the dismal performances of the Giants (just a year removed from a Super Bowl appearance) and, all too soon, the even more dismal performance of a Knicks team that openly cheated its fan base—the sorriest performance by a local basketball team in the 35 years in which I had paid attention.

So, if there is a connection, it is likely to be a thin one. In my own case, I can remember one particular time in my life when a sports team made something of a difference in my overall mood.

It was in September and October 1967. I was in Vietnam on my second tour as a reporter. More than 500,000 U.S. troops were in the country, and I was in a terrible mood. I thought the war was stalemated, which meant we were eventually going to lose because it was their country, and sooner or later we would have to go home—those of us who would be lucky enough to get that chance. More, I hated what I saw about me every day—all the lying from the Saigon press officers—and I hated what it told me about my beloved country back home, which was, for me, becoming harder to love at that moment.

That happened to be, by chance, the year that Carl Yastrzemski played so brilliantly in September to lead the Red Sox to the pennant. So I would go every morning (there was, as I recall, a 12-hour time difference) to the AP office in downtown Saigon where the baseball news and box scores would come in, clicking slowly over the old-fashioned teletype. And I would watch for Yaz, and he never seemed to disappoint—3-for-5, one home run, three RBIs. And of course, a great catch.

I was joined there every day by Tom Durant, a Boston native who was over there working as a doctor. It was the beginning of a lifelong friendship with a man who was as close to being a contemporary saint as any man I've ever know. He devoted his entire career to bringing desperately needed medical care to people in Third World countries. Doc Durant died last year, and I, like thousands of others, mourned him; we were, it seemed, bonded by Vietnam, the 1967 baseball season and Yaz's ability, and thus able to feel a little better about our country. When we saw each other, even in the 1990s, we thought about Yaz in 1967. But moments like this are rare—a brief bit of sunshine in an otherwise difficult setting. If it's a fix, it's a momentary one at best.

In truth, our lives are what we make of them. We work hard and, at the end of the day, in a world that is often mundane, the ability to watch one or two sports games a week is a kind of blessing, a relief from what is often a difficult routine. But if we want any kind of real emotional balance, we must get it from our loved ones, family, friends, co-workers.

That's what I think is at stake here. The parallel between what sports does for the country now and what it did during World War II is, I think, the wrong one. The America of 1941-45 was more of a Calvinist nation, with far less in the way of entertainment. Baseball—poorly played as it was, with aging Veterans and lots of minor-leaguers—was a small bit of normalcy in a nation where almost everyone's life had been profoundly changed by the war. People's lives were much harder, and almost the entire nation was making a national effort which demanded considerable sacrifice. There was radio, but no television, and a family going off together to a movie was a rare treat. So it was completely different from the America that exists today. In those days, we badly needed every respite we could get from the reality of the war, especially in the first year when the news was systematically bad. We needed some limited degree of diversion.

But today it's completely different. We live in an entertainment society. There is little around us but diversion—even people trying to broadcast the news have to make it ever quicker, simpler and more entertaining in order to compete with rival channels. Many people have television sets with 200 channels. Video games and computer games abound. The sports glut remains exactly that—a glut. We watch what has become a never-ending season—football in the summer, baseball in November, basketball, it sometimes seems, throughout the year.

We lead lives surrounded by diversions. The manufacturers of our fantasies—in Hollywood with movies and television, and of course in the world of sports—are more powerful and influential than ever. Keeping the nation tuned to serious concerns is infinitely harder than it was 60 years ago. Diversion comes more readily.

After Sept. 11, there was a relatively short span of time when people cared about foreign news and were momentarily weaned away from their more parochial concerns. But now it's largely back to normal. There might be, in the back of the minds of millions of people, a certain uneasiness a year after Sept. 11, because we know that America is no longer invulnerable, and that we can be attacked.

But in truth, the events themselves touched a very small percentage of the population. Unlike World War II, we operate with an elite, highly professional military that comes from very few homes. Almost no one else has been asked to sacrifice—there is no rationing, and the contemporary U.S. economy is so different from the one 60 years ago that the president's main request to the American people was to ask us to travel more, presumably because the airline industry was so shaky.

HOUSTON TEXANS FANS

Could it be the more obsessive the fan, the emptier his or her lives are?

As for the families who were actually touched by this tragedy, I would not presume to speak for them—they are eloquent enough in their own behalf. But the idea that their lives are in any way better because of what a given sports team did in the following months is barely worth mentioning.

In truth, our lives are what we make of them. We work hard and, at the end of the day, in a world that is often mundane, the ability to watch one or two sports games a week is a kind of blessing, a relief from what is often a difficult routine. But if we want any kind of real emotional balance, we must get it from our loved ones, family, friends, co-workers.

I am made uneasy by those who seem to need sports too much, these crazed superfans who bring such obsessive behavior to games where complete strangers compete. There is an equation at work here: The more obsessive they are as fans, the emptier I suspect their real lives are.

And so let me descend in advance from all the sportscasters and all the blathering that's going to go on in the next few days about the importance of sports after Sept. 11. Many of these sportscasters will push the importance and restorative qualities of sports. Let me suggest that we will do well in the current and difficult crisis not because the 49ers, Cowboys or Patriots do well, but rather if as a nation we are strong, wise and patient. That's all it really takes.

Sept. 11 is an experience rife with emotional discord. How does Halberstam attend to the conventions of writing and language in his post to create a particular tone and mood in accordance with a retrospective? What particular sentences and turns of phrase stand out as effective to you and why? How does Halberstam's tone affect you as a reader? Do you trust Halberstam? Why or why not? Are you convinced by his argument? What do you find compelling about his balance of tone with argument?

Halberstam writes about sport and 9/11 from the perspective of a seasoned sports writer who has seen both the world of sport and American culture change dramatically over the years. However, many of us were much younger when 9/11 happened. Write a reflective journal response (about 500 words) in which you reflect on the following: Where were you on Sept. 11? How old were you? Do you have any memory of the Yankees' World Series run? What other memories do you have of Sept. 11 and how do these memories relate to Halberstam's arguments about the limits and potentials of sport to distract and heal after a tragedy?

Watch the documentary *9 Innings to Ground Zero* and discuss as a class how the film relates to Halberstam's argument. Where do the two perspectives agree and where do they disagree? How do you feel about sport's role in historical moments like 9/11?

Halberstam argues that it is wrong to compare the relationship between sports and 9/11 to that of sports during World War II, citing how much has changed over the years, particularly Americans' availability to distraction and entertainment (mostly via television), and our overall ease of life compared to people growing up during the aftermath of World War II. Do you agree or disagree with Halberstam? In a small group, discuss the different perspectives on the use of sports and healing. Why can we or can't we compare the use of sports to heal during World War II to that of post 9/11? What are the limits and potentials of sport after a tragedy and how do your experiences shape your understanding of the situation?

This exercise will prepare you for Major Assignment #1: The Sports Memoir. Halberstam notes it is rare and limited when sports can have a meaningful experience for someone, citing his experiences as a journalist in Vietnam when he found respite in the Red Sox's race to the pennant with his colleague, Doctor Durant. Have you ever had a memorable or meaningful experience with sport? Why or why not? Write an essay in which you reflect on a time in which sports played a particularly meaningful role, either as a fan or a player. Where were you? How old were you? Who else was there with you? What did sports mean to you? What team in particular were you following/playing for? And why was sport so important to you at that time? If sports haven't been meaningful in your life, write an essay in which you reflect on why and how these ideas relate to Halberstam's arguments in his *Page 2* feature story.

In this speech, which won the 2008 Zeigler Award, Lucie Thibault outlines four inconvenient truths about the relationship between sport, its management, and globalization. The Zeigler Award is the most prestigious honor in the North American Society for Sport Management.

THE GLOBALIZATION OF SPORT: AN INCONVENIENT TRUTH

By Lucie Thibault

The purpose of the 2008 Earle F. Zeigler Lecture was to highlight some of the issues involved in the globalization of sport that affect the field of sport management. In particular, four issues were presented: a division of labor undertaken on an international scale where transnational corporations are drawing on developing countries' work forces to manufacture sportswear and sport equipment; the increasing flow of athletes where country of birth and origin are no longer a limitation on where an athlete plays and competes; the increased involvement of global media conglomerates in sport; and the impact of sport on the environment. The impact and inconvenient truths of these issues on sport management were addressed.

"When academics write about sports, they are capable of accomplishing the impossible: sucking all the pleasure and fun from the spectacle" (Foer, 2006, p. 86). I begin with this quotation because I believe that, that is, in part, what I am about to do in this paper. I chose to discuss the globalization of sport for the Earle F. Zeigler Lecture for a number of reasons. First, although the topic has been addressed by our colleagues in sport sociology (cf. Andrew & Grainger, 2007; Bairner, 2005; Hargreaves, 2002; Harvey, Rail, & Thibault, 1996; Maguire, 1999, 2005), it has not been extensively studied by sport management and sport policy scholars. Some exceptions include the work of Allison (2005), Henry and [the] Institute of Sport and Leisure Policy (2007), Houlihan (1994, 1999), Mason (2002), Mason and Duquette (2005), Means and Nauright (2007), and Wheeler and Nauright (2006). As well, a number of textbooks and chapters aimed at sport management students

From *The Journal of Sport Management* (2009).

on the importance of globalization in sport management have been published (cf. Fay & Snyder, 2007; Gratton & Leberman, 2006; Thoma & Chalip, 1996; Westerbeek & Smith, 2003). These works have all addressed issues of global governance and the marketplace in an era of global prominence. Second, it is clear that a number of controversial issues affecting professional and 'amateur' sports are global—for example, the use of performance enhancing drugs, the migration of athletes and coaches, the environmental impact, the use of developing countries' workforce for the production of sportswear and sport equipment, and the general commodification and commercialization of sports in society. Third, there are a number of sport organizations that yield a great deal of power in the world. Organizations such as the Fédération Internationale de Football Association (FIFA), the International Olympic Committee (IOC), and the National Basketball Association (NBA) play an important role in the 'new sport world order.' Finally, it is increasingly imperative for sport management students to understand globalization and its impact on sport as they embark on careers in the field.

Although globalization has led to positive outcomes in sport management, it also presents important drawbacks that must be understood and respected. At the very least, sport management students should be sensitized to issues of multilingualism, multiculturalism, and multidisciplinarity in the delivery of sport in a global context. Before addressing these issues, it is important to define globalization. For the purposes of this paper, I have relied on Robertson's (1992) interpretation of globalization, that is, the consolidation of the world into a whole space—in other words, a "global community" (p. 9). Robertson (1992) further explains that globalization is "the compression of the world and the intensification of consciousness of the world as a whole" (p. 8).

In the numerous works on globalization, several factors have been identified as playing a key role in the increasing movement toward globalization (cf. Marchak, 1991; Robertson & White, 2007; Teeple, 2000; Thomas, 2007; Wolf, 2004). These factors include: pressures from transnational corporations, international capital, neoliberal economies, and right-wing governments where markets have become deregulated and trade relations among countries have increased (Marchak, 1991; Teeple, 2000; Thomas, 2007; Wolf, 2004). In addition, progress in communication technologies has enhanced the ability of exchange among individuals, organizations, and governments. All this, in turn, has contributed to globalization in the political, economic, social, and cultural spheres (Neverdeen Pieterse, 1994; Robertson & White, 2007). The focus of these spheres has been addressed in various contexts: politics and international governance, economics, business, media and technology, health, education, development, environment, and culture, to name a few (cf. Ritzer, 2007). Sport has not been excluded from these discussions of the application of the political, economic, social, and cultural spheres (cf. Andrews & Grainger, 2007; Giulianotti & Robertson, 2007a, 2007b; Harvey & Houle, 1994; Harvey et al., 1996; Taylor, 1988; Wright, 1999).

In the context of sport, Tomlinson and Young (2006) and others (cf. Wertheim, 2004; Westerbeek & Smith, 2003) remind us that the FIFA is more 'global' than the United Nations (UN) since the FIFA has a membership of 208 countries while the UN's membership is 192 countries (cf. FIFA, 2008; UN, 2008).[1] Along similar lines, the IOC is also larger in scope than the United Nations. Giulianotti and Robertson (2007a, 2007b) note that "Olympism has a global political reach, with 203 National Olympic Committees affiliated to the IOC, giving 11 more national members than the United Nations" (p. 108).[2]

Tomlinson and Young (2006) write "in participatory terms, the World Cup and the Olympics offer a platform to all nations, and most of all to small nations of the world, that is unrivaled by any other cultural or political body, even the United Nations" (p. 2). Sport is so prominent in the world that the Vatican set up a sports department in August 2004 under the leadership of the late Pope John Paul II. In the announcement of this sports initiative, a spokesperson from the Vatican notes that "the church…is called upon without doubt to pay attention to sports, which certainly can be considered one of the nerve centers of contemporary culture and one of the frontiers for new evangelization" (The Associated Press, 2004, paragraph 7).

In many ways, globalization has been beneficial for sport. Among the evidence, I note the spread of sports throughout the world: the diversity in athletes' origins participating in many of the professional leagues around the world (e.g., the Ladies Professional Golf Association, the Association of Tennis Professionals, the Women's Tennis Association, the NBA, and the English Premier League). Also noteworthy is the increasing number of countries participating in international sport events. For example, Azerbaijan, Kenya, the Former Yugoslav Republic of Macedonia, Uruguay, and Venezuela participated in their first Olympic Winter Games in 1998 in Nagano, Japan (cf. International Olympic Committee, 2008a). In addition, an increasing number of athletes are participating in a diverse range of sports often crossing some gender and religious lines and climate barriers. For example, Muslim women participating in sport such as rugby and football; the gold medal victory of Nawal El Moutawakel[3] from Morocco in 400-meter hurdles at the 1984 Olympic Games in Los Angeles; the participation of Jamaican athletes in bobsleigh at the 1988 Olympic Winter Games in Calgary; the Australian gold medal victory (i.e., Steven Bradbury) in short track speed skating at the 2002 Olympic Winter Games in Salt Lake City; and an increased access to winter sports in tropical climates (e.g., in the countries of Dubai, Indonesia, Malaysia, and Taiwan) via snow domes where sports such

---

1 These membership numbers are based on 2008 data.
2 As of May 2008, the IOC reported a total membership of 205 National Olympic Committees (NOC). Each NOC represents one country (International Olympic Committee, 2008b). Given the membership for the United Nations in May 2008 (i.e., 192 countries), the IOC has 13 more member-countries than the UN.
3 Nawal El Moutawakel was the first woman from Africa to win a gold medal at the Olympic Games. She was also the first Muslim woman and the first Arab woman to win gold at the Games (cf. Hargreaves, 2000).

as downhill skiing, snowboarding, and ice skating take place indoors. The evidence also includes the increasing opportunities athletes, coaches, and leaders have been able to access because of the global nature of sport.

In praising the virtues of globalization and sport, Wilsey (2006, p. 47) argues that football (i.e., soccer) is "unique in its ability to bridge differences and overturn national prejudices." As evidence, the author uses one example of the collaboration that took place among the two host nations for the 2002 FIFA World Cup. It is no secret that the occupation of South Korea by Japan between 1910 and 1945 led to strong tensions between the two countries. As Wilsey (2006) explains,

> In less than half a century South Korea had gone from not allowing the Japanese national team to cross its borders for a World Cup qualifier, to co-hosting the tournament … Give the world another 50 years and we might see the Cup co-hosted by Israel and Palestine. (p. 47)

On the topic of relations between Israel and Palestine, grassroot sport programs such as Building Bridges Basketball Camp and Playing for Peace have been developed as strategies towards peace, collaboration, and unity among youth of these nations (Ford, 2006a, 2006b; International Platform on Sport and Development, 2005; Quinn, 2006). There is no shortage of examples of the 'power' of sport to bring people together. Several authors have discussed the global appeal of sport and the power of sport to transcend borders, culture, language, gender, race, religion, and socio-economic status (cf. Andrews & Grainger, 2007; Miller, Lawrence, McKay, & Rowe, 2001; Thoma & Chalip, 1996; Wertheim, 2004). As Miller et al. (2001) explain, "sport is probably the most universal aspect of popular culture" (p. 1). Along similar lines, Riordan and Krüger (1999) argue that defenders or promoters of sport, at the turn of the twentieth century, could not have predicted the power sport leaders and sport organizations would have in influencing "social and cultural life, in politics and economics" (p. ix). In a concrete example of the power of international sport, several sport researchers would identify the 1995 Rugby World Cup held in South Africa where Nelson Mandela shared in the victory of the South African Springbok team against the New Zealand All Blacks (cf. Crawford, 1999; Moodley & Adam, 2000; Steenveld & Strelitz, 1998). As Crawford (1999, p. 134) explains, "Mandela's presence and persona at the 1995 World Cup were a spellbinding moment, a fragment of transcendent time in which a country with a bitter history of racism, bigotry, and oppression displayed bright hopes and youthful optimism." South Africa Springbok's World Cup victory not only led to a successful nation-building achievement, it put the country of South Africa and the new anti-apartheid regime on the global map.

Sport has always included an international dimension but this dimension appears to have intensified. The evidence that sport is globalized is uncontestable. For example, Wright (1999) notes the increased involvement of global media conglomerates (e.g., Disney,

News Corporation, Time Warner) in acquiring sport properties (i.e., franchises, leagues, sport stadia); the growth of international sport management firms (e.g., IMG) and their involvement in all facets of sport events from the management of athletes, the creation of events, and the media production of these events; transnational corporations in the sport industry drawing on developing countries' work force to produce sportswear and sport equipment; international sport federations that are increasingly finding new sources of capital from the sale of broadcasting rights (e.g., IOC, FIFA, IAAF); and the increasing flow of athletes and coaches where country of birth and origin are no longer a limitation on where an athlete plays or where a coach coaches.

In the academic context, there has been an increase in sport management programs in universities and colleges worldwide and in the number of organizations at the continental and regional levels and within countries (e.g., North America, Europe, Australia and New Zealand, Asia). There has also been a proliferation in the number of journals related to the management and business of sport originating from various countries (e.g., Europe, Australia, and New Zealand, Egypt and Arab, Asia, France, Japan, Korea) (cf. Thibault, 2007). Evidence of the globalization of sport, it seems, is all around us.

As you have noticed, *the inconvenient truth* is part of the title of this article. What is *this inconvenient truth*? The *inconvenient truth* is that although there are many virtues associated with the global movement in sport, globalization has not been favorable for all. In fact, some argue that the globalization of sport has been achieved at the expense of individuals, organizations, and countries with limited resources (cf. Foer, 2006; Play Fair at the Olympics, 2004; Sage, 2005; Wertheim, 2004). The globalization of sport may, in large part, have been achieved on the backs of the poor.

> For all its virtues, globalization [is] not without its drawbacks: widening chasms between rich and poor societies, plummeting environmental standards and increasing dependence on outsourcing. Peril [is] riding tandem with so much promise. Which is to say, globalization is like sports: For all the winners there are necessarily, losers as well. (Wertheim, 2005, p. 79)

For the purposes of this article, I will address the inconvenient truths for the following four elements: a division of labor undertaken on an international scale where transnational corporations (TNCs) are drawing on developing countries' work force to manufacture sportswear and sport equipment; the increasing flow of athletes where country of birth and origin are no longer a limitation on where an athlete plays and competes; the increased involvement of global media conglomerates such as Disney, News Corporation, Time Warner, Vivendi Universal, and Bertelsmann AG in sport; and the impact of sport on the environment. There are many more issues related to the globalization of sport but I believe these issues capture fundamental problems and inconvenient truths associated with the globalization of sport. Labor issues are addressed in the first two elements of this article. The first part of labor issues is focused on developing nations' manufacturing of sportswear and sport equipment for consumers of developed nations.

LABOR ISSUES PART 1: THE USE OF DEVELOPING NATIONS' WORKFORCE BY TNC'S FOR THE PRODUCTION OF SPORTSWEAR AND SPORT EQUIPMENT

In the sport industry, the production of goods is largely achieved in developing countries through the use of subcontractors hired by major corporations such as Nike, Adidas, Puma, and Fila. The workforce responsible for the production of these sporting goods endures, to this day, pitiful working conditions. Even with public pressure originating from special interest groups such as the International Labor Organization, the Worker Rights Consortium, and Fair Labor Association based in developed countries (cf. Hussain-Khaliq, 2004; Sage, 1999, 2005), TNCs are still complicit in perpetuating the poor working conditions in the factories. Even though TNCs have developed codes of conduct and ethical guidelines, these codes and guidelines have not, for the most part, translated into real positive changes in the operations of subcontractors and the treatment of workers in developing countries (cf. Adams, 2002; Lim & Phillips, 2008; Maquila Solidarity Network, 2008; Play Fair at the Olympics, 2004). TNCs have to assume part of the responsibility for the low wages, long hours, lack of job security, and dismal and dangerous working conditions. As noted in the Play Fair at the Olympics (2004) report:

> If (labour) exploitation were an Olympic sport, the sportswear giants would be well represented among the medal winners. While the industry can boast its commitment to some impressive principles, enshrined in codes of conduct, its business practices generate the market pressures that are in reality leading to exploitative labour conditions. The consequence is that millions of workers are being locked into poverty and denied a fair share of the wealth that they generate. (p. 4)

In addition, the employees of these factories do not have the time to participate in sports nor do they have the resources to buy the products they create. As Sage (2005, p. 363) notes, "it is their labor that allows all of us to play, watch, coach, and administer sports. Their labor, in effect, is the very foundation of our sporting experience." This fact is often forgotten as we individually and collectively benefit from our involvement in sport.

Transnational corporations in the sport industry have experienced important increases in their profits in recent years (cf. Laurent, 2008; Ram, 2007; Rusli, 2007). These TNCs have also been involved in multi-million dollar deals to sponsor sport teams, leagues, and/or events and pay athletes millions of dollars to endorse their brands and products. While these TNCs are investing in the marketing of their brands, they have been slow to invest in the enhancement of working conditions and wages of employees in the factories. In fact, some argue (cf. Lim & Phillips, 2008; Maquila Solidarity Network, 2008; Play Fair at the Olympics, 2004) that the [traditional] business model is encouraging the status quo. As outlined in the report Play Fair at the Olympics (2004), the business model is

> based upon ruthless pressure on prices, a demand for fast and flexible delivery, and a constant shift in manufacturing locations in pursuance of ever-cheaper production costs. Global sportswear companies link millions of workers to consumer markets via long supply-chains and complex networks of factories and contractors. Market power enables global companies to demand that their suppliers cut prices, shorten delivery times, and adjust rapidly to fluctuating orders. Inevitably, the resulting pressures are transmitted down the supply-chain to workers, leading to lower wages, bad conditions, and the violation of workers' rights. (p. 5)

In their study on Nike and its corporate social responsibility initiatives, Lim and Phillips (2008, p. 152) also conclude that the implementation of the code of conduct "was hampered because Nike utilized the market-oriented production system." They further explain the importance of partnerships between suppliers and contractors in order to encourage compliance with Nike's code of conduct. The production of sport-related goods is a complex process involving a number of stakeholders. In their position at the top of the production chain, TNCs operating in the sport industry have the power to make a difference in improving the work conditions of employees who produce the sportswear and sport equipment. Unfortunately, evidence of achieving this is very limited. This issue will be further discussed at the end of the article. In the following section, the migration of athletes is examined as another labor issue in the globalization of sport that is worthy of consideration.

LABOR ISSUES PART 2: THE MIGRATION OF ATHLETES

In the context of a global economy, the free movement of workers between countries is not unusual. In fact, in many cases, it is encouraged. In sport, the migration of athletes refers to the movement of athletes from one country to another, generally to access more resources whether it is financial compensation or better coaching, equipment, and support services for their sport involvement (Bale, 1990; Bale & Maguire, 1994; Lafranchi & Taylor, 2001; Weston, 2006). Migration may also occur to facilitate the athlete's achievement of his/her ultimate goal of being selected to a country's Olympic team or signing on to a professional league. In the recruitment of international athletes in the National Collegiate Athletic Association (NCAA), Weston (2006) writes:

Player movement in international athletics is, essentially, sports' version of free trade. The global connection through sport and the increasing presence of international athletes are generally welcome and beneficial. The expanded market of talent increases the quality of competition for the consumer fan and the strength of athletic programs at colleges and universities. (p. 831)

Although athlete migration has been favorable for the coaches, teams, leagues, organizations, and nations benefiting from the access to better talent, it has also been identified as problematic (Bale & Maguire, 1994; Bale & Sang, 1996; Lafranchi & Taylor, 2001; Milanovic, 2005; Nafziger, 1988; Weston, 2006). For example, concerns over the massive exodus of Kenyan athletes to other countries and the drain on their talent pool have been raised by Kenyan officials when eight Kenyans migrated "to the affluent Persian Gulf nations of Qatar and Bahrain…Qatar and Bahrain lured the athletes with promises of generous benefits and lifetime pensions" (Carlson, 2004, p. D1). When a developing country's investment in its sport system are reaped by other countries (often affluent developed nations), it is disconcerting. Although Kenyan athletes who migrated have personally benefitted from the opportunities offered by Qatar and Bahrain, Kenya's sport system was 'deskilled' with the loss of these athletes (Maguire & Bale, 1994).

Increasingly, countries' sport leaders appear to be involved in the recruitment of athletes from other countries in order to be competitive in international sport events.[4] For example, prior to the 2006 Torino Olympic Winter Games, leaders from the Former Yugoslav Republic of Macedonia were recruiting Canadian talent (with Macedonian heritage) to field their Olympic team (Kingston, 2005). Citizenship and affiliation are, it appears, easily exchanged for the right sport skills and abilities. As noted by Weston (2006), the IOC has a rule that addresses nationality where athletes are required to "be citizens of the country which they represent in the [Olympic] Games. Despite this, application of nationality rules becomes dubious when countries grant citizenship to star foreign athletes on the eve of the Games" (p. 837). Along the same lines, Nafziger (1988) also identifies as problematic, "the growing practice of states to grant 'quickie' citizenship to star foreign athletes" (p. 79). Athlete migration has led, in some instances, to what Maguire and Bale (1994, p. 282) term the "deskilling of 'donor' countries." They argue that "Latin and Central American countries…regularly experience the loss of baseball and soccer player to the USA and Europe" (p. 282). They further explain:

Less developed countries have invested in nurturing athletic talent. Once this talent reaches maturity, more economically developed leagues,

---

4. Migration of athletes may originate from different sources. For example, the choice to migrate may come from the individual who moves to another country in order to train and compete, and perhaps to represent that country in international competitions while migration in other cases, may be based on the active recruitment of talent by leaders of other countries' sport federations (cf. Bale & Maguire, 1994; Carlson, 2004).

such as Major League Baseball, cream off the best. Native audiences are thus denied direct access to native talent nurtured and developed in their countries. (Maguire & Bale, 1994, p. 282)

As further evidence of the impact of athlete migration, the Greek softball and baseball 2004 Olympic teams are examples where most of the athletes on both teams were born in the United States. Even though the United States did not qualify for baseball for the 2004 Olympic Games, American baseball players were well represented. Twenty were Americans (with Greek heritage), one was Canadian (with Greek heritage), and two were Greeks (Carlson, 2004; The San Diego Union-Tribune, 2004). For softball, the situation was similar. Fourteen athletes were Americans while two were Greeks (Softball West Magazine, 2004). These athletes all became Greek citizens in time for the Olympic Games and they were excused from Greece's 2-year required military service (Carlson, 2004). Although this provided the chosen athletes with opportunities to participate in the Olympic Games, Greek-born athletes (i.e., domestic athletes developed in Greece) were essentially overlooked when team members were selected.

In the case of professional baseball, and Major League Baseball in particular, questions about siphoning talent out of the country or what has often been called 'poaching' along with exploitative practices in recruiting players from Central and South America have been raised (Bretón, 2000; Maguire & Bale, 1994). The unequal access to resources in Central America and South America relative to the United States has, in some cases, facilitated the migration of athletes and has, as well, perpetuated these inequities. For example, Miguel Tejada, initially shortstop for the Oakland Athletics,[5] came from very poor circumstances in the Dominican Republic. As Bretón (2000) explains,

> Knowing he had no alternatives, the Athletics acquired Tejada's considerable talent for $2,000. By comparison, Tejada's white American teammate, Ben Grieve, received a $1.2 million signing bonus. Similarly, the Texas Rangers acquired Sammy Sosa's services in 1986 for $3,500— the exact amount the Brooklyn Dodgers paid to sign Jackie Robinson in 1946. (p. 14)

Furthermore, Bretón (2000) reports the following statement made by Dick Balderson, vice-president of the Colorado Rockies at the time of publication, "instead of signing four [American] guys at $25,000 each, you sign 20 [Dominican] guys for $5,000" (p. 14). As is the case for labor issues that occur in the sporting goods industry, standards for the acquisition of talent in developed countries are not maintained when talent originates in developing countries.

---

5. Following his tenure with the Oakland Athletics, Tejada played for the Baltimore Orioles (2004-2007) and for the Houston Astros (2008-) (Major League Baseball, 2008).

The true (e.g., monetary) value of the acquisition is not fully recognized and shared with the athletes, their clubs, teams, leagues, and/or sport system. Equitable exchanges of resources are not occurring. Although athletes may personally gain, the real beneficiaries are typically the professional leagues and teams in developed countries. From a global perspective, the acquisition of talent by developed nations' leagues and teams is largely carried out at the expense of developing nations' sport systems. The depletion of athletes with promising talent from developing countries is rarely replenished, in any form, by the organizations responsible for its depletion. Athletes are poached to enhance the quality of a sport team and league in affluent countries.

In other cases, the internationalization of leagues such as the NBA or football in Europe may have enhanced the profile of teams in these leagues among fans, media, sponsors, and advertisers across the globe, however, it may have undermined the success of domestic leagues in certain countries, for example, the Chinese Basketball League (Yao Ming) and the Brazilian Football League (Ronaldo Luís Nazário de Lima). Related to professional basketball, Wertheim (2004) explains that even though the internationalization of the NBA has greatly enhanced its prominence in the global marketplace, this prominence has not translated into similar success for other professional basketball leagues. Wertheim (2004) writes:

> Stern evangelizes that the NBA's worldwide sprawl is a blessing to leagues in other nations—his rising tide lifts their boat—but it doesn't always play out that way. It's not only that the U.S. has become the destination of top Chinese league players…but also the increase in NBA telecasts and webcasts siphons fans from the CBA [Chinese Basketball League]. Why pay 40 yuan ($5 U.S.) to watch the Beijing Ducks play the Guandong Southern Tigers when you can stay home and watch decidedly superior NBA games for free on television or broadband? Chen Quanli, head of CCTV's [television network of the People's Republic of China] sports division, claims that ratings for NBA games outdraw the CBA's 3 to 1. (p. 79)

As for professional football (i.e., soccer), Foer (2004) explains that approximately 5,000 Brazilians have contracts to play football outside of Brazil. Wertheim (2004) argues that Brazil is the largest producer of football talent in the world, but as he explains,

> European leagues, taking advantage of the downtrodden South American economy, have aggressively pursued all the best players. Brazilian teams, often owned by multinational corporations, have been all too happy to sell stars overseas for transfer fees that can top $10 million—and it's not as if that money goes back into the team. So while Real Madrid fans can

cheer for Ronaldo [Ronaldo Luís Nazário de Lima], clubs in Brazil have second-rate rosters playing before disaffected crowds. (p. 80)[6]

In the American context, there have been important increases in the level of participation from international student-athletes in NCAA competitions. For example, in 2005, Weston (2006) reports that "in NCAA tennis, 63 of the top 100 Men's single players, and 47 of the top 100 women players were international student-athletes" (p. 841). Although more opportunities have been available to international athletes to train and compete in U.S. colleges and universities,

Weston (2006) notes where concerns have been expressed by Americans about their diminishing domestic opportunities in college and university tennis and the possible link between these diminishing opportunities and poor rankings of American athletes in professional tennis.[7]

Related to the migration of athletes, foreign ownership of professional sport franchises has also generated a great deal of controversy. Vecsey (2007) writes:

> When the Glazer [Malcolm Glazer] family from the United States took control of Manchester United in 2005, many loyal fans rushed the city walls with pitchforks and pots of boiling oil in a vain attempt to save the purity of British soccer. Yet the foreign hordes of investors keep arriving, bringing dollars or rubles or even Thai baht or Icelandic krona to the flourishing Premier League, by far the best soccer league in the world. (p. D4)

Fans were very vocal in expressing their concerns because they believed foreign ownership would compromise the cultural and social identity of their sport, their teams, and/or their leagues. There are several examples where public concerns about foreign ownership of sport teams have been expressed. For example, when the Seattle Mariners (MLB) was purchased by Japanese Hiroshi Yamauchi in 1992; when the LA Dodgers (MLB) was purchased by Australian Rupert Murdoch in 1998; when the Montréal Canadiens (National Hockey League) was purchased by American George Gillett in 2001; when Chelsea Football Club (English Premier League) was purchased by Russian Roman Abramovich in 2003; when Manchester United (English Premier League) was purchased by American Malcolm Glazer in 2005; and when Liverpool FC (English Premier League) was purchased by Americans George Gillett and Tom Hicks in 2007 (cf. Bonham & Hinchey, 2008; Howell, 2005; McRae, 2008; Rovell, 2008; Vecsey, 2007; Weiner, 2008).

---

6 Between 2002 and 2007, Ronaldo Luís Nazário de Lima played for Real Madrid. Since 2007, he has played for AC Milan.

7 In her study, Weston (2006) refers to the Association of Tennis Professionals' rankings reported on August 21, 2006 and the Sony Ericcson Women's Tennis Association Tour rankings reported on August 26, 2006.

The next topic to be addressed in this article relates to the role media have played in the globalization of sport.

GLOBAL SPORT-MEDIA COMPLEX

Some researchers have termed the interrelationship between TNCs, media, and sport organizations as the global sport media complex (cf. Jhally, 1989; Miller et al., 2001; Raney & Bryant, 2006; Rowe, 1996; Scherer, Falcous, & Jackson, 2008). Others have called it the sport media nexus (cf. Grainger, Newman, & Andrews, 2005; Messner, 2002; Nicholson, 2007), the golden triangle (cf. Honeybourne, Hill, & Moors, 2000; Nixon, 2008), or the love-match (cf. Rowe, 1996). In my class, I call it *ménage à trois*. For me, *ménage à trois* seems to capture well the interplay of media, TNCs, and sport as all three 'players' are involved in the most intimate relationships...and they all benefit from what they bring to the relationship. Media have the expertise and technical equipment to produce sport into a package that can easily be consumed by spectators. Media are also involved in providing important financial resources to sport in the form of broadcasting rights. TNCs provide sponsorship money to sport organizations in exchange for visibility of their products and they also buy advertisement time and space from media to ensure visibility of their products. In turn, with the resources from broadcasting rights and from sponsorships, sport organizations are able to invest in developing a better product that will have more appeal to audiences favoring mutual and reciprocal benefits to all the 'players' in the *ménage à trois*.

There are several examples where sport has changed to accommodate media's interest (cf. Miller et al., 2001; Nixon, 2008; Rowe, 1996), for example, stoppage in play to allow commercial breaks in telecasts of events, changes in sport rules to enhance the appeal of the sport for fans, for sponsors, and for media (mixed martial arts is a good example), and the creation of new sports (and/or events) to target new audiences for TNCs and media (extreme sports, ESPN's XGames).

In addition, several global media conglomerates are increasingly involved in the acquisition of sport properties (teams, leagues, stadia) (cf. Gerrard, 2000, 2004; Grainger & Andrews, 2005; Harvey, Law, & Cantelon, 2001; Law, Harvey, & Kemp, 2002; Wright, 1999). As examples of media conglomerates involved in the business of sport, we could include: Disney (based in the U.S.), News Corporation (based in Australia), Time Warner (based in the U.S.), Vivendi SA (based in France), Viacom/CBS Corporation (based in the U.S.), and Bertelsmann AG (based in Germany). Media's involvement in the business of sport can be problematic on several levels. As a number of media conglomerates increase their ownership of sport properties, we may see a decrease in the diversity in sport and sporting heritage. In addition, while media conglomerates increasingly gain control of sport properties, we can foresee a situation where only sports that can be commodified and commercialized will thrive. The value of sport will be determined by the size and composition of audience available for media, advertisers, and sponsors. As well, critical accounts of sport and the reporting of controversial stories may disappear as media that own the sport teams have no interest in supporting negative coverage.

The final issue I want to address is the environment in the context of the globalization of sport.

ENVIRONMENT

Sport makes a significant impact on the environment. A study was undertaken at the Centre for Business Relationships Accountability, Sustainability and Society at Cardiff University in Wales where the ecological footprint of rugby supporters was assessed during one game (Wales against Scotland) of the 2006 Rugby's Six Nations tournament. Although the researchers (Centre for Business Relationships Accountability, Sustainability and Society, 2007; Collins, Flynn, Munday, & Roberts, 2007) acknowledge the important economic benefits of this event for the Cardiff economy, they also point out the significant environmental cost paid by the city. Their research demonstrates that the "energy and resources used by 85,499 rugby supporters…resulted in an ecological footprint equivalent to the area of 3,578 rugby pitches" (Centre for Business Relationships Accountability, Sustainability and Society, 2007, paragraph 5; Jones, 2007, paragraph 6). Furthermore, the researchers argued that the largest impact on the ecological footprint resulted from supporters' food and drink consumption. A total of 66.5 tons of waste were generated during the event of which approximately 1% was recycled (Centre for Business Relationships Accountability, Sustainability and Society, 2007; Jones, 2007). The ecological footprint was further affected by the travel to, and from, Millennium Stadium. The researchers estimated a total of 24.3 million kilometers travelled by the supporters for the game. This translated into an average of 284 kilometers per supporter. Based on the number of sport events held throughout the world, our ecological footprint related to sport is immense and, for the most part, goes unnoticed.

Another example where sport has not been so kind to the environment is in downhill skiing. In preparation for the Nagano 1998 Olympic Winter Games, the Fédération Internationale de Ski (FIS) wanted to extend the length of the men's downhill course by 120 meters (395 feet), however, Japan and Nagano officials did not want to extend the course because it would be damaging to an ecologically sensitive area of the mountain. In the end (after a 5-year impasse blamed on "cultural differences" by the IOC), the Nagano Organizing Committee agreed to extend the start line by approximately 85 meters (i.e., 279 feet) (New York Times, 1997a, 1997b, 1997c). Initial concerns for vegetation and wildlife were set aside to ensure a longer downhill ski course for athletes.

Still on the theme of winter sports, is the building of snow domes to allow individuals living in countries where they do not experience the 'real' winter to practice sports such as downhill skiing, snowboarding, and skating. There are approximately 50 snow domes currently operating in 20 countries (UK, Indonesia, Taiwan, Malaysia, China) (Wilson, 2005). These facilities cover the space of 3 football fields and use the equivalent of 15,000 domestic refrigerators to keep the dome's temperature between −1° and −7° Celsius to support snow-making equipment that make 30 tons of snow every night to maintain snow levels in the facility (Agence France-Presse, 2005).

In another example of sport's impact on the environment, golf has been a concern. Even though golf is often associated with the great outdoors and individual's harmony with nature, the development and maintenance of golf courses negatively affects wildlife and vegetation, not to mention the depletion of water resources required for the upkeep of the greens (cf. Maguire, Jarvie, Mansfield, & Bradley, 2002; Wheeler & Nauright, 2006). Golf courses are usually built in, or near, ecologically sensitive areas (e.g., forests, marshes, lakes, rivers, fields) and then, once developed, chemicals such as fertilizers and pesticides are used to maintain the greens, further damaging the environment. As explained by Maguire et al. (2002), "building a golf course involves the clearing of natural vegetation and destroys natural landscapes and habitats. Trees, shrubs, hedgerows and plants are destroyed, hilltops are bulldozed and valleys are filled in to create an artificial golf landscape" (p. 93). The impact of golf on the environment has led to the development of an organization, Global Anti-Golf Movement, in 1993 (cf. Global Anti-Golf Movement, 2004; Maguire et al., 2002; Wheeler & Nauright, 2006) to increase awareness among the public about the negative impact golf has on the environment. As part of their manifesto, the Global Anti-Golf Movement (2004) states,

> In the face of growing criticism of the adverse environmental impacts of golf courses, the industry is promoting the notion of "pesticide-free," "environmentally-friendly" or "sensitive" golf courses. No such course exists to date, and the creation and maintenance of the "perfect green" comprising exotic grass inevitably requires intensive use of chemicals. (paragraph 6)

These are just a few examples of how the globalization of sport has had negative consequences for the environment. Several other examples could be used to further illustrate cases where the environment is consistently compromised to accommodate participants' involvement in sports.

DISCUSSION

In choosing labor, media, and environmental issues as evidence of some of the inconvenient truths of the globalization of sport, I am not suggesting that we stop taking part in sport, that we stop buying sportswear and sport equipment, that we prevent athletes from migrating to other countries, that we stop building sport facilities, or that we stop holding sport events. The point of this article is to increase awareness regarding the perils of globalization. In developed countries, the level of consciousness about the 'other side' of the globalization of sport is not always high as individuals (including sport management students and scholars) are bombarded by positive examples and outcomes of globalization. I am calling for increased sensitivity regarding the cost of globalization for individuals in developing countries, for their sport system, and for their country.

It may be inconvenient for us to ask, "What are we willing to give up to protect sport and the sport industry and to ensure a more globally egalitarian situation with respect to sport?" In other words, are we (in developed nations) willing to share the wealth with all countries and organizations involved in all of the labor used in sport? Should rich professional sport leagues in developed countries invest a portion of their profits in the countries where they acquired talent for their teams/leagues? These profits could be invested in the sport system to ensure talent development and ongoing support for the countries' sport systems.

Should sport management students and scholars be sensitized to the impact sport has beyond economic and financial terms of developed countries' sport teams and leagues? How do we ensure that these students understand the impact that sport has on developing countries, on sport systems from poorer countries, on workers producing our sportswear and our sport equipment? What choices and decisions can we make as consumers, as sport participants, as teachers, as researchers, as sport leaders to redress the imbalances that have occurred in sport as a result of globalization?

Can we exercise pressure on TNCs and media conglomerates to change their labor practices? Otherwise are we not complicit in perpetuating the perils of globalization based on our inactions? As a collective, we would not endure the working conditions and human resource practices of subcontractors involved in the production of our sporting goods—so what are we doing to change these poor labor practices? We need to ask ourselves, what role can we play in mobilizing the stakeholders involved (TNCs, governments, sport organizations, media, sponsors, advertisers, and individuals) to effect real change? Can we leverage sport sponsors to support sport systems beyond the borders of their head offices? For example, can the IOC solicit from its TOP 12 sponsors support for the sport systems of developing countries to reduce the sport performance and the resource gaps between developing and developed nations?

As discussed earlier, globalization has led to prosperity for many sport stakeholders, for example, media conglomerates, professional sport teams, franchises, and leagues, the IOC, and sport-related TNCs. The question we must ask, particularly with the inconvenient truths, is…has globalization deepened inequality or has it reduced it? Who has benefited from the economic wealth and growth originating from the globalization of sport? Who have been "winners" and who have been "losers"?

Has economic growth been used to benefit those who do not have access? How has access been defined and who has defined what sport is important? For example, in global initiatives where sport is used for development, who defines sport? Is it defined locally or by developed countries coming in to "help"?

Are sport organizations in developed nations increasing their wealth at the expense of developing countries' sport systems? What can we do as teachers and researchers to ensure this imbalance is redressed? Should we ensure that globalization of sport is critically discussed within the sport management curriculum. I would also suggest we encourage sport management students to critically investigate the *inconvenient truths* when pursuing their research. Has the globalization of sport meant that the unique cultural experiences of sport in various countries such as Afghanistan (e.g., buzkashi), Australia (e.g., Australian rules football), Bangladesh (e.g., kabaddi), Brazil (e.g., capoeira), Canada (e.g., lacrosse and ice hockey), China (e.g., table tennis), Cuba (e.g., baseball), India (e.g., field hockey), Jamaica (e.g., cricket), Japan (e.g., sumo), Korea (e.g., taekwondo), Lithuania (e.g., basketball), New Zealand (e.g., rugby union), and the United States (e.g., baseball) are valued equally by those of us in sport management? Should we and our students be sensitized to social and cultural differences between countries' sport priorities and systems?

The *inconvenient truths* regarding the globalization of sport need to be exposed and strategies to address the negative consequences of globalization of sport have to be devised and implemented. To conclude, as we reflect on the power of sport, we need to keep a critical lens on our understanding of the interrelationships between all the stakeholders involved in globalization.

Works Cited

Adams, R. J. (2002). Retail profitability and sweatshops: A global dilemma. *Journal of Retailing and Consumer Services, 9*, 147–153.

Agence France-Presse. (2005, April 26). Dubai desert gives way to ski resort. *Aljazeera.net/English*. Retrieved May 24, 2008, from http://english.aljazeera.net/ archive/2005/04/200849152045820278. html

Allison, L. (Ed.) (2005). *The global politics of sport. The role of global institutions in sport*. London: Routledge.

Andrews, D.L., & Grainger, A.D. (2007). Sport and globalization. In G. Ritzer (Ed.), *The Blackwell companion to globalization* (pp. 478–497). Malden, MA: Blackwell Publishing.

Bairner, A. (2005). Sport and the nation in the global era. In L. Allison (Ed.), *The global politics of sport. The role of global institutions in sport* (pp. 87–100). London: Routledge.

Bale, J. (1990). *The brawn drain: Foreign student-athletes in American universities*. Champaign, IL: University of Illinois Press.

Bale, J., & Maguire, J. (1994). *The global sports arena: Athletic talent migration in an interdependent world*. London: Frank Cass.

Bale, J., & Sang, J. *Kenyan running. Movement culture, geography and global change*. London: Frank Cass.

Bonham, D., & Hinchey, D. (2008, July 18). Boardroom sports: Foreign funds could back teams. *Rocky Mountain News*. Retrieved August 17, 2008, from http://www. rockymountainnews.com/news/2008/jul/18/foreign-funds-could-back-teams/

Bretón, M. (2000). Fields of broken dreams. Latinos and baseball. *ColorLines, 3*(1), 13–17.

Carlson, P. (2004, August 8). Flag relay. For Olympians in training, flexibility is everything. Especially when it comes to citizenship. *Washington Post*, p. D01. Retrieved November 2, 2004, from http://www.washingtonpost.com/wp-dyn/ articles/A48948-2004Aug7.html

Centre for Business Relationships Accountability, Sustainability and Society. (2007, February 9). *Rugby internationals leave large environmental footprint*. Cardiff University. Retrieved May 24, 2008, from http://www.brass.cf.ac.uk/news/

Collins, A., Flynn, A., Munday, M., & Roberts, A. (2007). Assessing the environmental consequences of major sporting events: The 2003/04 FA Cup Final. *Urban Studies, 44*, 457–476.

Crawford, S. (1999). Nelson Mandela, the number 6 jersey, and the 1995 Rugby World Cup: Sport as a transcendent unifying force, or a transparent illustration of bicultural opportunism. In R.R. Sands (Ed.), *Anthropology, sport, and culture* (pp. 119–135). Westport, CT: Bergin & Garvey.

Fay, T.G., & Snyder, D. (2007). A North American perspective on international sport. In J.B. Parks, J. Quarterman, & L. Thibault (Eds.), *Contemporary sport management* (3rd ed.) (pp. 163–188). Champaign, IL: Human Kinetics.

Fédération Internationale de Football Association (FIFA). (2008). *About FIFA Associations*. Retrieved May 6, 2008, from http://www.fifa.com/aboutfifa/federation/associations.html

Foer, F. (2004). *How soccer explains the world. An {unlikely} theory of globalization*. New York: Harper Perennial.

Foer, F. (2006). The goals of globalization. *Foreign Policy, 153*, 86–87.

Ford, C. (2006a). Peace and hoops: Basketball as a role player in sustainable peacebuilding. *Willamette Law Review, 42*, 709–736.

Ford, C. (2006b). Hooping with the enemy. A group of visionary risk-takers offer a most unlikely solution to the violence in the middle east. *ESPN.com–The Magazine*. Retrieved May 22, 2008, from http://sports.espn.go.com/espn/eticket/story?page=playingforpeace&lpos= potlight&lid= tab5pos1

Gerrard, B. (2000). Media ownership of pro sports teams: Who are the winners and losers? (case study). *International Journal of Sports Marketing and Sponsorship, 2*, 199–218.

Gerrard, B. (2004). Media ownership of teams: The latest stage in the commercialisation of team sports. In T. Slack (Ed.), *The commercialisation of sport* (pp. 247-266). London: Routledge.

Giulianotti, R., & Robertson, R. (Eds.) (2007a). *Globalization and sport*. Malden, MA: Blackwell.

Giulianotti, R., & Robertson, R. (2007b). Sport and globalization: Transnational dimensions. *Global Networks, 7*, 107–112.

Global Anti-Golf Movement. (2004). The global anti-golf movement manifesto. Retrieved August 19, 2008, from http://www.antigolf.org/english.html

Grainger, A., & Andrews, D. (2005). Resisting Rupert through sporting rituals?: The transnational media corporation and global-local sport cultures. *International Journal of Sport Management and Marketing, 1*, 3–16.

Grainger, A.D., Newman, J.I., & Andrews, D. (2005). Global adidas. Sport, celebrity, and the marketing of difference. In J. Amis & B.T.B. Cornwell (Eds.), *Global sport sponsorship* (pp. 89–105). Oxford, UK: Berg.

Gratton, C., & Leberman, S. (2006). Sport in the global marketplace. In S. Leberman, C. Collins, & L. Trenberth (Eds.), *Sport business management in Aotearoa/New Zealand* (pp. 89–105). Victoria, AUS: Thomson Dunmore Press.

Hargreaves, J. (2000). *Heroines of sport. The politics of difference and identity.* London: Routledge.

Hargreaves, J. (2002). Globalisation theory, global sport, and nations and nationalism. In J. Sugden & A. Tomlinson (Eds.), *Power games. A critical sociology of sport* (pp. 25–43). London: Routledge.

Harvey, J., & Houle, F. (1994). Sport, world economy, global culture, and new social movements. *Sociology of Sport Journal, 11*, 337–355.

Harvey, J., Law, A., & Cantelon, M. (2001). North American professional team franchises ownership patterns and global entertainment conglomerates. *Sociology of Sport Journal, 18*, 435–457.

Harvey, J., Rail, G., & Thibault, L. (1996). Globalization and sport: Sketching a theoretical model for empirical analyses. *Journal of Sport and Social Issues, 23*, 258–277.

Henry, I. P., & [the] Institute of Sport and Leisure Policy. (2007). *Transnational and comparative research in sport: Globalisation, governance and sport policy.* Abingdon, UK: Routledge.

Honeybourne, J., Hill, M., & Moors, H. (2000). *Advanced physical education and sport. For AS level.* Cheltenham, UK: Nelson Thornes.

Houlihan, B. (1994). *Sport and international politics.* Hertfordshire, UK: Harvester Wheatsheaf.

Houlihan, B. (1999). Policy harmonization: The example of global antidoping policy. *Journal of Sport Management, 13*, 197–215.

Howell, J.W. (2005). From SBC Park to the Tokyo Dome: Baseball and (inter)nationalism. In M.L. Silk, D.L. Andrews, & C.L. Cole (Eds.), *Sport and corporate nationalisms* (pp. 227–251). Oxford, UK: Berg.

Hussain-Khaliq, S. (2004). Eliminating child labour from the Sialkot soccer ball industry. Two industry-led approaches. *Journal of Corporate Citizenship, Spring* (13), 101–107.

International Olympic Committee. (2008a). *Nagano 1998 Did you know? For the first time.* Retrieved May 22, 2008, from http://www.olympic.org/uk/games/past/innovations_uk.asp?OLGT = 2&OLGY = 1998

International Olympic Committee. (2008b). *The Olympic Movement. Who is the Olympic Movement?* Retrieved May 14, 2008, from http://www.olympic.org/uk/organisation/index_uk.asp

International Platform on Sport and Development. (2005, September 1). News International Platform on Sport and Development Middle East update. Retrieved May 22, 2008, from http://www.sportanddev.org/en/news/middle-east-update.htm

Jhally, S. (1989). Cultural studies and the sports/media complex. In L.A. Wenner (Ed.), *Media, sports, and society* (pp.70–96). Newbury Park, CA: Sage.

Jones, G. (2007, February 10). Rugby game leaves 'eco-footprint'. *BBC News.* Retrieved May 24, 2008, from http://news.bbc.co.uk/2/hi/uk_news/wales/6348223.stm

Kingston, G. (2005, February 10). 'Poacher' countries take aim at Canadian athletes. *The Vancouver Sun*, p. E1.

Lafranchi, P., & Taylor, M. (2001). *Moving the ball: The migration of professional footballers.* Oxford, UK: Berg.

Laurent, L. (2008, February 26). Puma still has teeth. *Forbes.com.* Retrieved August 17, 2008, from http://www.forbes.com/markets/2008/02/26/puma-earnings-sportsmarkets-equitycx_ll_0226-markets17.html

Law, A., Harvey, J., & Kemp, S. (2002). The global sport mass media oligopoly. The three usual suspects and more. *International Review for the Sociology of Sport, 37*, 279–302.

Lim, S.J., & Phillips, J. (2008). Embedding CSR value: The global footwear industry's evolving governance structure. *Journal of Business Ethics, 81*, 143–156.

Maguire, J.A. (1999). *Global sport: Identities, societies, civilizations.* Cambridge, UK: Polity Press.

Maguire, J.A. (Ed.) (2005). *Power and global sport: Zones of prestige, emulation, and resistance.* Abingdon, UK: Routledge.

Maguire, J., & Bale, J. (1994). Postscript: An agenda for research on sports labour migration. In J. Bale & J. Maguire (Eds.), *The global sports arena. Athletic talent migration in an interdependent world* (pp. 281–284). London: Frank Cass.

Maguire, J., Jarvie, G., Mansfield, L., & Bradley, J. (2002). *Sport worlds: A sociological perspective.* Champaign, IL: Human Kinetics.

Major League Baseball. (2008). Player file: Miguel Tejada. Career Stats. Retrieved May 24, 2008, from http://mlb.mlb.com/stats/individual_stats_player.jsp?playerID=123173&statType=1

Maquila Solidarity Network. (2008). *Clearing the hurdles: Steps to improving wages and working conditions in the global sportswear industry.* Toronto, ON: Play Fair 2008 Campaign.

Marchak, P. (1991). *The integrated circus.* Montréal, QC: McGill-Queen's University Press.

Mason, D.S. (2002). "Get the puck outta here!": Media, transnationalism, and Canadian identity. *Journal of Sport and Social Issues, 26*, 140–167.

Mason, D.S., & Duquette, G.H. (2005). Globalisation and the evolving player-agent relationship in professional sport. *International Journal of Sport Management and Marketing, 1*, 93–109.

McRae, D. (2008, February 7). Mr basketball eager to conquer the lost frontier of Britain. *The Guardian.* Retrieved February 14, 2008, from http://www.guardian.co.uk/sport/2008/feb/07/ussport

Means, J., & Nauright, J. (2007). Going global: The NBA sets its sights on Africa. *International Journal of Sports Marketing and Sponsorship, 9*, 40–50.

Messner, M. A. (2002). *Taking the field. Women, men, and sports.* Minneapolis, MN: University of Minnesota Press.

Milanovic, B. (2005). Globalization and goals: Does soccer show the way. *Review of International Political Economy, 12*, 829–850.

Miller, T., Lawrence, G., McKay, J., & Rowe, D. (2001). *Globalization and sport. Playing the world.* London: Sage.

Moodley, K., & Adam, H. (2000). Race and nation in post-Apartheid South Africa. Patriotism, nationalism and non-racialism. *Current Sociology, 48*(3), 51–69.

Nafziger, J. A. R. (1988). *International sports law.* Dobbs Ferry, NY: Transnational.

Neverdeen Pieterse, J. (1994). Globalization as hybridization. *International Sociology, 9*, 161–184.

New York Times. (1997a, November 11) Olympics; A compromise sought for downhill course. *New York Times.* Retrieved May 24, 2008, from http://proxy.library.brocku.ca/login?url = http://search. ebscohost.com/login.aspx?direct = true&db = aph&AN = 29741942&loginpage = login.asp&site = ehost-live&scope = site

New York Times. (1997b, November 15). Olympics; Resolution seen on men's downhill. *New York Times.* Retrieved May 24, 2008, from http://proxy.library.brocku.ca/login?url = http://search.ebscohost. com/login.aspx?direct = true&db = aph&AN = 29743989&loginpage = login.asp&site = ehost-live&scope = site

New York Times. (1997c, December 2). Olympics; A compromise on downhill course. *New York Times.* Retrieved May 24, 2008, from http://proxy.library.brocku.ca/login?url = http://search.ebscohost. com/login.aspx?direct = true&db = aph&AN =29753858&loginpage = login.asp&site = ehost-live&scope = site

Nicholson, M. (2007). *Sport and the media. Managing the nexus.* Oxford, UK: Elsevier.

Nixon, H. L. (2008). *Sport in a changing world.* Boulder, CO: Paradigm.Paramount Pictures. (2006). *An inconvenient truth.* About the film. Retrieved May 24, 2008, from http://www.climatecrisis.net/aboutthefilm/

Play Fair at the Olympics. (2004). *Play fair at the Olympics. Respect workers' rights in the sportswear industry.* Oxford, UK: Oxfam GB. Retrieved January 12, 2006, from http://www.fairolympics.org/background/olympicreporteng.pdf

Quinn, M. (2006, January 20). News International Platform on Sport and Development Playing for Peace: Successful Middle East twinned school tournament. Retrieved May 22, 2008, from http://www.sportanddev.org/en/news/playing-for-peacesuccessful-middle-east-twinned-school-tournament.htm

Ram, V. (2007, November 8). Rosy outlook lifts adidas. *Forbes.com.* Retrieved August 17, 2008, from http://www.forbes.com/markets/2007/11/08/adidas-reebok-sportsmarkets-equity-cx_vr_1108marketsx12.html

Raney, A.A., & Bryant, J. (Eds.) (2006). *Handbook of sports and media.* Abingdon, UK: Routledge.

Riordan, J., & Krüger, A. (1999). *The international politics of sport in the 20th century.* London: E & FN Spon.

Ritzer, G. (Ed.) (2007). *The Blackwell companion to globalization.* Malden, MA: Blackwell.

Robertson, R. (1992). *Globalization: Social theory and global culture.* New York: Russell Sage.

Robertson, R., & White, K.E. (2007). What is globalization? In G. Ritzer (Ed.), *TheBlackwell companion to globalization* (pp. 54–66). Malden, MA: Blackwell Publishing.

Rovell, D. (2008, May 23). SportsBiz. Foreign ownership of U.S. sports teams – I'm predicting more. *CNBC.com.* Retrieved August 17, 2008, from http://www.cnbc.com/id/24790770

Rowe, D. (1996). The global love-match: Sport and television. *Media, Culture and Society, 18,* 565–582.

Rusli, E.M. (2007, December 20). Nike speeds ahead on global growth. *Forbes.com.* Retrieved August 17, 2008, from http://www.forbes.com/markets/2007/12/20/nike-athletic-closer-markets-equity-cx_er_ra_1220markets31.html

Sage, G.H. (1999). *Justice do it!* The transnational advocacy network: Organization, collective actions, and outcomes. *Sociology of Sport Journal, 16,* 206–235.

Sage, G.H. (2005). Corporate globalization and sporting goods manufacturing. The case of Nike. In D.S. Eitzen (Ed.), *Sport in contemporary society. An anthology* (pp. 362–382). Boulder, CO: Paradigm Publishers.

Scherer, J., Falcous, M., & Jackson, S.J. (2008). The media sports cultural complex. *Journal of Sport and Social Issues, 32,* 48–71.

Softball West Magazine. (2004, August). The Greek Olympic team has a U.S. flavor. *Softball West Magazine.* Retrieved May 6, 2008, from http://softballwest.com/articles/51/

Steenveld, L., & Strelitz, L. (1998). The 1995 Rugby World Cup and the politics of nation-building in South Africa. *Media, Culture and Society, 20,* 609–629.

Taylor, T. (1988). Sport and world politics: Functionalism and the state system. *International Journal, 43,* 531–553.

Teeple, G. (2000). What is globalization? In S. McBride & J. Wiseman (Eds.), *Globalization and its discontents* (pp. 9–23). Hampshire, UK: Palgrave.

The Associated Press. (2004, August 3). Pope promotes sports for Christianity. *NBC Sports*. Retrieved May 21, 2008, from http://nbcsports.msnbc.com/id/5592358/print/1/displaymode/1098/

The San Diego Union-Tribune. (2004, August 10). Greek Olympic baseball team. *The San Diego Union-Tribune*. Retrieved May 6, 2008, from http://www.signonsandiego.com/uniontrib/20040810/news_1s10greekbox.html

Thibault, L. (2007). Present issues in sport management and future research. *Proceedings of the 2007 International Sport Science Congress. Pursuing happiness through sport and leisure* (pp. 285–293). Seoul, Korea: Korean Alliance for Health, Physical Education, Recreation, and Dance.

Thoma, J.E., & Chalip, L. (1996). *Sport governance in the global community*. Morgantown, WV: Fitness Information Technologies.

Thomas, G. M. (2007). Globalization: The major players. In G. Ritzer (Ed.), *The Blackwell companion to globalization* (pp. 84–102). Malden, MA: Blackwell Publishing.

Tomlinson, A., & Young, C. (2006). Culture, politics, and spectacle in the global sports events. An introduction. In A. Tomlinson & C. Young (Eds.), *National identity and global sports events* (pp. 1–14). Albany, NY: State University of New York Press.

United Nations. (2008). List of member states. Retrieved May 6, 2008, from http://www.un.org/members/list.shtml

Vecsey, G. (2007, October 26). N.F.L. tries to turn globalization into a team sport. *The New York Times*, p. D4.

Weiner, E. (2008, March 7). Sports. American sports may soon face a foreign invasion. *The New York Sun*. Retrieved on May 6, 2008, from http://www2.nysun.com/article/72504?page_no = 2

Wertheim, L.J. (2004, June 14). The whole world is watching. *Sports Illustrated, 100*(24), 72–86.

Westerbeek, H., & Smith, A. (2003). *Sport business in the global marketplace*. Hampshire, UK: Palgrave Macmillan.

Weston, M. (2006). Internationalization in college sports: Issues in recruiting, amateurism, and scope. *Willamette Law Review, 42*, 829–860.

Wheeler, K., & Nauright, J. (2006). A global perspective on the environmental impact of golf. *Sport in Society, 9*, 427–443.

Wilsey, S. (2006, June). The beautiful game. Why soccer rules the world. *National Geographic, 209*(6), 42–48.

Wilson, A. (2005, October 22). Outside it's 80 degrees. Inside you get 23,000 sq metres of snow. *Financial Times*, p. 7.

Wolf, M. (2004). *Why globalization works*. New Haven, CT: Yale University Press.

Wright, G. (1999). The impact of globalisation. *New Political Economy, 4*, 268–273.

Invent What arguments does Thibault present in favor of the impact of globalization of sport? What arguments does she pose as concerns for the globalization of sport? Make a list and note supporting evidence used to back these claims then reflect on your opinions. Given Thibault's inconvenient truths, do you think globalization has been good or bad overall for sport and why?

Collaborate In small groups, divide Thibault's inconvenient truths about globalization and sport and research one of these issues more fully. Find three to four sources cited by Thibault in the section and read and annotate them. What new and different evidence do these sources present on the issue? What evidence do you see Thibault citing? What important evidence does she omit and how might fuller engagement with these other sources expand your understanding of this "inconvenient truth"?

Compose Write a one-page precis of Thibault's speech. What are her key points and evidence? How do you capture the core essence of Thibault's speech in one page?

Alexander Wolff is a senior writer for Sports Illustrated *who has also written several books on basketball, including* Big Game Small World, *a* New York Times *notable book that also ranks on* Sports Illustrated's *Top 100 sports books.*

SPORTS SAVES THE WORLD

By Alexander Wolff

VANCOUVER – I ran into Johann Olav Koss again in February 2010, at the Olympic oval in Richmond, B.C. The sight of Koss, then a temporary coach with Norway's speedskating team, transported me back 16 years instantly, happily.

I can't help it: Listmaking is a male thing, even more a sportswriterly thing, and I fastidiously rank Olympic Games. With its glitch-filled first week, the trucked-in snow and the fatal crash of a Georgian luger, the Vancouver edition will forever be an also-ran. The Winter Games of 1994, on the other hand, still surmount my desert-island all-time top five list of Olympics. Lillehammer abides with me not just because Koss won three gold medals and set three world records in three races; Dan Jansen finally skated to a gold himself; and 100,000 Norwegians camped overnight in the snow so they could cheer cross-country skiers with cowbells the next morning. It was the harmonious vibe, the intimate scale, the clean Scandinavian lines of the venues, even the crisp weather—as if the Norse gods had dropped a membrane over the town, sealing it off from the world's impurities.

The only breach of this hermetic idyll was on the pedestrian mall of Lillehammer's main street, where a few people solicited for a charity called Olympic Aid. They invoked Sarajevo, the Yugoslavian city that had hosted the Winter Games a decade earlier and, as a result of the war in the Balkans, remained under what would be the longest siege in modern history. The looping anthem of Sarajevo's suffering, Albinoni's Adagio in G Minor, haunted me every time I walked by. It seemed to whisper that, even as nature re-created a little patch of Eden for the playing of games, mankind still ginned up reminders of its fallen state.

From *Sports Illustrated* (2011).

And then the Perfect Olympics delivered its own latter-day god, a man to go forth into the Imperfect World and set it right. I'd watched Koss skate his triple at the Vikingskipet Oval. I'd heard him pledge his bonus money to Olympic Aid and challenge his countrymen to give 10 kroner each for every Norwegian gold medal, inspiring his government and fellow citizens to give $18 million over 10 days (page 70). For this as much as anything else, SI named Koss its 1994 Sportsman of the Year, an award he shared with U.S. speedskater Bonnie Blair. My colleague E.M. Swift wrote the story about the Olympic champion from Norway with a "headful of dreams and almost a lifetime in which to accomplish them."

We were now 16 years into that life left to live. When I saw Koss at the Richmond Oval, I asked, How goes the battle?

Sport, Koss replied, is doing nothing less than trying to save the world. Olympic Aid, since renamed Right To Play, now reaches 700,000 children in 20 countries during any given week. But Koss's outfit is only one player among hundreds in a burgeoning global movement. Today the field known generally as Sport for Development and Peace (SDP) extends well beyond nongovernmental organizations (NGOs) such as Right To Play. It attracts growing support from foundations and corporations, while governments and international agencies are eager to serve as partners to groups on the ground. And as the effectiveness of programs is more precisely measured, SDP's value as a tool for good is becoming more widely acknowledged. Even the stodgiest onlookers agree that sport "plays the hidden social worker," in the words of former champion miler Sebastian Coe, now chairman of the London 2012 organizing committee.

That is a good thing, for almost half the world's population is considered poor, and a full 1.4 billion people—one fifth of humanity, including more than half of all Africans—are extremely poor, living on less than $1.25 a day. As maladies of plenty such as obesity, diabetes and heart disease afflict the developed world, and elite pro sports reek of excess, SDP is a sobering counterpoint, spreading health messages, pacifying communities in conflict, preparing refugees for resettlement and providing what experts consider the simplest means of promoting development: improved status for women. At the turn of this century, when the U.N. drew up its Millennium Development Goals to cut extreme poverty in half by 2015 and eliminate it entirely by '25, Koss and Right To Play led the way in determining how sport could best help.

On the morning of the 2010 Olympic opening ceremonies, across Vancouver at a symposium at the University of British Columbia, the former Canadian ambassador to the United Nations, Stephen Lewis, delivered a confession. Lewis, who had served the U.N. secretary general as an anti-AIDS adviser, had long been skeptical of the value of sports. But SDP had won him over. "[Koss] understood early that you could use play to convey messages that aren't available anywhere else," Lewis told his audience. "Sport has become a development philosophy. Who would have imagined that to be possible? What began as an instinct has now become a profound social cause."

I wanted to see how, exactly. So after the dousing of the Vancouver flame, I lit out for far corners of this Imperfect World in search of other friends of sport who, like Koss, had broken from their bubbles to heed the Adagio call of Lillehammer.

RIO DE JANEIRO

It's not a classic hillside slum, but Complexo da Maré is easily one of Rio's largest favelas—a sprawling neighborhood of 135,000 people hard by the route visitors will travel between the airport and the beaches when they come to this city for the 2014 World Cup and the 2016 Olympics. Rival drug gangs recruit kids as foot soldiers and sort out differences with gunplay. Luke Dowdney has driven me into the favela beneath weltering electrical wires and past huddled walk-ups. He parks our car and we stroll a block. A boy of no more than 15 preens in an intersection, automatic weapon slung over one shoulder.

Dowdney, a former British universities light middleweight boxing champion, came to Brazil in 1995 to study street children in the northern city of Recife for his dissertation in social anthropology. He was haunted by the murder of two kids he had grown close to and by the words of a 12-year-old drug trafficker who told him, "I'm going to die young, but I'm going to live well." One day a group of glue-sniffing boys asked him to show them some boxing moves. "When they'd get in a stance, they'd leave the glue behind," says Dowdney, 38, "and a light went off in my head."

In 2000, Dowdney founded a boxing and martial arts program in Maré called Luta Pela Paz, or Fight for Peace, and five years later he opened a training and educational center. On its first floor, boys and girls practice boxing, wrestling and the Brazilian martial art capoeira. In a suite of second-floor classrooms the same kids learn computer skills, citizenship and conflict resolution; they also practice martial arts in a third-floor matted dojo. Boxer Douglas Noronha, whose brother was shot to death in '01, is one of about 4,600 young Cariocas to go through the program. "You'd think I'd have become more violent," he tells me. "In fact, I've become a more controlled person. It's all about the self-confidence and discipline of not finding yourself in a position where, before you know it, somebody's got a gun."

Dowdney introduces me to another fighter, Roberto Custódio, who was 14 when his father was ordered out of the favela by a drug trafficker who was jealous of his relationship with a local woman. When he returned to look in on his family, which he supported as a bus driver, the drug lord settled the matter in his usual way, with bullets.

Figuring that fitness and martial arts would help him square accounts with his father's killer, Roberto turned to Luta Pela Paz. Then the unexpected happened. The program transformed his blood lust into something altogether new. As he developed the discipline that boxing demands—and took the academic classes required of all participants—relatives marveled that his anger gradually drained away. Last October, Roberto, now 24, won the light welterweight gold medal at the Brazilian championships, and he is likely to qualify for the London Olympics as a welterweight. "Our program isn't just about getting rid of energy," Dowdney tells me. "It's also about rigor and values. The disciplined fighter will always beat the overwrought fighter. Luta means fight, but it also means struggle, in a good way."

Dowdney hopes to develop a funding stream from a new line of fight wear and lifestyle clothing called Luta (luta.co.uk). "If the line hits, it becomes the engine," says Dowdney, who runs a second Fight for Peace center in East London that has trained 1,700 boxers. "We're not about being a traditional charity. It's like boxing: You get out what you put in. If you're not trained, you don't win. That's life. You've got to step up."

Last spring, as a crew filmed a commercial for the Luta brand in a ring set up in a warehouse at the edge of the favela, a gunfight broke out between police and traffickers. The film crew dove under the ring for cover. That's what favela dwellers such as Roberto Custódio deal with. Says Dowdney, "Luta is about celebrating the real heroes in the favelas, young people born into extraordinary adversity who get painted as victims when they're actually aspirational heroes."

PORT ELIZABETH, SOUTH AFRICA

Tommy Clark figured his sojourn in Zimbabwe to play pro soccer after college would be a joyous homecoming. He'd spent part of his teens in that southern African nation while his father, former Scotland international Bobby Clark, coached Highlanders F.C. in Bulawayo. But what he found upon returning in 1992 left him mystified and heartbroken. Seven of his dad's finest players—seemingly invincible footballers whom Tommy had idolized—were dead or dying. Worst of all, no one dared say why. "I was there for a year," says Clark, who also taught school and coached, "and I didn't have a single conversation about HIV."

Clark hit upon the idea of using soccer to break down this wall of silence and educate Africans about HIV. He embarked on a medical career, with a residency in pediatrics and a fellowship in HIV research in the U.S. In 2002, Clark launched Grassroot Soccer with three ex-Highlanders, including Ethan Zohn, the Survivor: Africa champion who donated a chunk of his $1 million prize money to the cause. Today the organization operates in South Africa, Zambia and Zimbabwe and shares curriculum and resources with partners in nine other African countries. Studies confirm that graduates of the program wait longer to engage in sex; have fewer partners; and are more willing to talk about HIV with peers and relatives, take an HIV test and stay on treatment if they test positive. Those proven results have attracted such patrons as Elton John, whose AIDS foundation contributed $1.4 million last year to fund the program in Zambia. There's no way to tie the 50% drop in the HIV infection rate among South African teens from 2005 to '08 directly to Grassroot Soccer, but foundations are showing their confidence in the program with more grant money. This week the Clinton Global Initiative announced a $1 million commitment to a Grassroot program for South African girls.

Among the organization's most effective tools are the voluntary counseling and testing tournaments that it uses to reach the men who drive the disease. Clark invited me to a tournament in Motherwell, a township in the South African city of Port Elizabeth. For years locals had hidden behind euphemisms, saying of an HIV-positive woman, "She has a House in Veeplaas," a play on the name of a local neighborhood. But there had been a breakthrough a week before my visit, when South African president Jacob Zuma—a father of 22 children by multiple wives—announced the results of his own HIV test. (They were negative.)

The grounds outside a school teemed with players who ducked into a makeshift clinic between games, and Grassroot personnel touted a post tournament dance contest to flush more prospects out of a nearby supermarket. By the end of the day 289 more people knew their HIV status. "Five years ago, if you'd bring up HIV, everyone would shut down," one of the tournament workers, 27-year-old Mkadi Nkopane, told me. "Now a 10-year-old will tell you of an uncle or mother who's positive. The stigma will always be there, but it's much less now."

As the game that launches countless conversations in Africa, soccer is a natural idiom to cut through the taboos surrounding one of the continent's most pressing problems. In one popular drill, each soccer ball stands for a sexual partner. A player dribbling two balls is easily chased down by a defender who represents the AIDS virus; a player dribbling only one ball eludes that defender much longer, and a memorable point is made. Grassroot Soccer distributed thousands of "red cards" during the 2010 World Cup to help teenage girls, who can be up to eight times more likely to become infected than their male counterparts, use sass and humor to fend off unwanted sexual approaches. "The culture soccer creates around this topic is our 'secret sauce,'" says Grassroot Soccer COO Bill Miles. "By focusing on intergenerational sex and multiple partners, you try to shift social norms. And if you shift social norms, you change the epidemic."

Clark and his fellow ex-Highlanders work in part to honor the dead of Bulawayo—men such as the former star of the Zimbabwean national team who was refused service by bank tellers because of the stigma of AIDS, and the ex-player who trained as one of Grassroot Soccer's first coaches only to die before he could work with kids. "We're trying to be both bold and humble," says Clark, 40, whose program is nearly halfway toward its goal of a million youth participants by '14. "We ask for millions of dollars, and we're trying to change behavior and norms on a huge scale. But we also know we're not always going to have the answer, and that there may be a better answer tomorrow."

TEL AVIV, JERUSALEM AND THE WEST BANK

When it ventures to global trouble spots, basketball can flash a kind of diplomatic passport. In South Africa, hoops comes without the racial baggage of soccer (a largely black sport) or rugby (mostly white). In divided Cyprus it's loved equally by citizens of Turkish and Greek descent. In Northern Ireland it's regarded as neither a Gaelic game by Protestants nor a game of the British garrison by Catholics. All of which helps explain the success of Peace Players International (PPI), which has spent the past decade using basketball to build bridges among young people in divided communities.

In the Middle East such efforts face a challenge of another magnitude. Upon launching there in 2005, PPI easily found Israeli Arabs to mix with Jewish kids in its programs. But Palestinian parents in the Israeli-controlled West Bank balked at letting their boys and girls travel to Israel for integrated play. Meanwhile, poor coaching and inadequate facilities in the West Bank led kids there to fear that their lack of hoops competency would only bolster Israeli stereotypes of worthless Palestinians.

On a brilliant spring day in 2010, Brendan Tuohey flashes me a smile as he oversees a PPI youth tournament in a Tel Aviv park. "Five years ago we decided to build up the skills of Palestinian kids," says Tuohey, a former player at Colgate whose brother Sean had the idea for the organization. "It's a big breakthrough that players from [the Palestinian city of] Ramallah chose to get on the bus to come here today."

Some parents on both sides of the Israel-Palestine divide still hesitate to let their kids enter PPI's programs—Jews out of safety concerns and Arabs because of cultural norms for girls. But the chance to get good coaching at no cost, plus uniforms and occasional travel, has enticed some 5,600 participants. "They all come for sport," PPI Middle East director Karen Doubilet tells me. " 'Meet the other side' is just something they put up with in order to do what they really want to do."

Children ages 10 to 14 participate in PPI's "twinning" program, in which Jews and Arabs at first practice regularly in their home communities, then combine into mixed teams under two coaches (one Arab and one Jewish) and meet weekly throughout the school year. At 15 they're eligible to become PPI coaches themselves; last season two teams of 15- and 16-year-old Arab and Jewish girls competed in the Israeli first division under the PPI banner. Meanwhile, in hoops-deprived parts of the West Bank such as Ramallah and nearby refugee camps, PPI continues to offer its "single-identity" program to boost the level of Palestinian basketball, provide constructive outlets for kids' energy and train coaches as leaders.

Once PPI gets them, most participants buy into the coexistence component. It's based on a curriculum, developed by a U.S.-based conflict-resolution think tank called the Arbinger Institute, that supplies strategies for exploring why one side stigmatizes the other and how to change those attitudes. "After Arbinger they might still clique up," says Heni Bizawi, who has played and coached in the program, "but according to different variables, like Jaffa versus Jerusalem instead of Arab versus Jew."

Peace Players has helped make a fan of Raneem Nashef, a 12-year-old Arab who lives in the West Jerusalem enclave of Beit Safafa. She'll wake up early to watch TV broadcasts involving her favorite player, Omri Casspi, the Jewish Israeli who plays for the Cleveland Cavaliers. Her mother, Lubna, who grew up despising the yellow and blue of Maccabi Tel Aviv, Casspi's old club, catches me by surprise: "My daughter feels Casspi represents her. She knows he comes from her part of the world."

In the seemingly intractable Arab-Israeli conflict, progress is measured in tiny steps. "A lot of people in my school don't like Arabs and don't know that I play PPI," says Naomi Goldstein, 14. "I don't tell them."

Amir Abu Dalu, 19, an Arab who's now a PPI coach, also keeps his counsel: "Otherwise I might get in trouble."

But a tiny step is a step just the same. First a bus ride, then a basketball game, ultimately the realization that someone you thought was your enemy makes a pretty good teammate. "In basketball it's easy to communicate," says Dalu. "You can play a game and connect, just like that."

TORONTO

Johann Olav Koss runs Right To Play out of Canada's largest city, and University of Toronto professor and former Olympic distance runner Bruce Kidd has been a reliable sounding board for him. I've turned up at Kidd's office because SDP is one of his academic specialties, and I'm looking for a sense of where the movement has been and where it might go.

In the 19th century, English-speaking exporters of sport, freighted with ulterior motives such as imperialism and evangelism, held attitudes strikingly different from those of Luke Dowdney, Tommy Clark and Brendan Tuohey. The Victorians took their "Games Ethic" from the playing fields of Eton and sent it overseas to "civilize" the ancestors of many of the very people engaged by SDP today.

Fast-forward to 1987, to Kenya and the Eastlands of Nairobi. A Canadian environmental worker named Bob Munro looks on as a handful of kids play with a soccer ball made of discarded shopping bags tied with bits of string. "Clean up the field," Munro tells them, "and I'll give you a real ball." Soon Munro launches the Mathare Youth Sports Association (MYSA), a soccer league with a blunt message: If you do something, MYSA does something; if you do nothing, MYSA does nothing. To join elite teams, players must pledge to perform thousands of hours of community service together each season. Those who organize cleanups, counsel peers in AIDS-prevention activities and coach or referee younger kids become eligible for scholarships. Teams can't take a field unless they clear it of trash—but earn points in the standings for doing so. Today MYSA, which is owned and run by the youths themselves and was nominated for a Nobel Peace Prize in 2003 and '04, touches 25,000 young Kenyans at any given time with nested-in-sport programs in community building, health education and environmentalism.

Kidd points out that the recent rise of SDP coincides with the fall of apartheid as much as it follows from the efforts of Koss and MYSA. Activists who had led the international sports boycott that helped bring down the South African regime—Kidd among them—essentially asked, "What do we do now?" They rallied to the answer that came back from their allies in the new Africa: "Help us build sport."

Today even those in sport's sunlit uplands are responding to that cry. When he stood before the IOC in Singapore in 2005 to deliver the final pitch for London's 2012 Olympic bid, Sebastian Coe pledged millions in aid for SDP to benefit 12 million people in 20 countries. The IOC chose London over Paris, Moscow, Madrid and New York City in large part because of that commitment to "legacy." In its winning bid for the 2016 Olympics, Rio also distinguished itself over rivals such as Chicago with a superior commitment to grassroots sport. With the most recent World Cup and Commonwealth Games having taken place in South Africa and India, respectively, and the next World Cup and Olympics ticketed for Brazil, a legacy component for the developing world is the new normal for major global events.

But Kidd is among many students of the movement who sound cautionary notes. "It's woefully underfunded and highly uncoordinated," he tells me. "And it's completely unregulated and largely isolated from mainstream development efforts." At international conferences dedicated to SDP, delegates from the developing world complain about Westerners who parachute in with things that aren't wanted or needed. As Right To Play spearheads the handoff of responsibility to locals, such as a 500-person team in Liberia led by a former refugee who first encountered SDP in a displacement camp, Kidd credits Koss with leading a move away from "a top-down, we-know-what-you-need approach with First World volunteers."

Before the Brazilian national soccer team visited Port-au-Prince in 2004 to play its Haitian counterparts, organizers proposed offering free tickets to those who turned in a firearm, only to cancel the plan at the last minute out of security fears. Even so, without a long-term violence-reduction campaign, such an event would have been a one-off with limited impact. "More attention has to be paid to context," Kidd tells me. "It's got to be sport plus. Sport plus education, sport plus health, sport plus peace-building." For all its networking and digital platforms, SDP's biggest challenge may be coordination. "In Zambia, I saw kids in slums who'd been trained five or more times by different NGOs, while just outside the city there was nothing," Kidd says. "NGOs aren't just fighting for donors, they're fighting for kids."

Or as Eli Wolff of Brown University's Sport and Development Project, who also coordinates the International Sport for Development and Peace Association, puts it, "There's been this boom, lots of networks and groups, but not really a professionalization of the field. There's no credentialing process or quality control, the way there is for teachers or lawyers. And there's the question, Is it effective?"

It's a familiar demand in sports: Show me the numbers. Is a program actually creating a positive outcome or just coinciding with it? "Because there's so much evidence that participation is a good thing, it's easy to assume that programs work," says Amy Farkas, a former sport-for-development specialist with UNICEF. "It's a lot easier to simply justify your program's existence than to do the hard work of justifying the impact of the intervention. That's why all sport-for-development programs need rigorous monitoring and evaluation."

Kidd believes the clamor for M & E, as it's known, can be taken too far. "People who have personal trainers, who choose schools for their kids based on athletic opportunities, tell us, 'Prove it! Prove that sport has benefits!'" he says. "That's where Johann has made a huge contribution. He continues to argue on the rights-based front."

But practitioners of all types recognize that funders are increasingly insisting on proof of results. "You're tempted to do sport for sport's sake, because it's fun," says Miles, the Grassroot Soccer executive. "We like it. But you have to show donors the outcomes."

CHICAGO

The Beyond Sport Summit is a three-day mixer for all sides of SDP's triangle—problem, practitioner and patron. It's a place to shake loose funding and inspire others, and it serves as the Grammys of the field, a place to call attention to deserving programs. Dowdney, Clark and Tuohey turned up for the 2010 edition in Chicago, but so too did scores of first-timers, many with little more than a notion and a dream.

Since its founding in 2008, Beyond Sport, a London-based firm that helps match practitioners with corporate sponsors, has had a particular eye for the modest initiative that would have an enormous impact if only it could be replicated or scaled up. But even Beyond Sport can't recognize every worthy project. Cambodia, for instance, is a country whose 40,000 amputees, victims of some of the millions of mines laid during a decade of war, were long considered unemployable. Now more than 60% of the players in the Cambodian National Volleyball League-Disabled (CNVL-D), mostly demobilized soldiers from both sides of the conflict, hold jobs. Even more notably, with its sponsors and broad fan following, the league has so transformed public attitudes that many disabled Cambodians, athletic and not, now wear shorts to show off their prostheses. A league like the CNVL-D could flourish in virtually any post conflict part of the world.

Moving the Goalposts is another initiative ready for its scale-up. It offers soccer to Kenyan girls, who are much more likely than boys to be HIV-positive. The program distributes packs of sanitary pads imprinted with health messages, but it operates only in the coastal region of Kilifi—which invites the question, What if it had the funding to expand throughout sub-Saharan Africa?

Similarly, in barely five years Globalbike has touched the lives of some 400,000 people by supplying bicycles to frontline aid workers in Africa and Asia. A microfinance loan officer serving village artisans in Ethiopia, an engineer working to ensure clean water in Bolivia, a health worker delivering vaccines in Zambia—each can see three times as many people and carry five times as much equipment by bike as on foot. A U.S.-based pro cycling team spreads word of Globalbike's impact so far, which suggests what could be accomplished if tens of thousands of bikes were delivered to the field.

No one in the developing world wants to depend on Western aid, so much buzz in the halls and breakout rooms in Chicago was about programs that have come up with their own revenue streams—groups such as Grupo Desportivo de Manica in Mozambique, a soccer club turned community hub that is building Futeco Park, three pitches girdled by 1,500 trees flush with mangos, lychees, oranges, avocados, guavas and papayas, which members will harvest and sell to fund the club's activities.

Indeed, there's a salutary realism amid all the idealism. John Sugden, an English sociologist who pioneered the "twinning" concept 25 years earlier with a mixed-faith soccer team in Belfast during the height of the Troubles and who is now the director of Football 4 Peace, doing in the Middle East with soccer what PPI does with basketball, puts it both wryly and well: "It's not as if you can sprinkle the pixie dust of sport and everything's going to be fine."

But sport does have its bewitching power, and for evidence a skeptic need only look at South Africa. Even in solitary confinement Nelson Mandela knew that many of his fellow black nationalists played soccer during their captivity on Robben Island. As he heard how the future leaders of his country brought the game to life with their own meticulously run Makana Football Association (MFA), Mandela recognized that soccer brought them to life—and he could imagine them in turn taking the obligations of democracy seriously. Since the fall of apartheid, former MFA players, referees and officials have served as South Africa's president, defense minister, minister for safety and security, deputy chief justice and sports minister, as well as provincial premiers and members of parliament. In prison Mandela began to recognize a truth he would articulate decades later as a free man: "Sport can create hope where once there was only despair. It is more powerful than governments in breaking down barriers. Sport has the power to change the world."

Mandela would demonstrate this masterfully as president of the new nation. Aware of the hold of rugby on the Afrikaaner imagination, he enlisted white captain François Pienaar to help him rally citizens of all races around the national team, the Springboks—long a symbol of white-minority rule—for the 1995 World Cup, which South Africa hosted and won. Says team manager Morne du Plessis of the story told in the film Invictus: "The very game that kept us apart for so long, he used to unite this country."

Thus modern South Africa owes its existence as a functioning, multiracial democracy partly to the braiding together of two epic sports stories—one from a largely black game, the other from a historically white one. Considering that sport, through the international boycott, helped do away with apartheid, it's not a bad showing for a few decades' work in one small corner of the globe.

Emmanuel Madonda grew up in Durban, South Africa's fourth-largest city, and now works for the Laureus Sport for Good Foundation. "I was 14 at the time of the '95 Rugby World Cup, and it was a pivotal moment for my country," he tells me during a break in the conference. "But even more powerful is the ongoing delivery of programming, of working deeply with young people. In Zulu we have this concept of ubuntu: 'I am because you are.' That is the essence of it."

Today sporting ubuntu extends from the street kid in Rio who, thanks to boxing, is transformed from avenging tough into potential Olympian; to the African AIDS orphan who, thanks to soccer, has a better chance of living long enough to raise children of her own; to the Arab girl in West Jerusalem who, thanks to basketball, feels bound to the fortunes of a Jewish Israeli player in the NBA. Yes, we look up to Mandela and Pienaar, and to former NBA star Dikembe Mutombo, the Congolese seven-footer who built a $29 million hospital in his hometown of Kinshasa and received Beyond Sport's Humanitarian in Sport Award. We will always look up, because as fans it's in our nature to do so.

But as human beings there's something else in our nature, which leads us to look around. Our eyes meet those of others, whom we engage as opponents, teammates, collaborators, neighbors and there-but-for-the-grace-of-God versions of ourselves. As Mutombo told the gathering in Chicago, quoting a proverb of his people: "When you take the elevator to the top, please remember to send it back down so someone else might use it."

 What is Wolff's argument regarding sport and development? What key evidence does he use in support of this argument and how do rhetorical choices like arrangement, tone, and use of nonrhetorical appeals (interviews and testimony, for example) support his overall purpose? Are you convinced by the sport for development and peace platform by the end of his article? Why or why not?

 Pick one sport development and peace organization profiled in Wolff's piece and spend 10 or so minutes researching more about the platform. Look up the organization's website, its mission statement, any released research or statistics connected to the organization, and testimonies. Spend a few minutes writing down your reactions to the information. Do you think the program is effective? Why or why not? What most interests you about this organization? If you could research the topic more fully, what would you be interested in exploring?

 As a class, look up the 2015 Millenium Development Goals. Divide these goals among small groups. In your group, spend about 10-15 minutes researching the Internet for examples of how certain sport organizations are trying to tackle your specific development goal through a sport for development and peace platform. What similarities and differences in the approaches do you notice? Where are these organizations geographically focused? What demographics are they concerned with and why? Share your results as a class.

 Write a one-page precis that provides an overview of one organization's approach to sport for development and peace. Include key information such as relevant statistics and mission statements. You might also consider including visuals for supporting evidence. Finally, what questions or concerns do you have about the organization's approach to sport for development and peace? Note: The Explore and Collaborate exercises above will be good preparation for this activity.

David Tannenwald is a case writer at the John F. Kennedy School of Government at Harvard University. In small groups, read Tannenwald's overview of sport in developing in the Harvard Kennedy Review here: http:// harvardkennedyschoolreview.com/the-power-to-change-the-world-the-role-of-sport-in-development/. Then, watch the documentary *Right to Play*. Synthesize your developing understanding of the role of sport in development and peace and write a collaborative short response (500-word) that demonstrates your evolving understanding of the growing sport for development and peace movement working across Tannenwald, Wolff, and the documentary.

Brazilian street artist Paulo Ito created this mural on the doors of a schoolhouse and posted it online three weeks before the start of the 2014 FIFA World Cup tournament in São Paulo. Ito made a clear political statement with striking imagery; the mural depicts a young Brazilian child, crying, with nothing to eat but a soccer ball. According to an interview with Slate magazine, Ito explained, "The truth is there is so much wrong in Brazil that it is difficult to know where to start. [. . .] I didn't mean [to say] nobody is doing anything against poverty, but we need to show the world or ourselves that the situation is still not good."

WORLD CUP 2014 MURAL

BY PAULO ITO

The 2014 World Cup was a controversial event given Brazil's tenuous economy and high poverty and unemployment. Ito is being deliberately provocative with his mural. Freewrite for five minutes on your impression of the mural. In what ways is this mural like other sports editorial cartoons? What is its argument? How does it get the message across? Who is the argument intended for and why did he paint it (where was it painted, who sees it, what was Ito's intended outcome)? What alternative depictions of the controversy could you imagine? Are they as persuasive as this mural? Why or why not?

This photo rapidly went viral in the days preceding the opening ceremonies to the 2014 FIFA World Cup in Brazil. In a small group, discuss the following questions: Why do you think the mural went viral? What makes the mural particularly compelling or provocative? How does it affect you as a viewer? How does the place and location of the mural enhance or detract from its meaning? How do you understand the relationship between politics, sport, and social media given Paulo Ito's viral mural?

Read the following article by journalist Stahl in *Slate* magazine here: http://www.slate.com/blogs/the_spot/2014/05/20/paulo_ito_world_cup_a_brazilian_street_artist_has_created_the_world_cup.html. How do Stahl's arguments presented in this article correspond or differ with your's and your group's ideas about the image? Has it changed your thinking about the relationship between politics and major international sporting events? Note: This is a good follow-up exercise to Collaborate above.

This exercise will prepare you for Major Assignment #6: The Sports Editorial Cartoon. There is a long history of using editorial cartoons to make political commentary about sport. Read the Opper Project's concise Introduction to editorial cartoons: http://hti.osu.edu/opper/editorial-cartoons. Then draw an editorial cartoon that captures your own perspective on mega events like Olympics and the World Cup, and write a one page cover memo detailing a rationale for the compositional choices you made and how they help to forward an argument using visual and alphabetic mediums.

MAJOR ASSIGNMENTS

MAJOR ASSIGNMENT #1: THE SPORTS MEMOIR (MEMORY AND INVENTION)

BACKGROUND

Many of the readings in this textbook reflect on the idea of athletic identity; that is, these readings explore the relationship between sport, identity, and other social categories such as race, class, gender, sexuality, and disability and the ways in which these relationships inform our understanding of normal and exceptional bodies in culture.

ASSIGNMENT

In thinking about the impact of sport on your life, particularly during childhood, write a memoir that details your experiences with sport and makes a claim about what your interactions with sport say about you as a person today. Identify a specific audience for your memoir: general public, your classmates, an instructor, a friend or parent, or other applicable audience who might be interested in reading about your experiences. Structure your memoir in a way that will appeal to this audience. Throughout your memoir, use vivid description, plotting and scene staging, and character development to tell a compelling narrative about at least one significant sporting moment, memory, or broader theme drawn from your experiences with sport. The objective is to craft a narrative that will leave a lasting impression on your audience and that teaches them something about the complex and intricate relationship between sport and identity.

From *The Social Value of Humor* (New York: State University of New York, 1983): 113-20.

QUESTIONS FOR INVENTION

The following questions are intended to offer ideas for brainstorming a response to the prompt. You do not need to answer all the questions or proceed in order. Instead, select and respond to questions that seem particularly apt to your experiences with sport and your audience. Then, choose an organizational pattern for your memoir that helps make the message clearer and more focused for your audience.

- What are some of your earliest memories about sport? Did you play more than one sport? Did you play individual or team sports? Did you specialize early, or play competitive sports? Did you have positive or negative experiences associated with sports as a child? Which sports are particularly memorable and why? Have your parents shared any of their own sporting experiences with you as a child, and did they participate in your sporting experiences either as a coach, trainer, mentor, etc.?

- Have you gravitated toward specific sports as you have grown older? Are there sports you no longer care for? Why? Among your friends, are you particularly good/bad/indifferent at sports? What sports do you wish you could have played as a child? What sports do you wish you could have avoided as a child?

- How do the sports you played reflect your personality, interests, ideas, and values? Have you adapted your sports participation to reflect who you are—for example, changing from a team to an individual sport or vice versa, wearing a certain special charm or partaking in certain "pre-event" rituals such as listening to a specific song, wearing those "lucky dirty" socks, or styling your hair a certain way?

- What major lessons about culture and identity have you learned from sport?

ABOUT MEMOIRS

A memoir is a kind of essay where the author writes about himself or herself to communicate to the audience a story that reflects an important aspect of the author's life. Yet, unlike autobiography, which is viewed as a more objective "truthful" genre, memoir is often understood as a literary form, highly informed by stylized writing and interpretation. That is, not unlike a movie "inspired by true events," the memoir takes some creative license to reflect on the cultural and personal significance of particular events, in this case sport. As you brainstorm and begin drafting your sport memoir, keep in mind the narrative should:

- Have an interesting title that alludes to the overall message or emotion you wish to impart on your audience.

- Focus on a set of clearly defined and well-connected moments and or memories in your life that pertain to sport in order to convey a specific message and/or emotion to the audience.

- Use the textual conventions of narrative and descriptive writing modeled in the suggested readings: plot, scene, setting, character development, descriptive writing, and detailed experience, in order to explain the significance of sport in your life to your audience.

- Use concrete details to appeal to the audience's senses and emotions.

- Reflect on your experiences to help the audience understand how sport affected you and why these experiences should matter to them as well.

- You may wish to include visuals in your essay as support: photographs, clip art, drawings, editorial cartoons, or other graphics to help illustrate the sporting memories you have discussed.

SUGGESTED READINGS FOR THE ASSIGNMENT

Introduction
Heywood, excerpt from *One of the Guys*
Carlos, "The John Carlos Story"
Giamatti, "Hyperbole's Child"
Thompson, "The Kentucky Derby Is Decadent and Depraved"

MAJOR ASSIGNMENT # 2: ANALYZING SPORTS JOURNALISM (INTERPRETATION AND ANALYSIS)

BACKGROUND

Sports journalism has a long and interesting history in America. How journalists covered the sports beat in the early twentieth century—simply "reporting" game statistics—has radically transformed in the twenty-first century into a much more "personal interest story" and political commentary approach—hence *ESPN's Page 2*, Grantland, and 30 for 30 series, for example. While sports journalists strive to the tell the facts to their readers as best they are able, they are often still crafting arguments about sport and its athletes and their larger cultural significance, importance, or danger. Think about news coverage surrounding the "doping controversy" in baseball, cycling, and football, or the obsession with athlete's off-the-field conduct, as a few examples. Or consider how discussions around "pay for play" often have more interest in debating the meaning of "amateurism" than they do with the logistic, legal constraints, and ethics of compensating athletes. Sports journalists, in other words, are now expected to not only report on the technicalities of a given sports event, but also discuss the larger significance of sport and its athletes to American culture and identity.

ASSIGNMENT

Choose one or two feature articles or opinion editorials from this reader and read them closely several times before writing an essay that analyzes the ways in which the text(s) forward a particular argument about sport's cultural significance. You might, for example, look closely at a single feature article and analyze how the author shapes his or her argument using certain facts, arrangement techniques, and other rhetorical conventions such as tone, style, voice, credibility, and emotion. Or, perhaps you might compare and contrast two feature articles, or a feature article and an opinion editorial, discussing a similar issue, and perhaps arriving at different conclusions. For example, you might consider how Forde and Branch discuss the increasingly important "Pay for Play" debate; or, you might look at how Macur and Behar discuss the impact of modern science and genetics on sporting culture and the implications for youth and elite athletes. What are the central facts used to report each story? What research, evidence, and claims are used by each author to support their argument? How does working within the confines of a feature article or opinion editorial inform the author's choices about which claims to make and how to make them? In what ways are the texts' coverage of the issue similar? In what ways are they different? What might account for these differences in coverage? How does the author's own background and interests inform her or his approach to story? What images are attached to the feature stories and how do these images help frame the author's arguments? What about the titles? What other stylistic devices do the authors use to convince the readers of their argument?

QUESTIONS FOR INVENTION AND RESEARCH

1. *Sourcing:* Look up the websites of the original publication venues for your selections. What type of approach to sports journalism, for example, is ESPN known for? What about *Sports Illustrated*? How do the motives of sports journalism powerhouses like ESPN and SI differ from the type of coverage of sports in *The Atlantic* and *The New York Times*? How does audience drive these differences in sports journalism approaches? Is one approach more liberal, for example? Is one more "neutral" and another more "critical" or "conservative"?

2. *Perspective:* Where do you get your news about sports events? Do you look to different media outlets for local, national, and international sports events? How do your own interests in sports shape what kinds of sports journalism you read? How has reading different kinds of sports journalism texts for this assignment changed your views about the genre? About sports? About the significance of sports in American culture?

3. *Evidence:* What two or three facts, claims, or quotes from each piece stand out to you as central to their author's argument? How are these effective or not in helping the author achieve her or his purpose? How does the presentation of these facts or claims shape your understanding of the issue as a reader? How might you integrate these facts, claims, or quotes directly into your own essay to help build support for your own argument about the rhetoric of sports journalism coverage?

SOME SUGGESTED READING CLUSTERS FOR ASSIGNMENT

Sports and Science
Behar, "Will Genetics Destroy Sports?"
Macur, "Born to Run? Little Ones Get Test for Sports Gene"
*See also accompanying readings in affiliated exercises.

Pay for Play
Branch, "The Shame of College Sports"
Forde, "The Myth of the Exploited, Impoverished Athletes"
*See also accompanying readings in affiliated exercises.

Sports and Culture
Halberstam, "Sports Can Distract, But They Can't Heal"
Wolff, "Sports Saves the World"
Telander, "Senseless"
Foer, "How Soccer Explains the American Culture Wars"

Sports and Fandom
Garofalo and Waldron, "If You Build, it They Might Not Come: The Risky Economics of Sports Stadiums"
Thompson, "The Kentucky Derby Is Decadent and Depraved"
Williams, "The Crowd at the Ball Game"
Serazio, "Just How Much is Sports Fandom Like Religion?"

Sports and Gender
Levy, "Either/Or : Sports, Sex, and the Case of Caster Semenya"
Pappano and McDonagh, "Women and Men in Sports: Separate Is Not Equal"
Nelson, "Stronger Women"

MAJOR ASSIGNMENT #3: ANALYZING SPORTS MEDIA (INTERPRETATION AND ANALYSIS)

BACKGROUND

Their powerful images and provocative advertisements abound in today's society and are increasingly inseparable from everyday communication and cultural practices. They are also connected to large markets. An advertisement spot for the Super Bowl, for example, commonly boasts around a $4 million dollar price tag. Similarly, athletes receive millions of dollars in endorsement monies to sponsor products like soft drinks, shoes, clothing, and even watches. Thus, sports advertisements actively shape and drive consumer desires by linking certain cultural values and practices to sports culture and its products—the Nike Air Jordan, for example—or by using the ethos of celebrity athletes to endorse everyday products—like Maria Sharapova's support of the Canon digital camera. That is, sports and their athletes, entangled in a web of capital, media, and advertising, actively shape our understanding of culture and identity through the messages and arguments they convey and the values and products they do (and do not) endorse.

ASSIGNMENT

Choose a sports media image (magazine cover, iconic sports image) or advertisement (print or commercial) to analyze and write an essay that argues for an interpretation of the text. Review your text(s) closely, several times, making notes about what you observe. You may also choose to take screenshots of "evidence" to insert later in your essay. In your analysis, focus on rhetorically analyzing the text to discover how it reflects aspects of American culture, identity, and values. The goal of the assignment is to make an argument for a particular interpretation of the sports media image. To do so, you want to closely examine the rhetorical choices used to shape the text's message and composition. As you write your essay, consider your argument: Why is this sports media image or ad significant? For whom? If an ad, what is it selling, and what message does it attach to the product? If a cover or iconic image, what values are being sold through the framing of the athlete? What is it that you want to argue about concerning sport, culture and identity based on your analysis of this image? Include a clear thesis that helps control the organization of the essay and allows for you to make further claims about the textual strategies used in the text.

QUESTIONS FOR INVENTION

- *Genre:* What kind of sports media image am I analyzing?

- *Rhetorical Situation:* What is its purpose? Who is its audience? And what is the broader social and cultural context in which the image circulates?

- *Textual Properties:* What compositional choices are used in the image that support the text's broader purpose? What do you see in the text? What don't you see? What can you infer from these observations? How might the choices to use certain compositional elements and not others shape the overall meaning of the image?

- *Significance:* Why is this text significant? For whom?

SUGGESTED IMAGES FROM THIS BOOK

Newsweek, "Girls Rule!"
Leibovitz, "LeBron and Giselle"
LeBron, "#WeAreTrayvonMartin"
Dominis, "1968 Olympic Black Power Salute"
Ito, World Cup 2014 Mural

MAJOR ASSIGNMENT #4: SPORTS MEDIA AND IDENTITY (ANALYSIS AND INTERPRETATION)

BACKGROUND

As this reader's introduction, filmography, and readings suggest, sports, athletes, and their fans have long been a source of fascination and vexation in American culture. Where some believe athletes should be role models and activists—like John Carlos's involvement with the 1968 Olympic Project for Human Rights—others believe athletes threaten our cultural values—doping, dog fighting, domestic abuse. Similarly, sports fans have their own identities and rituals that seem perplexing and extreme for those not interested in the "beer and circus" of sports. The media plays a central role in shaping our understanding of athletes' and fans' social roles and identities. Which athletes—the hero or villain; the "out" or the "sex kitten"—and which fans—the soccer hooligan or the women's basketball fan—and how the media frame these identities as "good" or "bad" shape how we interpret and understand the cultural role of the athlete or sport's fan in American culture.

ASSIGNMENT

Choose a type of athlete or sport's fan identity and research representations of this type in at least three different media, finding images, stories, memoirs, or other takes on this athlete type not necessarily discussed at length in this book. You might, for example, explore the way in which LGBTQI athletes are portrayed by the media, or the correlation between gendered stereotypes and women's basketball fans. Or, you might look at female athletes and their complicated relationship to mass media. What about male athletes and the different identities afforded them by media? Or consider how the media handles discussions of disability and athleticism? Or, perhaps you are interested in differences in media coverage between athletes from ethnic minority backgrounds, particularly black athletes, and white athletes? As you identify representations of your athlete or sport's fan type, also consider people's responses to these interpretations. For example, how might local newspaper reviews, journal articles, blogs, magazine covers, and advertisements reinforce particular ways of seeing and understanding these athletes or fans as a "type"? You might also consider primary research, conducting surveys and interviews to better understand how different demographics talk about athlete identity. When you have finished gathering your data, analyze your findings and develop a thesis about the differences media make in both the representations and audience responses to your chosen athlete identity. Explain, illustrate, and defend your thesis with evidence from your research. [Note: You may present your findings in any mode, media, and genre you find persuasive for your purpose. You might also consider this an individual or collaborative assignment, depending on your instructor's requirements.]

QUESTIONS FOR INVENTION AND RESEARCH

- What category or type of athlete or fan do you want to know more about?

- What cultural, historical, and/or geographic context would you like to know more about in studying its athletes or fans?

- What media are you most interested in studying: sports media, literary journalism, opinion editorials, magazine cover images, advertisements, video games, local news stories?

- What do the media you have chosen have in common regarding representational practices of your athlete? What is different about the representations?

- Where are you most likely to find responses to the representations you've identified? Which responses are most likely to help you understand the difference media make in representing your athlete type?

- What modes and media most effectively help you craft a compelling argument about the impact of media on the representation of your athlete type: website, vlog, traditional essay, wikipedia entry, zine?

- How can you combine images, words, and possibly sound as well as various font types and color and other design elements to underscore your argument and make it more effective?

- How might you consider the value of your argument for public audiences interested in knowing more about your athlete type?

- What is the purpose of your argument?

- How might you incorporate citations and other textual cues that acknowledge sources of information and help you build authority and credibility?

SUGGESTED READINGS

Nelson, "Stronger Women"
Storey, "The Case Against the Special Olympics"
Levy, "Either/Or : Sports, Sex, and the Case of Caster Semenya"
Serazio, "Just How Much is Sports Fandom Like Religion?"
Butterworth, "Militarism, Public Memory, and the Pro Football Hall of Fame"

SUGGESTED IMAGES

Dominis, "The Black Power Salute"
LeBron, "#WeAreTrayvonMartin"
Leibovitz, "LeBron and Giselle"
Newsweek, "Girls Rule!"

MAJOR ASSIGNMENT #5: THE PERSUASIVE RESEARCH PAPER (RESEARCH AND ARGUMENT)

BACKGROUND

Many of the readings discuss controversial issues dealing with the world of sport, its athletes and fans. Some writers, such as John Carlos, argue that athletes are a platform for social change; whereas other writers, like Rick Telander and Taylor Branch, in this reader demonstrate the darker side of sports, including urban and inter-racial violence and the exploitation of college sports. Still, other readings, like Pappano and McDonagh, Levy, and Nelson have examined the controversial and complex nature of gender and sport—what really makes a woman a woman and a man a man, and should we segregate sports or not? For this assignment, you will conduct research about a sports issue and articulate your own argument about the topic.

ASSIGNMENT

Write a persuasive research-based essay in which you argue for a particular understanding of a controversial sports issue. For instance, you might want to argue for or against the "Pay for Play" debate, providing new evidence and perspectives that extend beyond this reader. Or, perhaps you want to research the complexities of "coming out" as a LGBTQI athlete or how to create more equitable policy for athletes with disabilities. Or still, you might want to weigh in on the tricky relationship between sport, technology, and science, using Macur and Behar as starting points for thinking about how comfortable or not we are with the increasing technologization of sport.

QUESTIONS FOR RESEARCH, REFLECTION, AND INVENTION

Your instructor will help you decide how much research and how many sources are appropriate for this assignment in addition to selections from this reader.

- What are the main points you want to argue?

- What and how much evidence or research do you need in order to support these points?

- What are the counter-arguments to your claim? How will you acknowledge while effectively refuting these claims? Will you need to compromise between two opposing sides? Is there another perspective that hasn't been considered?

- Who is your audience for this essay and how does this shape what kinds of research and evidence you include?

- What medium do you think is the most effective for circulating your argument to your desired audience?

ABOUT PERSUASIVE WRITING

Writing an effective persuasive paper for your audience requires you to incorporate what rhetoric calls the three appeals, or types of persuasion: ethical (*ethos*), logical (*logos*), and emotional (*pathos*). Depending on your audience, genre, and purpose, you will want to vary these kinds of arguments accordingly. You also need to consider how ethical, logical, and emotional persuasion work dynamically. Consider, for example, the highly emotional advertisements for ASPCA. Seeing images of hurt animals overlaid with sad music (usually in a minor chord with sentimental lyrics) is a highly emotional argument; yet this is also a logical choice on the author's part because they recognize that they need to craft an ethos that matches the desired outcome and values they wish in their audience: caring, compassionate people willing to donate funds and support a cause. Thus, creating a good balance of persuasive appeals is important and, again, depending on your audience and genre, this will vary. At the risk of oversimplifying matters, for example, you might consider, if you are writing for a scholarly audience, how overly emotional arguments can actually work against your credibility with this readership. Instead, you might be using more citation and inclusion of research to build credibility and demonstrate logical argument.

SUGGESTED RELATED ASSIGNMENTS

- Major Assignment #6: The Sports Editorial Cartoon provides an excellent opportunity to translate and reconsider your developing argument and research on sport in Major Assignment #5 for a new multimodal rhetorical situation.

MAJOR ASSIGNMENT #6: THE SPORTS EDITORIAL CARTOON (TRANSLATION, REFLECTION, AND MULTIMODALITY)

BACKGROUND

Sports have a long history in newspapers as inspiration for cartoonists and visual artists who strategically cull the power of the visual to evoke witty commentary about sports' role in culture and society. As a graphic argument published in a mass medium (newspapers, news magazines, or the web, for example), the editorial cartoon is generally educational in orientation and usually, though not always, supports the publication source's viewpoint. It also uses visual and written content dynamically to create an overall message/argument about a given subject matter. For more information, you may wish to consult the Opper Projects website, particularly their Introduction to editorial cartoons: http://hti.osu.edu/opper/editorial-cartoons.

Drawing a sports editorial cartoon challenges you to think through the complexities of using words and visuals dynamically to create a compelling and educational argument about sport. It also invites further reflection about communication as rhetorical by considering how audience, genre/context, and argument work together to influence how a particular message is shaped. That is, in drawing your sports editorial cartoon, you must once again consider what your argument is, which publication source would support this viewpoint, and how you shape your particular word and image choices in the cartoon to align your argument with the publication's viewpoint and its readership. This exercise also offers an excellent opportunity for you to translate your researched argument from Major Assignment #5 into a multimodal format for another, perhaps more publically oriented audience.

ASSIGNMENT

In this assignment you will draw a sports editorial cartoon for a particular publication source and its readership demographic This might be your university student newspaper, one of your local city newspapers, or a national newspaper like *The New York Times* or the *Los Angeles Times*. Your cartoon should aim to teach the readership something about your topic, perhaps even making an argument, and should carefully use visual and written content dynamically to support an overall argument about sport that would be supported by the publication.

In addition, you will write a two to three page cover letter in which you address the specific rhetorical and compositional choices used in making the editorial cartoon and why you believe they are effective for your argument and its intended publication. The letter should be as specific as possible, drawing attention to particular visual and written strategies (satire, humor, analogy, metaphor, irony, hyperbole, litote, and caricature, for example) used to create your argument as you explain how and why the cartoon aligns with the publication's overall viewpoint and what its readership will learn about sport from your editorial cartoon. Your cover letter might also draw on examples of previously published editorial cartoons in your publication as evidence to support the compositional choices you make in your own editorial cartoon.

QUESTIONS FOR INVENTION

- What was the main argument of your researched persuasive essay on sport (Major Assignment #5)?

- Who would support this argument and why? How would you characterize the argument's overall perspective: objective, liberal, conservative, dissenting?

- How might you draw on research from Major Assignment #5 to help you make a specific, focused argument/educational statement in your editorial cartoon?

- What newspapers and other mass medium publications might support a similar approach to sport? How do you know? What content from their website, articles, past editorial cartoons suggest their perspective aligns with yours?

- What is the most practical and reasonable publication source for your cartoon and why?

- What is the purpose of your editorial cartoon? What will it teach the publication's readership and how is it different from previously published sports editorials and editorial cartoons?

- How will visuals and written content work together to create your message?

- What tone do you need to strike—will satire or humor or irony work best? What are the differences and how do you convey these using visual and written content?

- How does the title of your editorial cartoon convey its argument and enhance the meaning of the cartoon itself?

The Cover Letter

- What is your publication's viewpoint and how do you know? What evidence can you supply from the source's mission statement as well as articles, OpEds, and other editorial cartoons to demonstrate a particular perspective?

- Who is your publication's audience and how do you know? Can you find empirical data on the audience's educational, gender, and socioeconomic background for example?

- How does your argument try to teach this audience demographic something about sport and why is it important for them to know about your topic?

- What strategies do you use in your visual and written content to support your overall argument?

- How does the cartoon rely on both visual and written content to make a coherent argument about sport?

- What have you learned about communicating using visuals and new genres in this assignment? How was it different than writing a researched argument and what did you find valuable about the assignment in terms of thinking about writing and communication as rhetorical or audience-directed acts?

SUGGESTED READINGS AND ACTIVITIES:

You might look back to activities associated with the following selected readings for further help and preparation:

Hunter S. Thompson's "The Kentucky Derby Is Decadent and Depraved"
Forde's "Myth of Exploited, Impoverished Athletes"
Ito's World Cup 2014 Mural

FILMOGRAPHY

DOCUMENTARIES AND DOCUDRAMAS

League of Denial: The NFL Concussion Crisis (2013)
A frontline documentary investigating the mental health crisis that plagues the NFL, and the ongoing and controversial medical research surrounding concussions and long term brain health of football players.

Battle for Brooklyn (2011)
This award-winning documentary is an exposé on the rhetoric of development surrounding sports stadia. *Battle for Brooklyn* focuses in particular on one of the more controversial uses of "Eminent Domain" policy and its relationship to the Atlantic Yards development, a development project designed to help relocate the New Jersey Nets basketball team to New York. The documentary follows the story of activist David Goldstein throughout his eight year struggle to save his home and community from displacement should Brooklyn approve the development of Atlantic Yards.

Bigger, Stronger, Faster (2008)
In following a pair of siblings pursuing their bodybuilding dreams, and their tangle with performance enhancing drugs, director Chris Bell examines the impact of American sports' "win at all costs" mentality.

Black Athletes: Fact or Fiction? (1989)
This award-winning yet highly controversial NBC documentary, written and produced by journalist John Entine, author of *Taboo: Why Blacks Dominate Sports and Why We're Afraid to Talk About It* (2001), with Tom Brokaw, explores scientific research surrounding the idea that blacks are genetically superior to whites in athletics.

Fire in Babylon (2011)
Stevan Riley explores the historic rise of the West Indies cricket team during the national liberation movements of the 1970s and 1980s and the broader global context of apartheid South Africa and English race riots.

Hoop Dreams (1994)
This 1994 Sundance Film Festival Audience Award for Best Documentary winner follows the stories of two African-American Chicago high school students with dreams of making it to the NBA.

Pumping Iron (1977)
A docudrama on bodybuilding culture, featuring Mr. Universe, actor, and former California Governor, Arnold Schwarzenegger in competition for the 1975 IFBB Mr. Universe and Mr. Olympia competitions. The film helped popularize bodybuilding, the fitness craze of the 1980s, and the expansion of the commercial gym market. In also inspired two follow-ups, including Pumping Iron II: The Women (1985).

Pumping Iron II: The Women (1985)
An exposé into the world of female bodybuilding culture at the height of the American fitness craze in the 1980s, focusing in particular on exploring acceptable gender norms of the female bodybuilding physique. The film has received criticism for its inaccurate portrayal of female bodybuilding culture and has also featured in early scholarship on women, gender, and sport.

The Truth About Exercise (2012)
Renown British doctor, journalist, and TV personality Michael Moseley uses himself as test subject to discuss the implications of the latest science research on exercise, including breakthrough findings about why some people seem to respond to exercise better than others and why we may not need to exercise for the recommended 2 ½ hours a week to achieve the maximum health benefits.

Training Rules (2009)
A dramatic look at the Harris vs Portland case concerning Penn State Women's Basketball coach Renee Portland's "no lesbian" rule and its impact on Jen Harris and other teammates playing under a homophobic team culture.

Trobriand Cricket: An Ingenious Response to Colonialism (1976)
This ethnographic documentary reveals how the Trobiand Islanders of Papua New Guinea modified the British game of cricket in order to use the game as an expression of Trobiand culture.

The Fab Five (1991)
A look at the five freshmen of the University of Michigan's basketball team, their success, the scandal, and the historic "Timeout."

Undefeated (2012)
This Oscar winning documentary follows the lives of a volunteer coach and his aspiring team during a single season of a high school football team in an impoverished area in North Memphis, Tennessee.

9 Innings to Ground Zero (2004)
A retrospective narrated by actor Liev Schrieber recounting the role baseball played in uniting America and healing New York in the days following the terrorist attacks of Sept. 11, 2001.

The Marinovich Project (2011)
A cautionary tale about hyper specialization in youth sports told through the life experiences of Todd Marinovich, son of ex-professional football player turned strength and conditioning coach Marv Marinovich. The film recounts Todd's rise and fall through college and professional football, his struggle with drug addiction, and his efforts to find meaning in life beyond sports.

Right to Play (2012)
An ESPN "30 for 30" film featuring the pioneering humanitarian efforts of Norwegian speed skater Olav Koss, who is using sport as a powerful platform to improve the lives of disadvantaged youth around the world.

Renee (2011)
Dr. Richard Raskin was a respected surgeon and successful professional tennis player, happily married with a son when he decided to undergo surgery to become a woman. Renee is one of the first in-depth documentaries to address the complexities of transgenderism and sport.

The Two Escobars (2010)
An ESPN "30 for 30" documentary featuring the entanglement of Colombian drug lord Pablo Escobar and the untimely death of Colombian national player Andres Escobar.

Dogtown and the ZBoys (2001)
A look at the pioneering efforts of the Zephyr skating team, narrated by Sean Penn.

Murderball (2005)
This film documents the journeys of quadriplegic athletes in their efforts to compete in the Paralmypic Games in Athens, Greece.

Kicking It (2008)
A look at how an organization's creation of an "Homeless World Cup" uses soccer as a global tool to promote consciousness about homelessness and provide homeless persons with a second chance at rebuilding their lives through the power of football.

Unforgivable Blackness: The Rise and Fall of Jack Johnson (2004)
A look at the first African-American heavyweight boxing champion, Jack Johnson.

The Announcement (2012)
A retrospective on the days leading up to and the years following Earvin "Magic" Johnson's discovery and public announcement that he is HIV positive.

FEATURE FILMS

42 (2013)
A biopic of Jackie Robinson and his breaking of the "color line" in American baseball.

Personal Best (1982)
The story of a female track and field runner's journey to qualify for the 1980 Olympic Games and her awakening to an unlikely romance with her training partner.

Remember the Titans (2000)
A black coach struggles to earn respect and unite his biracial football team during the civil rights movement in the South.

A League of Their Own (1992)
The retrospective on the rise of the women's baseball league during the war era.

The Blind Side (2009)
An urban teenager finds an unlikely home in the Touhys and an unlikely career as a star football player.

Million Dollar Baby (2004)
A working class waitress finds hope and a future in the world of boxing under the mentorship of a jaded trainer.

Raging Bull (1980)
A dramatized portrait of Italian boxer Jake LaMotta and the demons he fought inside and outside of the ring.

Bend It Like Beckham (2002)
A young Sikh girl follows her dreams to play soccer against her orthodox parents wishes.

Hoosiers (1986)
A dramatization of a true story about an unlikely coach and his small-town Indiana basketball team's journey to the state finals in 1954.

The Sandlot (1993)
An homage to America's favorite pastime narrated through the eyes of a boy as he recounts a memorable childhood summer as the new kid on the block who's taken up by a group of boys who worship "the sandlot."

Rudy (1993)
A classic underdog story about character and persistence and one unlikely boy's dream to play for the Notre Dame football team.

We Are Marshall (2006)
In 1970, nearly the entirety of Marshall University's football team, its coach, and several of its fans were killed in a tragic plane crash. Picking up after the terrible events, the movie documents the

efforts of the new coach to rally the remaining freshman squad to compete in the 1971 season in honor of their teammates.

Field of Dreams (1989)
A timeless classic about a smalltown farmer who, after hearing a voice, builds a baseball diamond in the middle of his corn field which is then visited by the ghosts of the seven Chicago White Sox players banned from the 1919 World Series.

Invictus (2009)
A look at Nelson Mandela's unique approach to unite a post-apartheid South Africa by enlisting the help of the national rugby team in their journey to win the 1995 Rugby World Cup.

Little Giants (1994)
A determined tomboy sets out to overcome gender stereotypes by proving girls can play football too.

Ladybugs (1992)
When a coach finds himself handed a team of uncoordinated girls, he disguises his prolific son as "Martha" to help the team win a few games.

Mighty Ducks (1992)
A lawyer finds himself in trouble and sentenced to community service that includes coaching a misfit hockey team.

Jerry Maguire (1996)
A dramatized view of the corporatization of big sports and the sex, money, and lies that go into making athletes rich and famous.

Any Given Sunday (1999)
A behind the scenes dramatization of the politics, money, and power involved in big time football, and the sexist obstacles for women to be heard in an male-dominated industry.

Moneyball (2011)
Based on the same named bestselling book, *Moneyball* narrates one man's vision to quantify game statistics alters the history of the Oakland A's franchise and forever changes the way baseball fills a roster.

ACKNOWLEDGEMENTS

Beck, Robert. Cover image for *Newsweek*. Copyright © 1999 *Newsweek*. Used with permission. All rights reserved.

Behar, Michael. "Will Genetics Destroy Sports?" Reprinted from *Discover Magazine*. Copyright © 2004 by Michael Behar. All rights reserved.

Branch, Taylor. "The Shame of College Sports." Reprinted from *The Atlantic*, Sept. 7, 2011.

Butterworth, Michael. "Militarism, Public Memory, and the Pro Football Hall of Fame." From *Communication Currents*, 7.5 (2012). Reprinted with permission of the author.

Carlos, John with Dave Zirin. *The John Carlos Story*. Copyright © 2011 by John Carlos and Dave Zirin. Reprinted with permission of Haymarket Books. All rights reserved.

Foer, Franklin. "How Soccer Explains the American Culture Wars." From *How Soccer Explains the World: An Unlikely Theory of Globalization*." Copyright © 2004, 2010 by Franklin Foer. Reprinted with permission of HarperCollins. All rights reserved.

Forde, Pat. "Myth of Exploited, Impoverished Athletes." Reprinted from *ESPN.com*, July 18, 2011.

Garofalo, Pat and Travis Waldron. "If you Build it They Might Not Come: The Risky Economics of Sport Stadiums." From *The Atlantic*, Sept. 7, 2012.

Giamatti, A. Bartlett. "Hyberbole's Child." From *Rules of the Game: The Best Sports Writing from Harper's Magazine*. Eds. Matthew Stevenson and Michael Martin. Copyright © 2010 Franklin Square Press. Reprinted with permission. All rights reserved.

Halberstam, David. "Sports Can Distract, But They Don't Heal." From *ESPN Page 2*.

Heywood, Leslie. "One of the Guys." From *Pretty Good for a Girl*. Copyright © 1999 by Leslie Heywood. Reprinted with permission. All rights reserved.

Liebovitz, Annie. "Shape Issue" from *Vogue*, 2008. Photo copyright © 2008 by Annie Liebovitz. Reprinted with permission of Condé Nast. All rights reserved.

Levy, Ariel. "Either/Or: Sports, Sex, and the Case of Caster Semenya." Reprinted from *The New Yorker*, Nov. 30, 2009. Copyright © 2009 by Ariel Levy. Reprinted with permission. All rights reserved.

Macur, Juliet. "Born to Run? Little Ones Get Test for Sports Gene." From *The New York Times*, Nov. 30, 2008. Reprinted with permission. All rights reserved.